ANIMALS
FOR SHOW AND PLEASURE
IN ANCIENT ROME

ELK IN THE ARENA, FROM AN IVORY OF
ANASTASIUS, A.D. 517

ANIMALS FOR SHOW AND PLEASURE IN ANCIENT ROME

George Jennison

PENN

University of Pennsylvania Press
Philadelphia

Originally published 1937 by Manchester University Press
Printed in the United States of America on acid-free paper

10 9 8 7 6 5 4 3 2 1

Published 2005 by
University of Pennsylvania Press
Philadelphia, Pennsylvania 19104-4011

To
C. G. STONE
MY
FRIEND AND HELPER

CONTENTS

ILLUSTRATIONS

FOREWORD

FEW presents which could be made to Kings or other rulers were so cheap, so effective, or so highly appreciated as a gift of wild animals. They appealed to the curiosity of the people and filled them with wonder and awe. They were (and are still) a fount of perpetual interest and scientific study to the learned, and were a new source of pleasure and excitement to the " court."

The meanest chieftain in the poorest country of the uncivilized world could offer in this kind a tribute as fine as that of the most powerful monarch—a gift made more valuable by the glamour that clung and still clings to the distant and the unknown. The very presence of strange creatures, beauteous birds or ferocious beasts, was a living proof of the monarch's might and influence, so that it should not surprise us to find that from the earliest times, and almost without exception, a very fine zoological collection has marked the crest of power in every great nation and shrunk with it to its fall.

Exploration may be expected to add much to our knowledge of the zoological treasures of ancient nations and to give us a very good idea of their comparative importance in the world whenever indeed the finds can be dated with certainty.

Europe was a comparatively poor continent until the second century before the Christian era, whereas India and China had been wealthy and civilized for some thousands of years earlier. The influence of India in zoological matters was potent but indirect. The Celestial Empire, which had extensive trade relations with the whole of Eastern Asia, had little intercourse with the West, and the wonderful zoological

collections of the wealthiest country of the ancient world were
almost unknown beyond its frontiers.

Egypt was little if at all behind these Asiatic kingdoms
either in point of time or of importance.   In the second millen-
nium she was the paramount mistress of the whole of Syria
and of the islands in the eastern Mediterranean.   When her
power waned and the Assyrians, Babylonians, Medes, Persians
and Greeks in turn became paramount, Egypt remained wealthy
and retained that reverence for animals which, in the days of
renewed prosperity under her Greek rulers the Ptolemies, when
the worship of Dionysus was added to that of Apis, produced
those wonderful processions that modified so profoundly the
Roman games and animal shows.

PREFACE

THE Animals of the Ancient World have never been studied by a naturalist. To one who has spent a lifetime in practical contact with wild animals many things are clear and simple which are obscure to scholars, and many difficulties are apparent which scholars have not appreciated. Some of these can be exposed and explained.

Even a poor book which could throw light from an unusual angle would not be useless. I have endeavoured to make a good book and trust it may prove valuable.

My research has been aided by the voluminous notes of Friedländer [1] and the equally valuable though little known *Histoire des Ménageries de l'antiquité à nos jours* by Gustave Loisel,[2] Docteur-ès-Sciences, Paris, with its many references to French authorities, documents and treasures.

Such references as I give I have examined in the original tongues and pictures as far as possible, and from them I have made such deductions as seemed probable, relying for correctness on personal knowledge of the animals described.

I have to thank many classical scholars for assistance and advice, particularly Mr. C. G. Stone, to whom I dedicate this book.

I am grateful to the Manchester University Press for the care with which the book has been produced, and particularly

---

[1] *Roman Life and Manners under the Early Empire*, by Ludwig Friedländer. Authorized translation by Leonard A. Magnus, Ll.B., George Routledge & Sons, Ltd., London ; E. P. Dutton & Co., New York.

[2] Henri Laurens, 6, Rue de Tournon, Paris. 1912.

to Professor James Tait for much time and trouble generously spent on the proofs.

I have also to thank the General Editors of the Loeb Classical Library for permission to include a few translations from their series.

GEO. JENNISON.

DISLEY,

    CHESHIRE.

    August 1937.

INTRODUCTION

"IT cheers me to look at them," says Penelope in Homer of her geese ; and it is with that kind of interest in animals among the Greeks and Romans (principally the latter) that this book is mainly concerned. It is true that in their public entertainments the Romans combined in horrible ways the pleasure of watching wild creatures with their pleasure in spectacles of killing and torture. But even the " hunts " of the arena owed much of their attractiveness to the fascination of watching animals in swift and spirited activity ; and of course there is plenty of evidence that the Romans were as fond as other people of keeping animals as pets, or of just looking at them, without enjoyment of their agonies or of human agony. Penelope, again, no doubt had mixed motives in keeping geese ; and animals might be kept partly for their beauty or quaintness or affectionate ways, and partly for sale or for the owner's table, or for the sport that they showed, or for destroying vermin, or for the interest in breeding them and pride in their pedigrees.

Of animals kept for pleasure or shown at entertainments, those that were exotic for Greeks or Romans will be specially noticed in this book. And the term " exotic " covers both those that were not bred in the lands where they were owned or exhibited, and those that were bred there, but were of kinds recognized as being of foreign extraction. Something, too, will be said of the means of providing for this pleasure in watching animals.

The history of shows or collections of exotic beasts and birds in the Hellenic world or in Roman Italy naturally reflects in

I

some degree the history of Greek and Roman expansion and imperialism ; and the Roman animal-shows mirror something of the constitutional history of the Roman state, and at times the personal characters of individuals who ruled it. Some illustrations of this may be reviewed together here, though most of them will be mentioned separately in the different chapters of this book.

To the free city-states of Greece contacts with Asia and Africa brought some kinds of foreign animals, mostly birds. But it was only after the conquests of Alexander, and in one of the Hellenistic monarchies which arose out of his empire, that a very notable collection of animals was formed in the Greek world. This was the royal collection in Ptolemaic Egypt, gathered, it would seem, for the most part from Ethiopia and North Africa and from Syria and Northern Arabia. At Alexandria, moreover, there was a remarkable development of the Greek custom of making wild animals form part of processions in honour of Artemis or Dionysus. Religious processions were one of the chief forms of public entertainment among the Greeks ; and Ptolemaic ceremonies of this kind may have been influenced by Indian and native Egyptian pageantry. We have a record of an elaborate and varied zoological display in a procession at Alexandria under Ptolemy II. That we do not hear of any such collection owned by Seleucid kings, is perhaps due in part to the fact that the line of Seleucus, though an active, intelligent race, had on the whole less intellectual curiosity than the Ptolemies, the patrons of the Museum at Alexandria, and in part to the fact that the Seleucids, with their harassing work of trying to maintain their authority in their wide and heterogeneous dominions, had less money to spare for such things than had the rulers of the very rich and sheltered Egypt. The Seleucids kept war-elephants, which could be used for spectacular purposes ; and no doubt they were interested in the stocking of their hunting parks, and sometimes owned strange animals sent to them as curiosities, so that Seleucus I could give a tiger to the people of Athens. In 165 B.C. the Seleucid Antiochus IV gave *venationes* (spectacles of killing wild animals) on the Roman model at Antioch—an event at once significant of that king's eccentric taste for the externals of life at Rome where he had lived as a hostage, and symbolic of the new Roman supremacy over the eastern part of the Mediterranean world. On the other hand, in their animal shows the Romans seem to have added something of the Greek procession (πομπή, *pompa*) to the *venatio*. The shows of Alexandria probably had much influence on the elaboration of those of Rome.

As the wonderful display of exotic animals given by Ptolemy II was probably derived originally from modest exhibitions of local wild creatures at religious ceremonies in small Greek states or in Macedon, so the great animal-shows of Imperial Rome seem to have had their origin in the " hunting " of animals of the Latin countryside in the Circus Maximus at such festivals as the Floralia. The extraordinary development of the Roman taste for bloody spectacles may have been due, at first, partly to the unfortunate accident of the example of Etruria (whence gladiatorial shows were introduced into Rome), and partly to a self-conscious idea that such sights were right and proper for a martial people. But when this development had once begun, it continued because the nobles were competitively interested in pleasing the public which could elect them to magistracies, and also because it might be taken as a distinction in itself, or a point of *dignitas*, to outdo others, or not to be outdone, in the entertainments which one gave one's fellow-citizens ; while an expanding empire was furnishing the means of appealing to the public taste in novel ways, and the aristocracy could use the " patronage " (*patrocinium*) which it exercised over the more or less subject allies of Rome to induce them to contribute to the entertainment of the Roman People. In this way it came about that in the *venationes* of the Roman Circus foreign animals were seen more and more frequently from the end of the third century B.C., especially " African beasts," a term which came to mean " lions and leopards," or " leopards," or " leopards and other *variæ*, i.e. large spotted or striped beasts." The nearness of Africa to Italy, and the

B

fact that in the second century Rome was the dominant power in North African lands which were swarming with big game, had much to do with the history of the Roman animal-shows.

In the second century the Roman Senate, as a body led by conservative Elder Statesmen, made attempts to check the exploitation of Rome's imperial position by Roman individuals or classes. And this attitude of the Senate is reflected in a decree forbidding the importation of African beasts into Italy. But again, that this attitude could only delay for a time the tendencies to which it was opposed, is illustrated by the fact that the decree of the Senate here mentioned was overridden by a law, which a tribune carried in the Assembly of the Plebs, allowing the import of African beasts for shows in the Circus at Rome ; and probably that limitation was itself soon disregarded.

In the first century B.C. the transition from the aristocratic Roman Republic, with its weakly organized central government, to the strong central power of the early imperial age was marked by the rise of ambitious individuals, who aspired to win military successes and have power and influence in the State on a scale far greater than was possible for the ordinary noble whose offices and commands came to him in the regular working of the constitution. Thus it was that Pompey in 55 B.C. undertook to entertain the Roman People in a manner corresponding to his position as a Colossus of the Roman world, and his Games included an unprecedented show of animals, with many elephants, and hundreds of lions and leopards, and strange beasts never before seen at Rome. Cæsar, too, had to entertain the Roman public in ways that should express that he was Cæsar and unique ; and when his ambition had brought him to the attempt to found a monarchy in the Roman state, there was not only the general magnificence of the shows at his triumphs, but there was also, in particular, the escort of torch-bearing elephants for the Dictator, such as had accompanied Seleucid kings. And characteristic, perhaps, of Pompey was the failure in imagination that allowed elephants to be slaughtered at his Games in a way that shocked even Roman spectators ; and characteristic of Cæsar was the interest in technical skill that exhibited in the Circus fights of horse, foot and elephants in different combinations of those arms, and gave Rome its first spectacle of Thessalian bull-fighting.

Meanwhile, in the last half-century of the Republic, when the exploitation by the Italians of their Empire had become fast and furious, and at the same time Greek influences in arts, crafts and ideas were working strongly and widely in Roman society, it became fashionable to spend part of a fortune made out of the Empire on aviaries, fishponds, small parks stocked with wild animals for the pleasure of looking at them, and other devices of the sort ; and here the Greek names for such things in Varro's *De Re Rustica* are signs of the reception of Greek technique.

Of Augustus, who brought the Roman world out of wild disorder to stability, it may be reasonably supposed that he would not have appeared in public, as did his rival Antony, in a car drawn by lions with a courtesan at his side. But the summary which he left behind him of his *Res Gestæ* shows that he, like the great men of the preceding age, took a deep satisfaction in breaking records ; and he thought it worth while to tell posterity that he had given the Roman People, in his own name, or in the names of his sons or grandsons, twenty-six *venationes* of African beasts, with a total of about 3,500 animals of that class killed. The spirit of the average Italian, which was so strong in Augustus, and helped him so much in his work, came out in his sympathy with the popular taste for spectacles ; and he was careful to let the public see the strange animals that came to him from far countries, as gifts from Asiatic or African rulers who had heard of a new great potentate among the kings of the earth. In contrast with this spirit in Augustus was the irritable rationality of Tiberius, which made him abstain, when Emperor, from providing in any notable way for the people's fondness for shows.

How different Emperors after Tiberius sought popularity or their own amusement, or tried to express the magnificence of their rule or of their victories, or the greatness of the Empire, in the *venationes* and other animal-shows which they exhibited at Rome, will be noticed elsewhere.   In general it may be said that such displays were manifestations of the principle that the urban masses of the Empire should be provided with amenities of life at the expense of the imperial government or of the rich, while the entertainment of the public in the city of Rome with animals brought from different parts of the Empire, and sometimes from beyond its borders, was symbolic of the idea that the Empire was in the last resort the Empire of the Roman People.   The members of the senatorial aristocracy had still to celebrate *ludi* when holding the offices that bore at any rate the names of old Republican magistracies.   But in the earlier part of the imperial age, after the reign of Tiberius, the Emperors were naturally the principal providers of this sort of entertainment.   The capture of certain animals (elephants and lions are known instances) without imperial licence came to be prohibited.   Later, when Rome was no longer a place of permanent imperial residence, and less could be spared from imperial resources for the pleasures of the Roman populace, the burden fell more on rich nobles like Symmachus, though a visiting Emperor, or a military chief like Stilicho when invested with the consulship, might sustain it now and then.

In some ways the Roman Empire only elaborated the barbarity of the earlier Roman temper ; and the practice of collecting great numbers of animals in order to make their slaughter a spectacle still continued, and culminated in the killing of 11,000 beasts at Rome when Trajan celebrated his conquest of Dacia.[1]   Perhaps it may be said that the civilization of the Empire is rather to be seen in the multiplying of novel performances by tamed and trained animals ; but in the course of their training these creatures must often have suffered much. And again there were the spectacles of criminals thrown to the beasts, sometimes with extreme refinements of cruelty.   It will be remembered that the conflict between the Empire and the Church was partly fought out in the arena.

But one may find in the *venationes* an interest which is not

[1] But see chapter XIII.

painful by noting the kinds of animals that appear in them. While Africa and the East were still drawn upon for the Roman shows, and new kinds of exotic animals were imported from those regions (for example, tigers from India or Northern Persia, which were not seen at Rome under the Republic, and zebras which came in the reign of Septimius Severus), lions and leopards are rarely recorded in large numbers after the reign of Nero, though lack of specification may partly account for this ; Numidian bears are seldom mentioned, while the extension of Roman power in Europe had the effect of making brown bears more common in the Roman arena (possibly on one occasion polar bears were seen there), and elk and aurochs were sometimes shown. The continual hunting of destructive animals, such as leopards, for these displays may have benefited some parts of the Empire, as, according to Strabo, it made it easier for the Numidians to turn from a nomad life to agriculture.

Emperors and wealthy men owned collections of exotic animals ; in the grounds of his Golden House at Rome Nero kept animals—*pecudes* and *feræ*—" of every kind," as Suetonius puts it. There was a fashion of keeping tame lions or bears. One might own a pet (a parrot, for instance) that was the sign of trade with far-distant lands. Foreign kinds of birds that had first been bred in Roman Italy in the last age of the Republic were bred there more commonly now, and others began to be bred there. By the end of the first century A.D. one might see on an Italian farm peacocks, flamingoes, guinea fowl, and pheasants. And it was in Roman times, apparently, that the cat became a common domestic animal in Western Europe. The Roman Empire was the cause of some permanent changes in the distribution of birds and beasts.

A general comparison of Greco-Roman with modern methods in the capture, care, and training of wild animals is made difficult by the scantiness of our information on ancient technique in these arts, of which (as Sir Thomas Browne said about " quincuncial ordination ") " the Ancients practised much, discoursed little."

It may be noticed that the means of killing wild animals have changed far more than the means of taking them alive. The resources of the modern trapper do not include any that differ so much in effectiveness from the pits, nets, lassoes, the corrals, huts and boxes of ancient times,[1] as the rifle differs from the bow or the hunting-spear. And the ancients had the advantage, that more time could then be spent on the capture of wild animals than can be given to it now by those who go on expeditions for the purpose to remote parts of the earth.

In the transport of captive animals the slow rate of progress in ancient times may have been compensated by roomier cages than would now be thought necessary. But though something larger than the modern " travelling box " might be required, it is to be remembered that narrow quarters with change of scene and the incidents of a journey to keep an animal alert are better for it than a spacious prison with monotony.[2] On the other hand, under ancient conditions the conveyance of animals to Rome might be interrupted by a stop at one place lasting weeks or months. Probably the wastage of animal life during transport was greater than at present, even when communications in the Roman Empire were at their best ; it was certainly very great at the end of the fourth century A.D., when Symmachus was collecting animals for shows at Rome.

As regards the duration of life among wild animals kept as pets or curiosities, we have not the means of comparing the state of things in Roman Italy with that in modern England or Europe. There was certainly a great deal of taming and training of wild beasts in Italy under the Empire, both for public shows, and for the private entertainment of wealthy owners ; and

[1] Traps for wild animals are shown in the wall-paintings of palæolithic peoples, and plans duly oriented for drives on a large scale to the death-pits and palisaded enclosures. Nets were used in Egypt some thousands of years before Christ.

[2] For newly caught animals, if they were such as the Romans called *bestiæ dentatæ*, cages with iron bars would have been worse than useless ; the beasts would have broken their teeth on the bars and become battered wrecks.

trained animals might be expected to live longer than others owing to their having a more occupied life and receiving special care. Keepers and trainers (*magistri*) were probably often slaves, or, if free, foreigners. In the first and second centuries A.D. the *amphitheatrales magistri* at Rome may have been the leading lights of the profession ; but the traditions of their art probably came largely from the Greek world, and perhaps particularly from Alexandria.[1] The results obtained by the *magistri* of Roman times seem to have been on the whole neither more nor less remarkable than those achieved by modern European trainers. How ancient and modern methods of training would compare in point of severity cannot be told ; but in the ancient world there was no Society for the Prevention of Cruelty to Animals.[2]

[1] There was a famous native Italian " school " of snake-charming among the Marsi of the Abruzzi. It has been immortalized by Virgil (*Æn.*, VII, 750–60).

[2] Starvation and the whip are mentioned by Philo (*De Animalibus*, 90).

A WATER TRAP (*see p.* 145)

CHAPTER I

TAMED ANIMALS OF THE CITY-STATES
OF GREECE

THE commercial activity of the Greeks, their settlement in countries far from the Greek peninsula, and the lively curiosity of their minds, may seem to have been conditions favourable to the growth of large collections of exotic animals in the city-states of Greece. But, on the whole, these cities had neither the wealth, nor the imperial power over other lands, required for making such collections. And as gladiatorial shows were an Italian, not a Greek, institution, so the Greeks had not the Roman taste for watching wild beasts being killed in large numbers, though bull-fighting was a Thessalian sport, and cock-fighting and quail-fighting were popular in the Greek world.

But it was common enough among the Greeks to keep or make gifts of animals that could be treated as pets or be admired for their beauty ; and some of these, as the monkey and the peacock, were of exotic origin. Animals of imported kinds might be owned by temples or bred for pleasure or profit by private persons. Wild creatures, native or foreign, were exhibited by showmen or were to be seen in processions at religious festivals. There are (as might be expected) traces in Greek literature and science of close and sympathetic observation of animals, and some indications of skill in taming and training them. It is clear that Roman Italy, particularly in the last age of the Republic, was indebted to the Greeks (and not only to the Hellenistic monarchies, but also to the Greek city-states) both for new breeds of animals and for new methods in the care of them.

Pigeon-keeping in Greece, though it probably had its native origins, may have been considerably influenced by Asiatic methods and breeds. Thus the older Greek word for the house-pigeon seems to have been *peleias* (πελειάς, in Homer πέλεια), and this was also the name for the wild rock-dove, from which, presumably, the native domestic breed had been evolved ; but from the fifth century B.C. onwards, though the Dorians continued to call the house-pigeon πελειάς, and this usage had not been entirely dropped among other Greeks, the ordinary Greek word for the domestic pigeon was *peristera* (περιστερά), which, it has been suggested, is derived from the Semitic *perach-Istar*, meaning the bird of Ishtar.[1] White pigeons, according to one account, first came to Greece when birds of that kind escaped from the vessels of the Persian fleet that was wrecked on the promontory of Mount Athos in 492 B.C. White is an artificial colour among pigeons, easily maintained, but still artificial. The Persians, says Herodotus, would not have white pigeons in their own country, associating them with leprosy. But the fleets of the Persian king which were operating in the Ægean in the years before the Battle of Salamis were, of course, drawn from the Asiatic coasts of the Mediterranean. White pigeons had been bred for centuries in Assyria.

Athenæus, IX, 394d

Keller, Antike Tierwelt, II, 122

Athenæus, IX, 394e

Herodotus, I, 138

When the use of the word *peristera* for the house pigeon had become established, the distinction between *peristera* and *peleias* (the wild rock-dove) was drawn thus : " The *peristera* and the *peleias* differ. The *peleias* is the smaller bird, the *peristera* is the more suitable for domesticating (τιθασσὸν γίγνεται μᾶλλον). The *peleias* is dark (μέλαν), small, red-footed and rough-footed ; it is therefore not bred by owners (διὸ καὶ οὐδεὶς τρέφει)." This last statement does not exclude the possibility that the word *peleias* was used for the rock-dove

Aristotle, H.A., V, 544b, 2-5

---

[1] A well-known example of the connection between doves or pigeons and this great goddess, who was worshipped under various names in Western Asia and the Levant, is to be found in the doves of the Paphian Aphrodite.

(*Columba livia*), not only in its wild state, but also when the bird was semi-domesticated, as were the *columbæ saxatiles* of Roman Italy (see p. 104 below). It seems moreover that either of the terms *peristera* and *peleias* might be used generically for pigeon as well as to distinguish a particular species.

The passage quoted above on *peristera* and *peleias* [1] is followed by the statements, that the largest sort of pigeon is the φάττα (in Athenæus it is said to be the size of a bantam), that the second largest is the οἰνάς, which is a little larger than the περιστερά, and that the smallest kind of pigeon is the τρυγών. This would mean that the φάττα was the wood-pigeon (or ring-dove, *Columba palumbus*), and that the οἰνάς was the stock-dove (*Columba œnas*), so named from the wine-colour, the reddish purple, of its breast.[2] The τρυγών was the turtle dove.

Athenæus, IX,
394a

In this review of kinds of pigeon the word φάψ, which was the name of a pigeon of some sort, does not occur. But elsewhere Aristotle says that the οἰνάς is smaller than the φάψ. To reconcile this statement with the assertion that the οἰνάς was next in size to φάττα, the largest sort of pigeon, one would have to suppose that the word φάψ either meant just the same as φάττα or denoted some variety of wood-pigeon. It cannot be made out for certain whether Aristotle did or did not see any difference between φάψ and φάττα ; for though some manuscripts of the *Historia Animalium* make a list of pigeons begin " φάψ, φάττα," the two best manuscripts

Aristotle, *H.A.*,
VIII, 593a, 20

[1] The passage is misrepresented by Athenæus (IX, 394c), who gives it a meaning almost exactly opposite to that which it really bears. The discrepancies between our text of the *H.A.* and the account in Athenæus of what Aristotle says about pigeons may be due partly to careless note-taking by or for Athenæus, and partly to his use of a corrupt and interpolated copy of Aristotle's work.

[2] Ælian, after wrongly reporting Aristotle as saying that the οἰνάς was larger than the φάττα and smaller than the περιστερά, says that he has heard that at Sparta there were what were called οἰναδοθῆρα (*N.A.*, IV, 58). This apparently means that among the fowlers of Sparta there was a special line in taking οἰνάδες. That the οἰνάς was a favourite quarry with Greek fowlers is suggested by the remarks in *H.A.*, VIII, 539a, 18–22, on when and how it was taken.

omit φάψ here ; and no explicit comparison or contrast between φάψ and φάττα is anywhere drawn by him.

The use of pigeons as messengers does not seem to have been a very ordinary practice among the Greeks, but it was not quite unknown to them. A certain Taurosthenes of Ægina is said to have dispatched a pigeon from Elis to carry to his home the news of his victory at the Olympic Games ; and that he could draw on some experience of sending messages in this way is suggested by the detail that he chose for his purpose a hen bird taken from her callow brood. The most important pigeon-races to-day are commonly won by hens whose owners are careful that the birds should be sitting when the time comes for them to be packed for a race. They are far keener to return home than the cock birds, and far more reliable.

Ælian, Var. Hist., IX, 2

A pigeon-shooting contest is an event in the games at the funeral of Patroclus in the *Iliad*, the target being a τρήρων πέλεια tied by the leg, at the end of a cord, to a mast.[1]

Iliad, XXIII, 850–8

Assyria had been sending to Egypt at least as early as Tuthmosis III tribute in the shape of domestic hens, but whether the breeding of poultry was introduced into Greece from Asia

Radcliffe, Fishing from Earliest Times, p. 354, referring to J.E.A., IX, 1–4

---

[1] There is a curious story in Herodotus (II, 55–7), that an Egyptian woman, sold by the Phœnicians into slavery in Thesprotia, established the famous oracle at Dodona, and that from a confused tradition of her at first unintelligible speech had come the tale told by the priestesses at Dodona of a black Egyptian dove, which had flown to their country, and settling on an oak had spoken with a human voice, declaring that there should be an oracle of Zeus in that place. Behind this may lie an ancient belief that the voices of pigeons in the oak-woods of Dodona were prophetically significant, while the Egyptian element in the story may have been due to the arrival from the South every spring of flocks of dark stock-doves. It was told of the temple of Aphrodite at Eryx in Sicily that the pigeons frequenting it were absent for nine days every year, escorting the goddess on a visit which she then made to Africa, and that they were led on their return by a single purple pigeon (Ælian, N.A., IV, 2 ; Athenæus, IX, 394f). Possibly the facts represented here are a movement of pigeons from Eryx *northwards* (not to Africa) in the spring, and the appearance round the temple a few days later of pigeons from Africa with some specimens of the Senegal turtle-dove among them.

before the sixth century B.C. is not known ; there is no allusion to it in Homer or Hesiod.   But in the fifth century poultry-keeping was evidently very common among the Greeks, though at Athens in the time of Aristophanes " Persian bird " was still an ordinary name for the cock.   In particular, cocks were bred for cock-fighting, which was a favourite sport at Athens and elsewhere in the Greek world.   " The cock who fights only at home " (ἐνδομάχας ἀλέκτωρ, contrasted by implication with the bird that is taken out by its owner for matches) appears in an ode of Pindar written about 470.   And cock-fighting scenes were often represented on Athenian vases.   " The Greeks," wrote disapprovingly a Latin authority on agriculture, " trained all their most spirited birds for fights."   Leeks and onions were diet for a fighting-cock.[1]

The Rhodian, Tanagran, and Chalcidian breeds of poultry, and the skill of the Delian poultry-farmers, were specially famous.   In the fourth century B.C., when poultry-keeping had spread far to the west, the " Hadrian " breed of bantams, from the country of the Veneti in the north-east corner of the Italian peninsula, was known in Greece.

The farmyards of Homeric times had their domestic geese.   In the *Odyssey* an eagle flies past the palace of Menelaus at Sparta, carrying in its claws " a tame white goose from a yard " ; and Penelope in Ithaca had a flock of twenty geese, which it comforted her sad soul to watch.   Probably in the fifth century B.C. there was imported the Egyptian goose, which the Greeks called " foxgoose " (*chenalopex*) ; its eggs were thought very good.   Geese as pets were quite common.   Goose-farming

---

[1] In later times there were different versions of a quite unreliable story that the spirit shown by fighting-cocks had been held up as an example to the Greeks by some leader of theirs (Themistocles, according to Ælian ; Miltiades, according to Philo Judæus) in one or other of the Persian invasions: Philo, *Quod omnis probus liber*, 19 ; Ælian, *Var. Hist.*, II, 28.   Ælian says that in memory of this incident there was an annual day of public cock-fighting in the theatre at Athens.   According to Pliny (*N.H.*, X, 21(25), 50) there was in his time a yearly municipal spectacle of cock-fighting (*ceu gladiatorum*) at Pergamum.

was a business in Thessaly ; crane-farming also, probably conjointly worked.¹

It is not clear that any of the kinds of duck kept by the Greeks (νῆττα, mallard, *Anas boscas* ; φαλαρίς, or φαληρίς coot, *Fulica atra* ; βοσκάς, teal, *Querquedula crecca*) was of foreign origin. The duck was associated with Aphrodite ; νησσάριον (" duckie ") was a term of endearment, and figures of ducks ridden by Aphrodite or Eros have been found in Rhodes and Cyprus. Aristotle and Athenæus mention along with the ducks the κολυμβίς, which is probably the black-necked grebe (*Podiceps nigricollis*). A very small bird, a great diver, with eye alert for everything on every side, he is familiar but hard to catch, an ornament to any pond.

African guinea-fowl (μελεαγρίδες) were introduced into Greece perhaps in the fifth century B.C. They somehow became connected with Meleager, whether because the Greeks had found them associated in Africa with the Phœnician god, Melkarth, or by a corruption of μελαναργίδες, the " black-and-white " or " speckled " birds. They were kept at the shrine of Meleager in Ætolia,² and perhaps (as one Greek writer suggested) it was mainly from there that they spread to other parts of Greece. In the second century A.D. they were evidently much kept in Phocis, not far east of Ætolia, for geese and guineafowl are mentioned together as offered by the poorer sort of worshippers at a temple of Isis in the Phocian country. A pupil of Aristotle, Clytus of Miletus, introduces an excellent description of the bird by saying that guineafowl were kept on marshy ground near a temple of Artemis on the island of Leros not far from Miletus.

Peafowl were introduced from India into western Asia,³

Aristophanes, *Birds*, 707
Athenæus XII, 519a

Aristotle, *H.A.*, VIII, 593b, 19
Athenæus, IX, 395 cf.

Aristophanes, *Birds*, 565
Plutus, 1011, Menander, *Incert.*, 422.
Keller, *A.T.*, II, 229–30

Aristotle, *H.A.*, I, 487a, 23 ;
VIII, 593b, 19
Athenæus, IX, 395d

Keller, *A.T.*, II, 154

Athenæus, XIV, 655a

Pausanias, X, 32, 9

Athenæus, XIV, 655 c–f

---

¹ Plato, *Politicus*, 264c.

² As *meleagrides* were said to fight at the tomb of Meleager (for that seems to be Pliny's meaning in *N.H.*, X, 26 (38), 74, though he puts their fighting in Bœotia), so there were birds called *memnonides*, which were said to fly every year from Ethiopia to fight at the tomb of Memnon at Ilium (Pliny, *ibid.*, 26 (37), 74). These latter were probably ruffs (*Machetes pugnax*).

³ Solomon's " apes and peacocks " will be remembered.

Athenæus,
XIV, 655a,

and thence, at an unknown date, were brought to the temple of
Hera at Samos, where they were kept as the sacred birds of
the goddess. It was probably from Samos that peafowl were
first imported into Athens, about 450 B.C., perhaps by a certain
Pyrilampes. At any rate, thirty years later they were being
bred there by Demos the son of Pyrilampes, and were being

Athenæus,
IX, 397c
Ælian, N.A.,
V, 21
Keller, A.T.,
II, 149

exhibited to the public, on payment of an entrance fee, at the
New Moon—that is, on Hera's day. Visitors from other parts
of Greece were curious to see them, and purchased their eggs.
At first a pair of birds for breeding could be sold at Athens for
10,000 *drachmæ*, or about £330. But a comic poet of the fourth

Athenæus,
XIV, 654e

century says, with humorous exaggeration,

> Once a single pair of peafowl some one brought into this city,
> As a rarity and wonder ; now they're commoner than quails.

This poet, Antiphanes, has other lines on the peacock :

Athenæus,
XIV, 655b

> Far off, men say, in a city of the Sun
> Are phœnix birds, at Athens owls ; the isle
> Of Cyprus has the loveliest doves ; and Hera
> In Samos has the golden kind of bird,
> The peacock that we gaze on for its beauty.

Athenæus,
II, 58b

Peafowls' eggs were thought good eating. But it does not
seem that the birds themselves became a fashionably expensive
food among the Greeks as they afterwards were at Rome.

The pheasant—φασιανός or φασιανικός, the bird from the

Aristophanes,
Birds, 68
Athenæus,
IX, 387b

country about the river Phasis at the south-eastern corner of
the Black Sea—was known at Athens in the time of Aristophanes,
and might be served as a rare dish at a fourth-century Athenian

Aristotle, *H.A.*,
V, 557a, 12 ;
VI, 559a, 25 ;
Pseud.Ar.,*H.A.*,
IX, 633b, 2

dinner-party. But it remained a rarity. Aristotle knew something of the bird's habits and of the appearance of its eggs, but
it may be noticed that in the first of the passages in the *Historia
Animalium* where pheasants are mentioned, they are referred
to (in a way suggesting that they were not familiar to the
Greeks) as " the so-called Phasis-birds " (οἱ καλούμενοι
φασιανοί). Of pheasant-breeding in Ptolemaic Egypt something will be said in the next chapter.

Aristophanes,
Acharnians, 875
Athenæus, IX,
387f–388b

The *attagen* (francolin) which was found in Boeotia and
elsewhere in Greece in the time of Aristophanes, and had a

reputation as good eating, had perhaps been introduced, with its foreign-sounding name, from Asia Minor.

The flamingo, which the Greeks called "scarlet-wing" (φοινικόπτερος) is mentioned as a rarity by Aristophanes— "not one of the birds you ordinarily see," the Hoopoe says of it, speaking to two Athenians in the *Birds*. Probably Aristophanes, who dressed one of his Chorus in the *Birds* to represent a flamingo, had seen specimens brought to Athens from North Africa or the Western Mediterranean. He knew that it was a marsh-bird, and speaks of its lovely bright red colour. He makes it say "Tŏrŏtix tŏrŏtix," and had heard it therefore, though these birds, which often pass over Rome, rarely go as far east as Athens.

Aristophanes, *Birds*, 267–73

The Greeks came to know the African purple galinule, which they called *porphyrion*, and probably kept for its beauty, as it was kept later in Roman Italy. They noted the bird's dislike of being watched while it fed, its way of walking round before feeding, its habit of holding its food in its claw while it ate, and its fondness for dust baths. The story that it would hang itself if the mistress of the house where it was kept committed adultery, may have had its origin in the shyness of the bird, which might easily become wild and injure itself in the presence of a stranger.[1]

Athenæus, IX 388 c–d Ælian, *N.A.*, III, 42

So far as is known, the parrot (ψιττακός) was not seen in the

---

[1] Athenæus (IX, 388d) quotes Callimachus as distinguishing the *porphyrion* from the *porphyris*. But it seems possible that the word *porphyrion*, though it came to be reserved for the purple galinule, was originally used as the masculine form of *porphyris*, which was the name of a bird that was probably the common waterhen. Athenæus (IX, 388e) quotes allusions to the *porphyris* or *lathiporphyris* ("the porphyris that avoids notice") from Ibycus, an Italo-Greek poet of the sixth century B.C. Possibly by *porphyris* Ibycus meant the waterhen, and by *lathiporphyris* the purple galinule. In Aristophanes *porphyris* appears in a list of birds, and *porphyrion*, in another passage, as a bird that would be a suitable present for a boy (*Birds*, 304, 707). Aristotle (*H.A.*, VIII, 595a, 13) says that the *porphyrion* is the only bird that drinks κάψει, by pecking—*morsu*, as Pliny translates it (*N.H.*, X, 46(63), 129). But this applies both to the purple galinule and to the waterhen.

Hellenic world till after Alexander's invasion of India, though before that time readers of the work of Ctesias, who had been physician at the court of Persia in the last years of the fifth century B.C., would have learnt that there was an Indian bird called βιττακός, which had a human tongue and voice.[1] One of Alexander's officers, Nearchus, brought some live parrots to the West, and there were parrots among the exotic birds in the great procession at Alexandria organized by Ptolemy Philadelphus.

Among the wild birds of Greece that might be kept in captivity, and tamed and trained in one way or another, were quails (ὄρτυγες), which were kept for quail-fighting. There was also the game of quail-knocking, in which the quail's owner betted that it could not be made by taps on the head to leave a circle in which it had been placed. The well-known tale may be recalled, how Alcibiades addressed the Athenian Assembly with a quail under his arm, how it escaped, and how his audience went running after it for him.

Cranes were sometimes treated as pets, and so were sparrows ; and nightingales, blackbirds, pies, starlings, and so on, were no doubt often kept for their singing or " talking," as they were in Roman Italy. From Aristophanes we learn that a live chough (κολοιός) could be bought in the Athenian market for an obol, a crow (κορώνη) for three times that price.[2]

[1] The notice in Aristotle's *Historia Animalium* (VIII, 597b, 26–9) of the Indian ψιττακή, or " so-called human-tongued bird," belongs to a passage which is thought to be an interpolation in the text.

[2] The following notes on birds may be added :

(a) The *malacocraneus* described in Pseudo-Aristotle, *Historia Animalium*, IX, 617a 32–b5 may be identified, by its habit of perching " always in the same place," as the ortolan bunting.

(b) The κίγκλος of Pseudo-Aristotle, *H.A.*, IX, 615a, 21–4—a bird that is hard to catch, but easy to tame, and is as it were lame, having weak hinder parts—is the little dabchick, *podiceps ruficollis*. Its name, κίγκλος, was used as a slang word for a tramp, a good comparison, for the bird is a shuffling, stumbling, dejected-looking thing, and has no apparent home.

(c) The story in Ælian, *N.A.*, VI, 29, of the devotion of a tame eagle to a sick boy, who had owned and tended it since it was an

Arrian, *Ind.*, I, 15, 8
Ctes. *Ind.*, 3, ap. Photium

Nearchus, fr. 13
Athenæus, V, 201b

Aristophanes, *Birds*, 1298–9
Keller, *A.T.*, II, 163–4

Plutarch, *Alcibiades*, 10

Keller, *A.T.*, II, 186 (cp. 164, Fig. 47)
Athenæus, XII, 519a

Aristophanes, *Birds*, 17–18 (cp. 5)

Ælian, *N.A.*, XII, 9

The Greek types of hound, sheepdog and watchdog which were imported into Italy will be noticed in chapter VIII. No doubt in most substantial Greek households, in the town as well as in the country, there would be the large watchdog (οἰκουρός), which might be of a kind that was also used for shepherding, like the house-dog in the *Wasps* of Aristophanes. But small pet dogs (κυνάρια or κυνίδια) were also common.[1] They were often, it would seem, of a Maltese kind, with a long silky white coat. In a pseudo-Aristotelian passage of the *Historia Animalium*, it is said that the marten is the size of the smaller sort of Maltese dog (τὸ μέγεθος ἡλίκον Μελιταῖον κυνίδιον τῶν μικρῶν).

The weasel (γαλέη, γαλῆ) is usually said to have been kept in Greek houses for the destruction of vermin. But I have never heard of domesticated weasels ; and the γαλῆ in houses was probably the polecat (*Mustela putorius*), which in a domesticated state is the ferret. The αἴλουρος brought to market at Athens by the Boeotian in the *Acharnians* of Aristophanes, and mentioned by Aristotle, was probably the pine marten (*Mustela martes*). The ἴκτις, which was also on the Boeotian's list, and is described in the *Historia Animalium*, was the beech or stone marten (*Mustela fovina*). These animals would be valuable as pelts.

The name αἴλουρος (perhaps " wavetail ") was moreover given by the Greeks to the foreign animal the cat, which was generally rare in the Mediterranean world outside Egypt before the Roman imperial age. But vase-paintings supply evidence that it was kept in Greek cities of South Italy about the end of the fifth century B.C.

Margin notes:
Aristophanes, *Wasps*, 955–8
Keller, *A.T.*, I, 92–4
Pseudo-Aristotle, *H.A.*, 612b, 10–11
Ælian, *N.A.*, VII, 40

Theocritus, *ib.*, XV, 27–8

Acharnians, 879–80
Aristotle, *H.A.*, VI, 580a, 24–7
Ps.-Aristotle, *H.A.*, IX, 612b, 10–17

Herodotus, II, 66

Keller, *A.T.*, I, 77–8

eaglet, may be true, and the crowning touch, that when the boy died the bird threw itself into the flames of the funeral pyre, may record a fact. Birds do not know the danger of fire, and in bright daylight would not notice flames. In the late war our messenger pigeons homed into cotes blazing from shell-fire.

For a very exhaustive list of references to the birds of Greece the reader is referred to *Glossary of Greek Birds*, D'Arcy W. Thompson, Clarendon Press, Oxford.

[1] In St. Matthew xv. 27, the dogs that eat of the crumbs which fall from their masters' table are " the little dogs " (τὰ κυνάρια).

Harmless snakes might be kept in houses to destroy vermin, and their presence seems to have been felt as a kind of embodiment of the continuity of the family and as suggesting the presence of its dead. They were also kept in temples and used in mystery-rites. With Æsculapius, the god of healing, was associated, particularly at Epidaurus, the yellow *Coluber Æsculapii* or *flavescens*. And there is the well-known story in Herodotus, that in the temple of Athene on the acropolis at Athens was the " guardian " of the place, " a great snake," which was regularly fed with honey cakes, and that when Athens was being evacuated at the time of the invasion of Xerxes, the snake's honey-cake was left untouched, which was taken as a sign that the goddess herself had departed from the Acropolis, accompanying her people. Probably the rodents that usually ate the cakes had migrated, driven out by stress of hunger, and the snakes had followed them. I have kept very many snakes, nor ever knew one to eat cakes or drink milk.

The author of the ninth book of the Aristotelian *Historia Animalium* mentions incidentally " the hedgehogs kept in houses " as changing their positions with a change of wind.

Monkeys from North Africa were probably to be found in Greece from the seventh century B.C., if not from an earlier time. Semonides of Amorgus (*circa* 630 B.C.) says that the ugly, malicious, intelligent type of woman has the mind of a monkey. They became very common as pets. In a play of Eubulus, an Athenian comic writer of the fourth century, a character says, how much better it is for a human being to nurture another human being than to make a pet of a goose, a sparrow, or a mischievous monkey : its echo sounds in Rome after five hundred years.

The kind of monkey usually kept in Greece was no doubt that which is the only one fully described by Aristotle—the tailless barbary ape (*Macacus inuus*).[1] He calls it the πίθηκος,

Pausanias, II, 28, 1

Herodotus, VIII, 41

Pseudo-Aristotle, *H.A.*, IX, 612b, 7

Archilochus, 96 (in *Anthologia Græca*, ed. Hiller-Crusius) Semonides, 7, 71–82 (*ibid.*)

Athenæus, XII, 519a

Martial, VII, 87

Aristotle, *H.A.*, II, 502a, 16–b, 26

Bury, *History of Greece*, 2nd edition, p. 117. Vase of Arcesilas II

---

[1] This tailless ape, the Barbary Ape of naturalists (*Macacus inuus*), appears as a tame specimen on a ship at Cyrene *circa* 560 B.C. There are also Egyptian kites and apparently a tame cat, the Caffra Cat (*Felis caffra*) which is the supposed progenitor of our domestic cat.

and mentions two other kinds, the κυνοκέφαλος and the κῆβος. Of the κυνοκέφαλος (baboon) he says that it is larger, stronger, and fiercer than the πίθηκος, with face and teeth more like those of a dog. It is possible that he had not himself seen a baboon, and was drawing on descriptions of it. Of the κῆβος he only says that it has a tail. He may have used the term in the general way in which κερκοπίθηκος seems to have been afterwards used for tailed African monkeys. Later the name κῆβος or κῆπος seems to have been applied especially to the *Cercopithecus pyrrhonotus* (nisnas guenon or keb) of North-East Africa (see pp. 36, 55).

Towards the end of the fourth century B.C. Theophrastus writes as if it was the fashion to own a monkey which he calls a tityrus. The tityrus is shown on a vase as a thin tall tail-less monkey. The face is long and narrow, quite unlike that of any man-monkey, but as it is roughened on the cheeks and chin with a suspicion of a beard, the animal represented may be the orang utan from India, but not the chimpanzee, which never has hair on the chin. The chimpanzee was nearer to Greece, on the Upper Nile, but though reports of that monkey seem to have reached the Greco-Roman world in the form of stories about " satyrs," there is no evidence that specimens were brought down to the Mediterranean.[1] However, as tityrus monkeys are not mentioned again, it seems that the exceptional accident of Greek domination in India had caused traders to bring a caravan-load of them (whatever they were) to Greece. In 1928 a drought led to the capture of a large number of orang utans, which were sold at exceptionally low prices.

The harmless wild animals of the Greek country-side, and also the young of kinds which were not harmless when full-grown, were no doubt often taken alive to be kept as pets, and

Theophrastus, *Characters*, V, 9

Daremberg et Saglio, *Dictionnaire d' Antiquités*, s.v. *Bestiæ immanes*

Philostratus, *Apollonius of Tyana*, VI, 27, 241–2 Pliny, *N.H.*, V, 8 (8), 44 ; 46

---

[1] The story in Philostratus is of a satyr in the Nile country above the third cataract. It attacked women and was caught with wine. Man-like apes, and indeed all monkeys, are very fond of fermented liquors, and the story of monkeys raping women is a commonplace all across Africa to this day.

Theocritus,
XI, 40-1

especially as pets for boys and girls.   The eleven fawns and four bearcubs which the Cyclops is keeping for Galatea in the Idyll of Theocritus are, of course, a present on a Cyclopean scale.

Isocrates,
Antidosis, 213

Dancing bears were exhibited by showmen in fourth century Greece.   It has been noticed that in Xenophon's treatise on the chase there are directions for hunting the hare, deer, and

Xenophon,
Cynegetica,
II, I

boar, but not the bear, which is referred to only in a list of animals that might be found on one or other of a number of mountain ranges ἐν ξέναις χώραις—in foreign lands—the nearest range mentioned being that of Pindus, west of the Thessalian plain.   It has been inferred that in the fourth century B.C. there were no longer bears to be hunted in Attica or the Peloponnese.   But Xenophon does not mention wolf-hunting in his treatise ; and it is surely very unlikely that there were no more wolves in his day in the highlands of Southern Greece, or that no one hunted the wolves that there were. Pausanias, writing in the second century A.D., mentions bears

Pausanias, I,
32, I ; III, 20,
5 ; VIII, 23, 6

among the animals to be found on Mount Parnes in Attica, on Mount Taygetus between Laconia and Messenia, and in Arcadia.[1]   It is possible that there were more bears then in Greece than in the time of Xenophon, owing to the decline in the numbers and prosperity of the human population of the country.[2]

[1] To the imaginations of the Greeks of historical times, Arcadia had once been pre-eminently a country of the bear and the wolf. They thought of its name as meaning the bear-land, and there were the legends of how Callisto was changed into a bear and hunted by her son Arcas, and of the werewolf Lycaon.   So in the tales of the early wars between the Spartans and Messenians the Arcadian high-landers were imagined as clothed in the skins of wolves and bears (Pausanias, IV, II, I).

The girls who took part in the rites of the festival of Artemis of Brauron in Attica wore saffron robes and were apparently called " bears " (Aristophanes, *Lysistrata*, 645).   Possibly the saffron robe was here meant to imitate the straw colour of one variety of Greek bear.   Pausanias mentions "white" Thracian bears " which, he says, some people kept in his day (VIII, 17, 3).

[2] Aldrovandus, writing in the seventeenth century, says that Crete and England alone are without bears.

When it was that the lion disappeared from Southern and Central Greece, or whether there had ever been lions in the Peloponnese, cannot be told. To argue from the Nemean lion slain by Heracles would be rash ; and the representations of lions in Mycenæan art do not prove that the Peloponnese was then itself a lion-country. It is also uncertain in what regions of Greece or of the western coastland of Asia Minor men had the experiences that lie behind the references to lions in the Homeric poems. When Herodotus has told the story that lions attacked the camels [1] of the baggage-train of the army of Xerxes when it was passing through Macedonia, he takes the opportunity to remark that lions are not found in Europe except between the River Nestus, flowing through the territory of Abdera in Thrace, and the Achelous, the chief river of Acarnania, on the west side of Greece, north of the Corinthian Gulf. This statement as to the boundaries of the European lion-country seems to have become a commonplace. It is repeated by Aristotle in the next century. But if there were really lions in this area in the fourth century, they probably disappeared from it soon afterwards. It seems likely that in the first century B.C. there were no more lions in Europe, and few or none in Asia Minor, where in earlier times the lion had been associated with the great goddess Cybele. Cælius Rufus, who appears in Cicero's correspondence as so anxious to get leopards from Southern Asia Minor (see pp. 137– 140 below), does not show any hope of lions from that quarter.[2]

(margin note: Herodotus, VII, 125–6)

(margin note: Aristotle, H.A. VI, 579b, 5–8)

---

[1] There is an Arab saying that lions pray to God for strength before attacking the camel. In Africa lions evince a preference for zebra flesh.

[2] Xenophon (*Cynegetica*, 11, 1) says, " Lions, leopards, lynxes, *panthēres* (see Appendix, p. 184 below), bears, and other such wild beasts are taken in foreign countries, about Mount Pangæus, and Cittus beyond Macedonia, and on the Mysian Olympus, and on Pindus, and on Nysa beyond Syria, and on other mountain-ranges suited to supporting such animals." But though it is likely enough that there were still some lions in Xenophon's day on Pindus and in Macedonia, this passage cannot be adduced as evidence for that. It does not mean that *all* the animals mentioned were to be found on

Isocrates,
Antidosis, 213

Tamed and trained lions were being exhibited in Greece in the fourth century B.C. And in the next century Theocritus

Theocritus, II,
66–8

gives a glimpse of a procession in honour of Artemis with " many wild beasts " in it, " among them a lioness." It is not unlikely that some temples permanently owned a lion or lions.

Aristotle, *H.A.*,
VIII, 606b, 16

" Leopards," says Aristotle, " are natives of Asia, but not of Europe." The correspondence of Cicero shows that in the first century B.C. they were to be found in Southern Asia Minor—in Pamphylia, and the region where Caria, Phrygia,

Iliad, XXI,
573–8

and Lycia met (see pp. 137–140 below). Asiatic Greeks might hunt the leopard—there is a description of such a hunt in the Iliad. To Greece itself the leopard-skin would come by way of trade, and now and then a captive live leopard. The animal was associated in the Greek imagination particularly with Dionysus.

Athenæus,
XIII, 590a

The tiger sent by Seleucus as a present to the people of Athens towards the end of the fourth century was probably the first animal of its kind to be seen in Greece. And possibly no other specimen reached the Ægean area till Augustus received at Samos, in the winter of 20–19 B.C., a present of some tigers from an Indian king (see p. 67 below). The nearest region to Greece where tigers were to be found in ancient times was perhaps Eastern Armenia, about Mount

Virgil, *Ecl.*,
V, 29

Ararat ; the " Armenian tigers " in an Eclogue of Virgil will be remembered. But the two lands generally reputed as tiger-countries were Hyrcania (bordering the southern end of the

Pliny, *N.H.*,
VIII, 18(25), 66

Caspian) and India : *Tigrim Hyrcani et Indi ferunt*, says Pliny. And it is likely enough that the tiger which Seleucus gave to Athens was an Indian beast.

each of the ranges mentioned ; indeed Xenophon, by writing τὰ δ'ἐν τῷ Ὀλύμπῳ τῷ Μυσίῳ καὶ ἐν Πίνδῳ, τά δ' ἐν τῇ Νύσῃ κ.τ.λ., seems to be indicating that he does not mean that. It is most unlikely that there were leopards on Pindus or in Macedonia (see text above). Keller (*Antike Tierwelt*, I, 35) has made a slip in interpreting the passage ; Xenophon does *not* say that beasts caught elsewhere were preserved for hunting on Pindus or Pangæus.

Captive wild animals might be exhibited either in processions at religious festivals, or in the shows called θαύματα (" marvels ") given by animal-trainers. The animal-trainer, again, though he would in any case profess to work, in the Greek phrase, " not without some god," might be more or less of a religious " thaumaturge," or more or less secular in his profession. The ancients were quite as clever as the men of to-day in taming and training animals.

In πομπάι—processions at festivals—wild animals might be carried in cages or have sufficient training to walk quietly or even to draw vehicles. Often—perhaps usually—the processions in which they appeared were in honour of Artemis, the goddess of hunting and of wild creatures. An example has been given already from Theocritus (p. 24 above). In the second century A.D. Pausanias saw at Patræ a " most magnificent " procession, which was a regular feature in a yearly festival of Artemis. A maiden priestess rode at the end of it in a car drawn by stags. To train stags to go in harness would need very great skill. But we do not know for how long this had been done at Patræ before the visit of Pausanias ; the art of animal-training seems to have been much developed in the Greco-Roman world during the first century A.D. Moreover, Patræ had been made by Augustus into a Roman colony, with a population half Italian and half Greek ; and there is perhaps something more Italian than Greek about the ceremony which took place on the day after the procession—the burning alive of a great number of wild animals. Possibly an old local custom had been elaborated in a way that suited Roman taste. Edible birds, says Pausanias, wild boars, stags and roebuck (or perhaps imported gazelles ?—δορκάδες), wolf-cubs and bear-cubs, were driven into the flames. If any of the animals broke away, it was dragged back to the fire ; but no one, it was said, was ever harmed by the frightened beasts. This apparent miracle was due to the stupefying effects of the smoke, which, as I have seen in a fire, deprives animals of their energy.

Exhibitions of tamed wild animals are referred to by Isocrates, writing in the fourth century B.C., in support of his argument

Pausanias, VII, 18, 7

Isocrates, Antidosis, 211, 213

against those who undervalue education. " These men are aware that some people possess the art of training horses and dogs and most other animals, whereby they make some more spirited and others more gentle and others again more intelligent—and yet cannot see that human beings would respond to the same methods. . . . But most absurd of all, they see in the shows (ἐν τοῖς θαύμασι) which are held every year lions which are more gentle towards their tamers than some men are towards their benefactors, and bears which dance about and wrestle and imitate our skill . . . and yet they are not convinced."

Athenæus, XII; 520 c–f

What Isocrates says here about the training of horses may serve as a hint to recall the story, for which Athenæus alleges the authority of Aristotle, that at Sybaris horses were taught to dance to the flute, and that in the war between Sybaris and Croton the Crotoniates threw the cavalry of Sybaris into confusion by playing dance-music to it.[1] A similar anecdote is told of a war between the people of Cardia, a city on the Thracian Chersonese, and the Thracian tribe of the Bisaltæ, the Cardian horses having been trained, it is said, like those of Sybaris. It is possible that these tales have at any rate this foundation in fact, that horses were sometimes trained in this way among the Greeks. Certainly horses captured in battle and used in the opposing army have even in modern times obeyed their well-known trumpet-call despite every effort of their new riders.

The nearest thing to the Roman *venatio*—more or less skilful animal-killing as a spectacle—that the Greeks developed of themselves was apparently bull-fighting, which was practised in Thessaly. How Thessalian bull-fighting came to be exhibited in Rome in the first century B.C. will be noticed later (pp. 56, 59 below). Bull-fighting seems to have been especially popular in the Greek cities of the Roman Empire. Whether there was any historical connection between the sport

Friedländer, *Roman Life and Manners*, Engl. Tr., Vol. II, p. 71, with references to authorities in Vol. IV, pp. 526–7

[1] The horses " not only danced off the field (ἐξωρχήσαντο), but came over (ηὐτομόλησαν) to the Crotoniates, bringing their riders with them."

which the Romans found in Thessaly and the acrobatic tricks played with bulls in Minoan Crete, cannot be told, but it is not at all probable ;   in Crete the display was part of a religious rite. The Greeks of the plain of Thessaly were a people of horse-men, rich in herds ; it was natural that their bull-fighting should become largely a display of mounted cowboys' skill (pp. 59, 69 below). Bull-fighting on foot, with swords and lances, seems also to have been practised under the Roman Empire.

CHAPTER II

ZOOLOGICAL MAGNIFICENCE IN EGYPT
UNDER THE PTOLEMIES

THE conditions of wealth and power that were needed in the ancient world for making large collections of exotic animals were realized in Egypt under the Macedonian dynasty of the Ptolemies, which ruled that country for nearly three centuries between the death of Alexander and its annexation by Rome in 30 B.C. Those conditions were also realized more or less in other Hellenistic monarchies ; and though the Ptolemies could afford to spend more on such objects than other rulers, it may be assumed that they were not the only Hellenistic kings to keep as curiosities animals which were " exotic " at any rate from the Greek point of view.

Cf. Chandragupta;
Strabo,
XV, 1, 69

When Seleucus I presented a tiger to the people of Athens, he may well have kept at least one for himself. But there is a lack of definite evidence of zoological collections in the Hellenistic world outside Egypt. The elephants which were owned by the Seleucid kings and others were of course mainly valued as instruments of war, though they were also used for ceremonial purposes. It may be noticed that at the Games which Antiochus IV of Syria celebrated at Antioch about the year 165 B.C. in imitation of the Roman shows, though besides

Polybius, XXX,
25-6 (XXXI,
3-4)
Athenæus, V,
194c-195c

gladiatorial combats there were " hunts " (that is, displays of killing wild animals like the Roman *venationes*), yet in the procession on the opening day—where a display of zoological curiosities would have been in accordance with ancient custom —the only animals mentioned are elephants, horses, and oxen.

Allowing for the scantiness of our information, one may still

believe that Alexandria usually contained the largest and most
varied zoological collection in the Hellenistic world. For besides wealth and power, and a favourable position for collecting
animals from Africa or Western Asia, the Ptolemies had a   Strabo, XVII,
1, 5
marked family trait of intelligent curiosity, and they were
patrons of science.

Of Ptolemy II (283–246 B.C.) it is expressly recorded that   Diodorus, III,
36, 2–4
he was not only active in organizing the means of obtaining
elephants from Ethiopia, but also paid generously for difficult
captures of other beasts in that region, so that he made the
Greeks acquainted with animals that they had never seen
before, among them the chimpanzee. A gigantic snake,
45 feet long, was brought from the marshes of the Upper
Nile. Moreover, Athenæus has preserved a description (which
will be considered in detail below) of a very remarkable assembly of exotic animals forming part of a great procession
at a festival of Dionysus celebrated by Ptolemy II, probably
at the beginning of his reign. Some of these animals may
have been obtained by Ptolemy I, though the only zoological   Lucian,
Prometh. in
verb., 4
acquisition of that king definitely mentioned in our sources
was a Bactrian camel, perhaps a present from Seleucus.[1]

About the royal zoological collection at Alexandria after the
reign of Ptolemy II we have next to no evidence. Ptolemy III
(246–221 B.C.) was interested, like his father, in ways and means
of obtaining Ethiopian elephants, and he seems to have had
scientific tastes. After the battle of Raphia (217 B.C.), where
the African elephants of Ptolemy IV were badly beaten by the
Indian beasts of the Seleucid Antiochus III, the quest for
Ethiopian elephants seems to have been dropped ; but the
trading-posts which had been founded on the Red Sea coast
in connection with the elephant-hunts still remained. The
loss of Southern Syria under Ptolemy V, about the year 198,
may have made it rather more difficult to obtain Asiatic animals.
At any rate, in the latter half of the second century B.C. there

---

[1] Ptolemy II had been joint-king with his father from 285 to
283 B.C., and may then have been gratifying his taste for natural
history.

Athenæus,
XIV, 654c

was still a collection of animals, perhaps worth calling a zoological garden, at the royal palace at Alexandria, and it was
described by Ptolemy VII ; but all that we have of his description is a note on the pheasants kept there.   The giraffe exhibited at Rome by Cæsar in 46 B.C. presumably came from
Alexandria, and was perhaps a present from Cleopatra.   How
many of the animals killed in the Roman Shows of 29 B.C.,
after the annexation of Egypt, came from the collection of the
Ptolemies—if indeed any did—we do not know ; but it is not
unlikely that the one hippopotamus and the one rhinoceros,

Dio., LI, 22, 5

which are particularly mentioned by Dio as killed on this
occasion, had been taken thence.

Athenæus, V;
198d foll.

We may now return to the animals exhibited at Alexandria
under Ptolemy II.   The great procession already mentioned
took all day to pass through the Stadium of the city ; it was
headed by a representation of the Morning Star, and the
Evening Star came at the end of it.   Only the items of zoological interest concern us here.

After a representation of Dionysus returning from India
came the following animals :

(1) Elephants drawing chariots.   There were twenty-four
chariots with four elephants harnessed to each.   Where did
these beasts come from ?   It is improbable that Ptolemy II
had as yet organized the capture of African elephants from a
base on the Red Sea coast, and their subsequent training ; and
though some of the other animals exhibited on this occasion
certainly came from Ethiopia, it is not likely that he had at
this time as many as ninety-six elephants from that region.   It
seems more likely that they had been acquired with their
mahouts from India by Ptolemy I, and that Seleucus I had
permitted them to pass through his dominions to Egypt.   For
though Seleucus probably felt aggrieved by Ptolemy's occupation of Southern Syria in 301, yet he had owed his life and
his kingdom to the protection and help which he had received
from Ptolemy at an earlier time ; and just as he had not gone
to war with his old friend over Southern Syria, so, even after
301, he may have felt that he could not refuse a request from

Ptolemy for facilities for obtaining Indian elephants, though these were instruments of war. But after the deaths of Seleucus I and Ptolemy I it was the hostility between their successors that made the son and grandson of Ptolemy try to get elephants from Ethiopia. With the ships of the time, it was practically impossible to keep up a considerable force of elephants in Egypt by bringing the animals overseas from India, and there is no evidence that it was ever done by anyone. On the other hand, presumably Carthage would not allow the export of elephants to Egypt from the western half of North Africa.

More will be said later in this chapter about the elephant-hunting for the Ptolemies in Ethiopia, which seems to have begun about 275 B.C. Here it may be noticed that in the middle of the third century Antigonus Gonatas of Macedon alluded to the wealth of Egypt and its " elephants, and processions, and palaces," which, he said, had dazzled the Achæan Aratus.

Tarn,
*Hellenistic
Civilisation,*
2nd edition,
p. 57

Plutarch,
Aratus, 15

(2) Sixty pairs of he-goats, each drawing a chariot.

(3) Twelve pairs of *kōloi*, drawing chariots. The κῶλος may be the κόλος of Strabo, who describes it as between a stag and a ram in size, swifter than either, white in colour, and inhabiting the Scythian and Sarmatian country, north and north-east of the Black Sea. Hesychius says that the κόλος is a large goat without horns. The animal in question is the Saiga antelope (*Saiga tartarica*) obtained through one of the Greek settlements on the northern side of the Black Sea.

Strabo, VII,
4, 8

Cf. Herodotus,
IV, 29

(4) Seven pairs of *oryges*, drawing chariots. These were antelopes, either of the kind now known as *Oryx beisa*, or of that now called the White oryx (*Oryx leucoryx*). Aristotle says that the *oryx* is one-horned, an assertion probably due to reports of persons who had seen *oryges* on which had been practised the trick (known to-day among breeders) of binding together the soft and flexible horns of a young antelope, so that the two should grow into one (see below, p. 78). *Oryges* imported from North Africa were to be seen later in the arenas and parks of Roman Italy in the imperial age. The *Oryx beisa* is now to be found mostly in Abyssinia, but in the third cen-

Aristotle, *H.A.,*
II, 499b, 20

tury B.C. it may not have been uncommon in the deserts adjoining Egypt.

(5) Fifteen pairs of *boubaloi* in harness. The *boubalos* or *boubalis* was an antelope that in some way reminded the Greeks of a cow, and was probably therefore the Tora hartebeest (*Bubalis tora*), one of the many varieties of hartebeest in Africa. These animals could have been got from the deserts near Egypt. Hartebeest were common on the North African littoral until at least the end of the fourth century A.D.

Loisel, Vol. I,
f. p. 96,
Mosaic
" Hunting "
found at
Bona, Algeria,
1909, probable
date A.D. 350

(6) Eight pairs of ostriches in harness. These may have come from North Africa or from the Syrian desert, and the acquisition of them may have been facilitated by Ptolemaic control of the Cyrenaica or of Southern Syria. Xenophon reports that there were many ostriches in the desert on the left or Mesopotamian side of the middle Euphrates, along which the army of Cyrus marched on its way from North Syria to Babylonia. On the ostriches of Cyrenaica in late Roman times see pp. 115–116 below.

Ibid.

Xenophon,
Anabasis, I, 5, 2

(7) Seven pairs of *onelaphoi* in harness. The *onelaphos*, or ass-deer, was a kind of wild ass, and the origin of its name is probably discernible in the passage in which Xenophon describes the hunting of the wild asses which the army of Cyrus found in great numbers in the desert east of the middle Euphrates. These animals were much swifter than the horses of the mounted men of the army who chased them, but some of them were taken by the device of hunting them with parties of horsemen disposed at different points, and their flesh was " like venison " (παραπλήσια τοῖς ἐλαφείοις), but more tender. The *onelaphoi* in this procession are probably the Persian Wild Ass (*Equus asinus persicus*), a regal dish.

Ibid.

(8) Wild asses, drawing four chariots in pairs, and the same number of chariots in teams of four. These asses, of some kind distinguishable from the *onelaphos*, could have been obtained locally in almost any direction.

In each of the chariots drawn by the different animals above-mentioned was a small boy dressed as a charioteer with a small girl at his side.

(9) Six pairs of camels laden with spices. It was apparently Ptolemy II who introduced the camel into Egypt. He furnished with camel-transport the desert route between Coptos on the Nile and the northern Berenice on the Red Sea.

Tarn, *Hellenistic Civilisation,* 2nd edition, p. 159 Strabo, XVII, 1, 45

After these came Ethiopians with 600 tusks of ivory, 2,000 blocks of ebony, gold and silver vessels, and gold dust.

(10) Two thousand four hundred hounds, of Indian, Hyrcanian, Molossian, and other breeds. Indian hounds had been highly valued by the Persians ; four large villages in Babylonia, says Herodotus, were taxed only for the keep of the Indian hounds belonging to the Persian satrap of the country. An Indian king, Sopeithes, had shown Alexander the extraordinary courage of his hounds in a lion-hunt. The temper of the Hyrcanian breed may be judged from the idea in the West that it had a strain of tiger in it. The famous heavily built Molossian breed from Epirus need not be enlarged on here.

Herodotus, 192 Pollux, V, 43 Diodorus, XVII, 92 Strabo, XV, 1, 31 Gratius, 161–70

(11) After the hounds came a hundred and fifty men carrying "trees to which were attached wild animals and birds of all sorts."

(12) There followed cages in which were parrots, peacocks, guinea-fowl, pheasants, and "Ethiopian birds." The first four kinds have been noticed in the preceding chapter. The parrots in the Mediterranean world of the Roman Empire came, or were generally supposed to have come, from India. But it is possible that the parrots in this procession, or some of them, came from Ethiopia. On the peacock, guinea-fowl, and pheasant see pp. 15 and 16 above. In the latter half of the second century B.C. pheasants were kept at the royal palace at Alexandria.[1]

Athenæus, XIV, 654b

---

[1] Ptolemy VII (145–116 B.C.), in his notes on the royal palace at Alexandria and the animals kept there, mentioned " the pheasants called tetaroi," which had been not only procured from Media, but also bred at Alexandria (apparently by some earlier Ptolemy) by putting the eggs under guineafowl (if this is the meaning of νομάδας ὄρνιθας ὑποβαλών ; there would be no point in crossing pheasant with guineafowl), so that a large number of these birds had been raised for food. Ptolemy VII wrote as if the practice was a thing of the past in his time. He added that he had himself never tasted pheasant, but kept the birds as a treasure.

The " Ethiopian birds " may have included ibis, egrets, flamingoes—but the possibilities are innumerable.

(13) After other groups of animals unnamed in the summary of Athenæus, came sheep of different kinds : one hundred Ethiopian, two hundred Arabian, twenty Eubœan. Strabo alludes to the " white-fleeced " North Arabian and the " goat-haired " Ethiopian breeds of sheep.

Strabo, XVI,
4, 26 ; XVII,
2, 3

Loisel,
Histoire des
Ménageries,
Vol. I Egypt,
Garden of
Ammon

(14) Twenty-six white Indian oxen, perhaps zebus ; these had been bred on the shores of the Mediterranean since the days of Tiglath-Pileser ; some varieties, not all, were sacred.

(15) Eight Ethiopian oxen, probably of the race that had been famous since the days of Hat Shep Sut in the fifteenth century—they were remarkable for their size and horns of curious twist.

Cf. Frederic II
of Sicily
exchanging
with the Sultan
of Cairo a polar
bear for a giraffe
Cf. Pausanias,
VIII, 17, 3

(16) A large white bear. Though it is not quite impossible that this was a polar bear, it is more likely to have been an albino of the straw-coloured bear of Syria or " white " bear of Thrace.

(17) Fourteen leopards, probably from Africa or Syria.

(18) Sixteen *pantheres* or *pantheroi*. Perhaps cheetahs. See Appendix, pp. 184, 185.

(19) Four lynxes.

(20) Three cubs (ἄρκηλοι) ; leopard-cubs or cheetah-cubs.[1]

(21) A giraffe, which must have come from Ethiopia.

(22) A rhinoceros, definitely described as Ethiopian ; that is to say, it was of the two-horned African kind, not a one-horned Indian animal. It may be noticed that Strabo mentions only one horn on the rhinoceros which, he says, he had seen, that Diodorus, in trying to describe the Ethiopian rhinoceros, gives it only one horn, and that Pliny speaks of the *rhinoceros unius in nare cornus, qualis sæpe visus* (at Rome), without mentioning the two-horned African kind. Was it then usually the Indian, not the African, rhinoceros that was seen in the Mediterranean world from the time of Pompey

Strabo, XVI,
4, 15

Diodorus, III,
35, 2–3

Pliny, N.H.,
VIII, 20 (29), 71

---

[1] Ælian, *N.A.*, VII, 47, quotes Aristophanes of Byzantium as saying " the young of leopards are called σκύμνοι and ἄρκηλοί," adding that some say ἄρκηλοι are a different species from παρδάλεις.

(when the animal was first exhibited at Rome) to that of Vespasian ? Unlikely as it may seem, probably it was ; the Indian rhinoceros is very hardy, it thrives in very small quarters ; and my experience goes to prove that its expectation of life in captivity is double that of its African cousin. However, the two-horned rhinoceros did appear at Rome under Titus and in the Antonine age (see pp. 74, 86).

In the sixth century A.D. Cosmas Indicopleustes, who had seen a live rhinoceros in Ethiopia " at a distance," and a stuffed specimen at close quarters, duly ascribes " horns " to the beast.

Cosmas Indicopleustes, XI, 441b–c

(23) Somewhere in the procession there were twenty-four lions of great size (λέοντες παμμεγέθεις). These may have come from the Cyrenaica, or from the borderlands of Syria and Arabia, or from Mesopotamia. The idea mentioned in Diodorus, that the lions and leopards of the part of Arabia adjoining Syria were larger and stronger than those of North Africa, may have originated in the capture of some exceptionally large South Syrian or Arabian beasts. Diodorus also says that lions and leopards were more numerous in that region than in North Africa (Libya) ; and that notion may have been started at Alexandria because most of the lions and leopards seen there came from the neighbouring parts of Asia.

Diodorus, II, 50, 2

It may be remarked that the tiger is absent from this list ; and if it had appeared in the procession, it would surely have been mentioned both by Callixenus, the authority of Athenæus, and by Athenæus himself. Indian monkeys too are noticeable by their absence from among the named animals. The sea journey would probably have been fatal to them.

The modern value of the named animals may be estimated at about £44,500, of which £20,000 would be for the elephants on the assumption that they were not particularly fine beasts. The quarters of the whole collection would probably cover about 100 acres.

Apart from the recorded details of this procession, we have hardly any information about the strange animals which were brought to Alexandria in this age. Diodorus gives an account of the difficulty with which a great snake was captured in

Diodorus, III, 36–7

Ethiopia by hunters who hoped, not in vain, to be richly rewarded for it by Ptolemy II. After an unsuccessful attempt to take it in a contraption of nooses and ropes, they marked its lair, which they blocked up in its absence, and close by they prepared a hole in which they placed a purse bag of rushes. When the snake returned and could not get into its lair, it was driven by the raising of clamour and din towards the hole, and when it was there, the cords for closing the mouth of the bag were pulled. The captors managed to bring it alive to Alexandria, where it was kept on view at the royal palace. Diodorus says that it was made very tame by meagre feeding. A python will become tame without being starved ; but perhaps the effects of weakness were mistaken for tameness. The length of the monster is given as 30 cubits (45 feet) ; one cannot say that this is impossible, though I know of no snake alive or dead that has at all approached it.

Strabo, XVII, 1, 40 ; XVI, 4, 16

On the cebus or cepus monkey from Ethiopia, which was worshipped in Egypt at a place near Memphis, and was probably the nisnas guenon, more will be said when we come to its appearance in the Roman arena in 55 B.C. (see p. 55 below).

Diodorus, III, 35, 10
Cosmas Indico-pleustes, XI, 444c

Whether specimens of the Ethiopian hyena (" the animal which the Ethiopians call *crocotta* ") or of the warthog (if that is the *choirelaphos*, i.e. pig venison, which Cosmas Indicopleustes had " seen and eaten " somewhere) ever reached Alexandria in Ptolemaic times, we do not know.[1]   But the warthog is

Cosmas Indico-pleustes, XI, 444c ; 441c ; Hakluyt Society's translation, p. 363

[1] The *Corocotta* is mentioned at Rome in the reigns of Antoninus Pius and Septimius Severus (see pp. 84-5 below). The *Choirelaphos* (i.e. warthog) and the *Taurelaphos* (buffalo) appear in a list of Indian and Ethiopian animals in Cosmas Indicopleustes. He explains that the Indian *taurelaphos* is tame, the African kind wild. The latter is evidently the Cape buffalo (*Bos caffer*). He says that he has eaten the *Choirelaphos* ; there is no description of the animal, but there is a drawing which suggests strongly the wart-hog (*Phacochœrus africanus*). Pliny knew both this animal and the Indian horned pig, the *Babirusa*, but Cosmas never went within hundreds of miles of the known habitat of that curious creature.

Names of beasts compounded with -elaphos may in some cases indicate a resemblance of their flesh to venison, or their value as food.

not difficult to keep alive, and the young pigs are extremely small ; transport would be easy as compared with the removal of a giraffe. It may have appeared in Rome (see p. 71 below). The hyena would present no difficulties—it is even tameable.

It has been mentioned above that under Ptolemy II and Ptolemy III elephant-hunting in Ethiopia was carried on from the Red Sea coast. It may be that the comparatively powerful Ethiopian kingdom, or kingdoms, on the Nile would not permit the collection of elephants by military or semi-military expeditions passing by the route up that river, whereas the inhabitants of Northern Abyssinia and the adjacent regions were at this time in the condition of simple savages who could be persuaded by presents and subsidies to let the king of Egypt's men go about their business among them. At any rate, under Ptolemy II a fort or trading post called Ptolemais of the Hunts (ἐπὶ θήρας) was established on the Red Sea coast near Suakin. This apparently served as the base from which expeditions went up country to procure elephants in Abyssinia and the eastern Sudan. The animals captured were shipped from Ptolemais to the port of Berenice, which was founded in this reign on the coast in the latitude of Assuan. From Berenice they were taken to the Nile at Coptos (Koft) by a road constructed by Ptolemy II.[1] Under Ptolemy III another coastal base for expeditions into the interior of Ethiopia was established some 300 miles south of Ptolemais of the Hunts. This was Berenice the Golden, near Massowa, perhaps the Adulis of the later Axumite kingdom. It is possible that inland from Berenice the Golden another trading-post was founded at Koloë, which was later reckoned as three days' journey from Adulis.

Cf. Expedition of Queen Hat-shep-sut to Punt. Circa 1500 B.C.

Tarn, Hellenistic Civilisation, 2nd edition, pp. 214-15

Flinders Petrie, Koft, II, 64

Periplus Erythraei Maris, 4

----

[1] Myos Hormos (Kosseir), which was much nearer to Coptos than was Berenice, was also founded on the Red Sea coast under Ptolemy II, and at the beginning of the first century A.D. was the chief Red Sea port for the trade that passed through Coptos. But the difficulties of transporting elephants by sea would account for their being landed at Berenice rather than further north at Myos Hormos.

This attempt to maintain a force of elephants in Egypt by a supply from Ethiopia was not very successful. The natives of Ethiopia did not catch elephants for taming ; they hunted them only to kill, by hamstringing or by shooting them with big bows each worked by three men.[1] It is said that when some hunters were offered large rewards by the officers of Ptolemy III, if they would catch elephants alive, they refused to do so. Thus the kings' agents could not pick the animals most suited to their purpose from hundreds of thousands of beasts, as could be done in India ; they would have to take such young males as they could catch, whether in pits, or by driving a herd into a long depression prepared with banks and ditches to prevent escape, and their method of breaking depended more on starvation than on skill.

Agatharchides, De mari Eryth., 53 (Geographi Græci Minores, I, 144)

Pliny, N.H., VIII, 8(8), 25

The elephants thus taken must have been kept in the country till they were used to captivity and had learnt the obedience necessary for safety in ships. It is likely that the Ptolemies employed Indian mahouts ; and it has been suggested that the embassy sent by Ptolemy II to the Indian king Vindusara had for its object to obtain the services of men of this profession.[2]

Tarn, Hellenistic Civilisation, 2nd edition, p. 58 Pliny, N.H., VI, 17(21), 58

The voyage up the Red Sea was a perilous business. There were dangerous reefs and shallows along the coast, and we have an account of how the elephant-transports, riding deep in the water and propelled by sails, not by oars, might easily run aground by night and become total wrecks. Night-sailing on these voyages may have been due either (as our authority suggests) to the strength of the wind making it impossible to put into shore or anchor for the night, or to the fact that in the sultry heat of the Red Sea sailing by day was injurious to the

Diodorus, III, 40, 4–9

---

[1] The hamstringing method is described by Diodorus, III, 26, 2. Shooting with a heavy bow is still practised in southern Abyssinia (W. D. M. Bell, *Wanderings of an Elephant-Hunter*, 1923, p. 19). The six-foot bow of the Ethiopians on the Nile is mentioned by Herodotus, Strabo and Diodorus.

[2] The Carthaginians may have employed Indians in this service in the third century. The elephants in Carthaginian armies in the First and Second Punic Wars of Rome are spoken of by Polybius as being in the charge of Indians (I, 40, 15 ; III, 46, 7–8 ; XI, 1, 12).

health of the elephants ; for in sailing ships the wind that helps progress diminishes ventilation. The beasts would stand on the bottom of the vessel, uncovered except by light sheets to protect them from the sun.

The elephant attains its maximum size at about twenty years of age. Probably the animals caught for the Ptolemies were much younger, both for convenience of transport by sea, and because full-grown males would be likely to kill themselves during breaking. They would grow in Egypt, but in unskilful hands few would attain great size and many would die within twenty years ; so that annual hunts were needed to keep up the stock without much probability of improving it. It was the general belief among the Greeks and Romans that the African breed of elephant was smaller than the Indian. This is untrue ; the African breed is considerably the larger.[1] But (and this is how the belief may have started) the African elephants of Ptolemy IV at the battle of Raphia were mostly smaller than the Indian elephants of Antiochus III. This seems to show that not only were the African catchers less efficient than those in India (so that many beasts in Africa were lost at once), but also the Ptolemies' elephants were in less skilful hands than those of the Seleucids, so that there was more need of replacement in Egypt than in Syria, and, in consequence, a much higher proportion of immature beasts on the Egyptian side at Raphia than on the Syrian. In the elephant lines in India to-day, an animal with twenty years' service is exceptional, although the elephants employed there include females, which would have been almost useless for battle in ancient warfare. The male of the Indian race in my experience lives longer than the African, and is less likely to develop faults, in particular a weakness of the ankle-joints in one or more feet, which disables from service. This may help to explain

[1] Philostratus (*Apollonius of Tyana*, II, 12) says that as a Nisæan horse is to an African elephant, so is the latter to an Indian elephant. The weights would be perhaps 1,635 lb., 32 cwt., and 70 cwt. But Jumbo, the great African elephant of the London Zoological Gardens, weighed 130 cwt.

the fact that after fifty years of elephant-collecting only seventy-three beasts could be put into line of battle on the Egyptian side at Raphia (when all the available force of the kingdom was needed to avert a threatened invasion), whereas in the Seleucid army there were a hundred and two in action, and that Ptolemy's elephants were mostly smaller and weaker and, as Polybius correctly remarks, feared their stronger antagonists. A few big animals in the Egyptian force bore themselves well. The rest ran away ; sixteen were killed, and most of the others captured. Five only of the other force were killed or died of wounds. In spite of this débâcle, the battle ended in a victory for Ptolemy's army. But elephant-catching in Ethiopia for war purposes ceased after this experience.

Polybius, V, 84, 2–6 ; 86, 6

Nevertheless, the Egyptian trading-posts on the African side of the Red Sea were maintained, partly for the transmission of Indian merchandise to Egypt, and partly for the trade in ivory and other products of Ethiopia. A southern Arsinoe was founded, not far from the Straits of Aden. Thus there were still the means of obtaining strange animals from equatorial Africa. But how far they were taken advantage of, we do not know.[1]

Tarn, Hellenistic Civilisation, pp. 215–16, 2nd edition.

It seems that under the later Ptolemies there was some direct trade between Egypt and India, not through the medium of the South Arabian markets. This direct commerce increased very much after the annexation of Egypt by Rome, owing to the demand in the Roman Empire for Indian goods. We may take it that Indian parrots came in this way to Alexandria, and occasionally other Indian animals.

Ibid.

Visitors to Egypt were of course interested in the worship of local animals, and some of these animals aroused curiosity,

---

[1] Centuries later, about A.D. 520, caravans of upwards of 500 men were going once a year from the Axumite kingdom in Tigre (now part of Abyssinia) to a country called Sasu " near the Ocean," where gold was purchased by dumb barter for oxen, salt, and iron. The whole journey took six months (Cosmas Indicopleustes, II, 100b). Expeditions of this kind may have gone up-country from the Red Sea coast in the Ptolemaic period.

particularly the crocodile. We have a note sent up the Nile in 112 B.C., to the effect that the crocodiles were to be hungry on the arrival of a tourist of distinction, a Roman Senator. Strabo describes the feeding of a tame sacred crocodile by priests who opened its jaws and placed in its mouth the food offered to it by visitors.

Oxyrhynchus Papyri, I, no. 33, p. 127 Strabo, XVII, 1, 38

The Roman *venationes*, or displays of killing wild animals, seem to have been of Italian origin. The development of them would naturally be popular among a people which in the third century B.C. had learnt to delight in the gladiatorial shows that were introduced from Etruria. But there are hints that in the Roman shows of the later Republican period, animals were exhibited in processions, and that practice may have been suggested by spectacles seen at Alexandria or elsewhere in the Greek world. Moreover in the middle of the first century B.C. animals from Egypt (whether of Egyptian or of Ethiopian origin) were being exhibited as curiosities at Rome ; for example, the hippopotamus and the crocodiles which appeared in the shows of Scaurus in 58 B.C. In the early imperial age, Egypt seems to have been one of the chief sources of supply of animals for the Roman arena. And it is certain that the taming and training of animals at Rome owed much to experts from Alexandria.

CHAPTER III

THE ANIMALS OF THE ROMAN GAMES
(TO 30 B.C.)

Ovid, *Fasti*, IV, 681

Ibid., V, 371

THE exhibition of animals at the Roman Games probably had its origin in the " hunting " (*venatio*), or
baiting, of Italian wild creatures, in the Circus Maximus or elsewhere, as both an amusement for the spectators
and a religious or magical rite. In the time of Augustus, part
of the ritual of the Feast of Ceres was the turning loose of
foxes (apparently in the Circus) with firebrands tied to their
tails ; and this was probably a very ancient custom, which,
when the official Games of Ceres were established towards the
end of the third century B.C., was introduced into their programme. Moreover, in the Augustan age it was a tradition
that at the Feast of Flora hares and wild goats should be
hunted in the Circus, but not fighting beasts (*pugnaces feræ*).
Ovid asks the goddess Flora why in her honour " unwarlike
goats and the anxious hare are netted instead of Libyan
lionesses." And the goddess answers that her domain is not
the forest, but gardens and tilled fields, which " the fighting
beast " may not haunt. Here too the official Games (which
were first instituted for Flora in 238 B.C., and became annual
from 173 onwards) seem to have preserved a custom older
than they.[1]

---

[1] By the middle of the second century B.C. there were six annual
sets of official Games (*ludi*), the management of each being assigned
to one or two of the yearly magistrates—to the curule or plebeian
ædiles or to the city prætor. Of these annual Games (*ludi sollemnes*)
only one set, the *ludi Romani*, was of older origin than the middle of

This chapter will be mainly concerned with notices of animals imported into Italy for the Roman Games from the time of the Punic Wars to the fall of the Republic. But probably throughout this period a *venatio* at Rome would be usually supplied, either mainly or wholly, with Italian animals—deer, hares, wild goats, boars, bears, and bulls.[1] Varro, writing about 36 B.C., says that a gathering of " stags, boars, and other quadrupeds," seen on a friend's estate, was a spectacle no less fine than that in the Circus Maximus when the ædiles give *venationes* " without African beasts." And even when there were African or other imported beasts at a *venatio*, there may

Varro, *R.R.*, III, 13

the third century B.C. Another set of Games was established in 81 B.C., in honour of Sulla's victories ; and the victories of Julius Cæsar were commemorated for some time in the annual *ludi* which were instituted in 46. Besides these annual Games, special Games (*ludi extraordinarii*) might be celebrated by a magistrate or ex-magistrate in payment of some official vow taken for the welfare of the State or for success in its service, or they might accompany the dedication of a temple or other public building. Again, an individual might entertain the public with *ludi privati*, on such an occasion as the funeral of a member of his family (*ludi funebres*). Allowances were made from the State Treasury for official Games. But anyone who had the management of such *ludi* might also spend his own or borrowed money on them, and it became usual for the managers to demand subscriptions from provincials, who might also be put to expense and trouble in, for example, the capture of animals for transport to Rome.

The *venatio* was only one of several kinds of entertainment which might be offered to the public at *ludi*, other kinds being chariot-racing or horse-racing, gladiatorial combats, and dramatic and musical performances. It appears from a remark in Suetonius (*Div. Aug.*, 43, 1) that it was not at all usual to give a *venatio* by itself. The *venationes* at official *ludi* were mostly held in the Circus Maximus, in the valley between the Palatine and the Aventine, but some were given at the smaller Circus Flaminius in the Campus Martius. *Venationes* at private *ludi* might be given in the Forum Romanum or Forum Boarium, or in temporary amphitheatres elsewhere.

[1] It may be noticed that Pliny (*N.H.*, VIII, 45(70), 182) does not say that bull-fighting was first introduced into Rome as a spectacle by Julius Cæsar, but that Julius Cæsar was the first to exhibit at Rome the Thessalian method of bull-fighting on horseback.

well have been more from Italy except at shows of extraordinary magnificence. In Cicero's correspondence of the year 51 B.C., we find an ædile-elect in difficulties about getting more than 20 leopards for his *ludi*.

Cicero, *Ad. Fam.*, VIII, 9, 3

It so happens that the first exotic animals definitely recorded as a spectacle at Rome had not been brought to Italy for the Roman *ludi*. They were the four elephants captured from Pyrrhus when, in his second invasion of Italy, he was defeated near Beneventum by a Roman army under M.' Curius Dentatus (275 B.C.). These elephants appeared at Rome in the triumph of Curius. A Roman name for the elephant was " Lucanian cow," from the part of Italy, Lucania, where a Roman army had first to face war-elephants, in the earlier invasion of Pyrrhus.

Seneca, *De Brev. Vitæ*, 13, 3 Eutropius, II, ii, 14

Varro, *L.L.*, VII, 389, 39 Lucretius, V, 1302, 1339 Pliny, *N.H.*, VIII, 6(6), 16

Twenty-four years after the triumph of Curius, L. Metellus brought to Rome over 100 African elephants, which he had taken from the Carthaginians in his great victory over them at Panormus (Palermo) in Sicily (251 B.C.). The mahouts passed into the Roman service, and the captured animals were taken across the straits to Rhegium without mishap on a raft built on barrels, and were exhibited in all the towns that lay on the route to Rome. There, in order to allay the fears of the citizens, the bulky beasts were driven across the Circus by a few slaves armed only with blunt javelins. This dramatic exhibition may have been a clever trick in which the slaves acted an unimportant part. The mahouts were the real actors, in my opinion. Mingling unnoticed with the excited crowd, they could be relied on to keep a recalcitrant beast on the right path by shouting directions which the elephants would immediately obey. Whether this great herd was kept, is doubtful ; they would be an expensive luxury as a show, and, as will be seen later, the Romans never made much use of the elephant in war.

Seneca, *De Brev. Vit.*, 14, 2

Orosius, IV, 9, 15 Frontinus, *Strateg*, I, 7, 1; II, 5, 4 Zonaras, VIII, 14 Florus, I, 18, 28

We do not know when foreign animals were first exhibited at the Roman Games, but they had made their appearance there by about the beginning of the second century B.C. The ostrich from Africa (or perhaps brought from a Sicilian estate)

Plautus, *Persa*, 199

had been seen by then in the Circus, and had impressed the spectators by its wonderful speed.

Plautus, who mentions the ostrich, has a couple of lines which perhaps imply that soon after the Second Punic War African animals were being imported for public shows. In the *Pœnulus* (a contemptuous title—the Carthaginian whom they feared no longer) the poor foreigner is inquiring after two lost daughters. A joker professes to translate him :

> Non audis ? mures Africanos prædicat
> In pompam ludis dare se velle ædilibus.

Plautus,
Pœnulus,
1011-12

("Don't you hear ? He says he wants to supply the ædiles with African mice for the procession at the games.")

It has been suggested that in Plautus' time leopards may have been called *mures Africani*, as the elephant had been called *luca bos*, and the ostrich *passer marinus*. But the professed interpreter is representing his protégé as a seller of odds and ends, and the joke would seem to be in the absurdity of the idea that the small creatures which Pliny afterwards knew as *mures Africani* should be led in a procession. However, the more important question is, whether we can take this passage as evidence that African beasts were being ordinarily supplied by traders for the Roman official shows. And it does seem to imply that the ædiles were buying African animals for their Games. Besides, it is *a priori* likely that from the third century onwards traders and showmen were occasionally bringing leopards and even lions to Rome, and that the term "African beasts" (*Africanæ bestiæ*, or simply *Africanæ* [1]) early acquired the meaning, which it bore later, either of "leopards" or of "lions, leopards, and other large cats." Since the term is found in Livy in connection with a show of 169 B.C., it may be convenient to illustrate here the ways in which it was used.

Persa, loc. cit.

Pliny, *N.H.*,
XXX, 6(14), 43

Livy, XLIV,
18, 8

Augustus records that 3,500 *Africanæ bestiæ* were killed in his 26 *venationes*. Here the term must include at least lions and leopards. But that a single batch of animals described as

Mon. Anc.,
XXII (IV,
39-42)

---

[1] Under the Empire *Libycæ feræ* or *Libycæ* perhaps came to be the more usual term ; e.g. Symmachus (end of fourth century A.D.), *Epistulæ*, II, 46, 76 ; VII, 122.

Africanæ would usually consist wholly or mainly of leopards, or of leopards and other large spotted cats, is suggested by the fact that Pliny, in a passage where he is dealing with animals of the leopard class, mentions a decree of the Senate forbidding the importation of *Africanæ* into Italy. A number of lions not mixed with leopards, and exhibited at a single show, would probably be recorded as *leones*, not as *Africanæ*. But there seems to be no mention of lions *and* African beasts at a single show, though there are mentions of African beasts *and* bears. Lastly, it is clear from the way in which Augustus uses the term *Africanæ bestiæ*, that in his day it was not always confined to animals that had really been brought from Africa. It may be noticed, that Africa always remained, in the Roman imagination, pre-eminently the land of terrible beasts, and particularly the land of lions, even at a time when lions could be got by the Romans from their own Asiatic territory.[1] For a discussion of Latin words for leopard see Appendix I.

Pliny, *N.H.*, VIII, 17(24), 64

In the second century B.C. Rome was the dominant power in North Africa. The Numidian kingdom was her ally and client; so too was Carthage, till the outbreak of the war in which the Carthaginian state and city were destroyed, with the result that the former territory of Carthage became a Roman province (146 B.C.). Moreover, the power of Rome was expanding eastwards; she came to dominate the Balkan peninsula, where she annexed Macedonia in 146 B.C.; the kingdoms of Asia Minor were brought under her protectorate, and in 133 her province of Asia was formed out of the western part of the kingdom of Pergamum; and she became able to intervene decisively, when she chose, in the affairs of the Egyptian and Syrian kingdoms. Lastly, Spain was in her grasp, and was slowly being brought under control.

This development of Roman imperialism enabled Roman nobles, at the shows which they gave in their magistracies, or when they were fulfilling vows made in wartime, or were

---

[1] In an inscription of the imperial age, referring to a *venatio* at Panormus in Sicily, the phrase *orientales bestias* occurs. Dessau, *Inscr. Lat. Sel.*, 5055.

honouring their dead, more and more to entertain the people (in so far as the practice was not checked by a decree of the Senate to be noticed below) with " hunts " of wild beasts from foreign countries. The Roman liking for bloody spectacles had been already strengthened by the gladiatorial shows, which, according to tradition, had been first introduced from Etruria in 264 B.C.

Venationes are particularly recorded for the years 186 and 169 B.C. In the former year M. Fulvius Nobilior fulfilled a vow made for success in the Ætolian War by the celebration of games which lasted for ten days, and which Livy believed to have been almost up to the standard of the Augustan age in lavish variety. In this show, besides Greek athletic contests, which were then first seen at Rome, there was a *venatio* of lions and leopards. These animals are called by Livy *leones* and *pantheræ*, not *Africanæ*. Perhaps they had been collected from the East. (It may be noticed that Seneca thought that lions at this time were shown in chains ; they were still rarities.) Under the year 169 it is noted by Livy, as an indication of growing magnificence, that the curule ædiles gave a show in the Circus Maximus, at which appeared 63 " African beasts," 40 bears, and some elephants. The use of beasts for the doing to death of criminals in this age is illustrated by the ways in which Æmilius Paullus and Scipio Æmilianus punished men who had deserted from Roman armies to the enemy (168 and 146 B.C.).

The growth of the custom of giving *venationes* of imported wild beasts is betrayed by an attempt to check it. A decree of the Senate was passed forbidding the importation of " African beasts " into Italy. The danger that the beasts might escape and do damage, the undesirability of introducing into political life a new and expensive way of gaining irrelevant popularity, and the likelihood that the collection of wild beasts for Roman shows, at the request of Roman nobles, would often entail much hardship and expense on Rome's subjects and allies—all these things may have been in the minds of the Senators who voted for the decree. But the regulation made by the Senate was in part overridden by a law of the Plebs, proposed by a tribune

Livy, XXXIX; 22, 2

Seneca, *De Brev. Vit.*, 13, 5

Livy, XLIV, 18, 8

Valerius Maximus, II, 7, 13–14

Pliny, *N.H.*, VIII, 17(24), 64

Cn. Aufidius.   This law permitted the importation of *Africanæ* for shows in the Circus Maximus at Rome.   Its date cannot be fixed with any certainty.   A Cn. Aufidius was tribune of the Plebs in 170 B.C., and perhaps it was he who had this law passed, with the result that *Africanæ* were exhibited in the Circus by the ædiles of 169.   In time the decree of the Senate became wholly obsolete.

In the period from the end of the second century B.C. to the death of Julius Cæsar, the animal-shows reflect the further expansion of Roman power, the increasing exploitation of the Mediterranean world by the Italians, which now reaches its height, the growing spirit among Roman nobles of reckless competition and eagerness to outdo precedent, and, finally, the emergence, first of Pompey to a position of vast influence, and then of Cæsar to the supreme power of his dictatorship.

We may first notice the animals which are mentioned as having been exhibited at Games (*ludi*) in the first century B.C. before the great shows of Pompey in the year 55.

Pliny, *N.H.*, VIII, 7(7), 19

The first elephant-fights seen at Rome were part of a show given by C. Claudius Pulcher in his ædileship in 99 B.C. Twenty years later L. and M. Lucullus, as ædiles, exhibited a fight of elephants and bulls.

As regards the employment of elephants elsewhere than at *ludi*, it may be noticed that one of the very few records of their having been used by the Romans in war is the state-

Florus, I, 37, 5; (III, 2, 5) Orosius, V, 13, 2

ment of Florus that elephants terrified the enemy in the victory won by Cn. Domitius Ahenobarbus, in 121 B.C., at Vindalium (between Avignon and Orange) over an army of the Gallic tribe of the Allobroges.   The idea that elephants might have a useful effect on the Celtic mind seems to be traceable again in later stories of the invasions of Britain by Cæsar and Claudius (see pp. 58, 66 below).[1]   An abortive

Pliny, N.H., VIII, 2(2), 4 Plutarch, *Pomp.*, 14

attempt to use elephants for drawing the car in which a general rode in his triumph was made by Pompey in 81 B.C.   He was

---

[1] This idea may have been derived from the famous victory which Antiochus I won in 275 B.C. over the Gauls in Asia Minor by means of his elephants—the " elephant victory."

to celebrate a triumph for his campaign in Africa, whence he
had brought a large number of elephants taken from the King
of Numidia whom he had deposed ; and he wished to enter
the city in a car drawn by four of these animals. But the
gateway, it is said, was too narrow for them to get through ;
perhaps Pompey was persuaded that his idea was in bad taste
for so young a *triumphator*.

A lion-fight was shown at Games celebrated by " Scævola, $\quad$ Pliny, *N.H.*,
son of Publius " in his ædileship : that is, no doubt, by Q. $\quad$ VIII, 16(20), 53
Mucius Scævola, who was consul in 95 B.C., and whose ædileship
would have been in or about the year 101. According to Pliny,
it was the first fight " of a number of lions together " (*leonum
simul plurium*) to be exhibited at Rome. Whether Pliny's
phrase *leonum pugna* means that lions were made to fight lions,
or that men fought lions, is not clear ; but the latter interpre-
tation seems the more probable. Seneca believed that the first $\quad$ Seneca, *De
Brev. Vitæ*,
occasion on which lions were let loose unchained in the arena $\quad$ 13, 5
was at the great display of 100 maned lions, which Sulla had
procured, for the games which he celebrated in his prætorship
(93 B.C.), from his friend King Bocchus of Mauretania. They
were despatched by javelin-men (*iaculatores*), who had also
been sent by Bocchus. Probably nothing like this number of
lions had been seen together at Rome before. There is a $\quad$ Plutarch,
well-known tale of how Sulla, having failed in one attempt $\quad$ *Sulla*, 5
to gain the prætorship, declared that the People had wished
him first to take the curule ædileship, as in that office too he
would have celebrated games, at which his known friendship
with Bocchus (a result of the Jugurthine War) would have
enabled him to give a fine *venatio* of " African beasts."

Bears are mentioned as appearing in a *venatio* given by $\quad$ Pliny, *N.H.*,
L. Domitius Ahenobarbus in his curule ædileship of 61 B.C. $\quad$ VIII, 36(54),
A hundred bears were shown, with a hundred *venatores* to kill $\quad$ 131
them. The bears were said to have been Numidian, the
venatores " Ethiopians." Pliny says that he is astonished to
find the bears called Numidian, it being well known that bears
are not native to Africa (*miror adiectum Numidicos fuisse*, $\quad$ *Ibid.*, 58 (83),
cum in Africa non gigni constet). He repeats this statement $\quad$ 228

later, saying that in Africa there are no wild boars, stags, roedeer, or bears. He seems' to be wrong here about wild boars.

Herodotus,
IV, 191 ; II, 67

Is he also wrong about bears ? Herodotus, in the fifth century B.C., had mentioned bears among the wild animals of the western part of North Africa, and had said that they were

Strabo, XVII,
3, 7

to be found, though rarely, in Egypt. Strabo, writing under Augustus or Tiberius, says that the natives of Mauretania dress and sleep in the skins of " lions, leopards and bears " ; there is no reason why bear-skins should have been purchased from Spain; they are thick and hot, and cheapness alone suggests

Virgil, Æn,
V, 37
Juvenal, IV, 99
Martial, I,
104, 5

their use. The Roman poets, Virgil, Juvenal, and Martial, speak of Libyan or Numidian bears ; why should their testimony be rejected ? The " Oppian " of the *Cynegetica*, in the

"Oppian" *Cyn.*,
II, 460–6

early years of the third century A.D., mentions boar and bear as animals which the oryx is ready to fight ; and the oryx

Dio, LIII, 27, 6
LIX, 7, 3

seems to be the beisa antelope, only found in Africa. Dio's phrases about shows given in 25 B.C. and 37 A.D. (ἄρκτους . . . καὶ Λιβυκὰ ἕτερα θηρία, and, ἄρκτους μεθ' ἑτέρων Λιβυκῶν θηρίων) may mean only that " the other animals," not the bears, were African, but they may equally well mean that the bears were African also. Probably Pliny is mistaken about this. The belief that there were no bears in Africa may have been a popular one, due to the fact that, while bears were frequently exhibited at shows in Italy, these animals almost always came from Europe, and often from Italy itself, so that bears came to be definitely thought of as *not* " African beasts."

Pliny, *N.H.*,
VIII, 17(24), 64
Ibid., 26(40), 96

An unprecedented display of *variæ* (leopards, and perhaps other large spotted cats) was given by M. Scaurus as ædile in 58 B.C. A hundred and fifty of these animals were let loose together in the arena. At these Games, too, was seen the first hippopotamus brought to Rome, exhibited with five crocodiles in a temporary pond or tank. But the main part

Ibid., XXXVI,
15(24), 113 *seq.*

of the vast sums that were spent by Scaurus on his famous *ludi* seems to have gone on the magnificent theatre which he erected for the occasion.

The hippopotamus and crocodiles no doubt came from Egypt

with native keepers. The *variæ* probably came from Syria, where Scaurus had served in high commands from 65 to 59 B.C., first as Pompey's lieutenant, and then as acting governor of the new Roman province of Syria, which Pompey organised in 63. The annexation of Syria gave the Romans a second main source of supply of lions and leopards, besides Africa. Probably at this time, as four centuries later, in the Mesopotamian country adjoining North Syria lions swarmed in the reed-beds of the rivers. But transport from Syria to Italy would be longer and more expensive than from Africa.

Ammianus
Marcellinus,
XVIII, 7,

We now come to the animals exhibited in the great shows of Pompey, which he gave in the autumn of the year 55, to celebrate the opening of his theatre and the dedication of his temple to Venus Genetrix. These *ludi* were on a scale meant to be proportionate to the unprecedented influence of Pompey in Italy and the Empire—an influence which must have greatly facilitated the collection of animals for his Games. In Africa, the Numidian king at the time was either still the Hiempsal whom Pompey had put on the throne in 81, or Hiempsal's son, Juba, who was to take the Pompeian side in the civil war which broke out in 49. The East knew Pompey as the conqueror of Pontus, Armenia, the skirts of the Caucasus, and Syria, and as the organizer or reorganizer of the Asiatic part of Rome's Empire—a maker or destroyer or remaker of kingdoms, principalities, and cities. It is likely, too, that he had money out at interest in other parts of the East besides Cappadocia, whose king was deeply in debt to him. In Egypt, in the spring of this year 55, King Ptolemy Auletes had been restored to the throne from which his subjects had driven him, and his restoration had been due to the influence of Pompey, Cæsar, and Crassus, and to the action taken by Pompey's adherent Gabinius, the governor of Syria. These are the countries or regions from which came the animals mentioned in our records as shown in Pompey's Games—with the exception of a lynx from Gaul, perhaps a present from Cæsar. The piteous slaughter of some African elephants, the extraordinary numbers of lions and leopards exhibited, and a few rare animals

E

—these are the things mentioned in accounts of, or allusions to, these Games.

Seneca, *De Brev. Vit.*, 13,6
Pliny, *N.H.*, VIII, 7(7),
20–21
Dio, XXXIX, 38, 2–4
Cicero, *Ad. Fam.*, VII, 1, 3

The elephants were some twenty in number. Their drivers, when inducing them to go on board the ships that brought them from Africa to Italy, had promised that they should not be harmed. The promise was not kept. They were exhibited in the Circus on the last day of the shows, and Gætulians, from Africa, were set to kill them.[1] One animal roused the astonishment of the spectators by fighting on its knees when its feet were wounded, and snatching at its enemies' shields and tossing them in the air, so that they lay round it in a circle, *velut arte non furore beluæ iacerentur.* Another was killed by a single javelin that hit it under the eye. But on the whole the exhibition disgusted the spectators. The elephants caused some alarm by trying to break through the iron bars which penned them in. But above all they excited pity by their agonized trumpetings, so that the spectators rose and cursed Pompey for his cruelty. According to Dio, the slaughter had to be broken off; but the elephants which were not killed in the arena were despatched soon afterwards, Pompey having no use for them. Cicero wrote to a friend that the spectacle in the Circus had aroused both pity and a feeling that the elephant was somehow allied with man (*esse quandam illi beluæ cum genere humano societatem*).

Pliny, *N.H.*, VIII, 16(20), 53; 17(24), 64
Dio, XXXIX, 38, 2

The number of lions shown by Pompey in the Circus was, according to Pliny, 600, of which 315 were maned; this is probably more accurate than Dio's " 500 lions destroyed in 5 days." Moreover, 410 *variæ* (leopards and perhaps other large cats) were shown. The highest recorded figures for previous exhibitions of these animals had been Sulla's 100 lions, and the 150 *variæ* of Scaurus.

It is likely that Pompey's lions and leopards came partly from Africa, partly from the East, for in both quarters he had great influence. And it may be noticed here that we lack evidence as to the proportion which the number of African

---

[1] Seneca says that criminals were pitted against them; Pliny, with more probability, says that Gætulians were employe

lions and leopards appearing at Rome from this time onwards bore on the whole to the number from Asia. A Roman who was giving a *venatio* would be likely to get all or most of his beasts from countries where in one way or another he had some special influence. We know that Sulla's 100 maned lions came from Mauretania, as the result of his service in the Jugurthine War and his friendship with the Moorish king, Bocchus. It is probable, as we have seen, that the *variæ* of Scaurus came from Syria, where he had fought and administered for some years just before his ædileship, when he exhibited these animals. It seems certain that the large number of lions belonging to C. Cassius, which were found at Megara in 48 B.C., had been held up by the civil war on their way to Italy from Syria, where Cassius had been first Crassus' quæstor, and then, from 53 to 51, acting governor. It has already been pointed out that the phrase " African beasts," as used in the Augustan age and later, cannot be taken as reliable evidence that the beasts so called really came from Africa. In the *Historia Augusta*, in an account of some shows given by Probus (A.D. 281) —an account in which some of the details have a perhaps deceptive air of verisimilitude—100 *leopardi* are said to have come from Africa, and 100 from Syria. Towards the end of the fourth century A.D., Symmachus, in speaking of the lions which he hoped to get for a show, talks of a *Libyca congressio* ; but that does not make it *certain* that they really came from Africa. Claudian, writing in A.D. 399, expects Stilicho to get lions and leopards from Africa ; but—apart from the fact that lions usually came from Africa in the imagination of poets— Stilicho's power was exercised in the western half of the Empire, and his relations with the government of the eastern half were not such as would be likely to make the collection of Syrian or Mesopotamian lions easy for him. Nor can any inference on this point be drawn from Strabo's remark on the reduction in the number of wild beasts in Numidia by the time of Augustus, owing to collection for the Roman shows (a reduction which may have been made in many districts, and yet have left plenty of lions and leopards in North Africa) ; nor yet from the state-

Side notes:

Plutarch, *Brut.*, 8

Hist. Aug. Probus, 19

Symmachus, *Epp.*, II, 76

Claudian, *De Consul. Stilichonis*, III, 333 foll.

Strabo, II, 5, 33

Diodorus, II, 50, 2

ment of Diodorus that in the part of Arabia which borders on Syria lions and leopards are more numerous and larger and stronger than in Libya.[1] Only, it may be said that transport to Italy from North Africa would be on the whole quicker and easier than from Syria.

It remains to notice the rarities among the animals at Pompey's Games.

Pliny, *N.H.*, VIII, 19(28), 70

There was a Gallic lynx, then seen at Rome for the first time. Pliny calls it a *chama*, and says that the Gauls called it *rufius*, and that it has a wolf's shape and leopard's spots. It would have been too cowardly to show fight in the arena.

Ibid., 20(29), 71

A one-horned rhinoceros was shown—" such as has often been seen," says Pliny. He evidently knew of no earlier appearance of this animal at Rome. When Lucilius, in the second century B.C., compared a man to " an Ethiopian rhinoceros," he had probably only heard of the beast. No doubt Romans had seen it by that time at Alexandria. On the point that it seems to have been the one-horned Indian rhinoceros, not the two-horned African kind, that had often been seen at Rome when Pliny wrote, see p. 34 above.

Lucilius, *Sat.*, 159 Marx

---

[1] A poem on hunting written early in the third century A.D. (the *Cynegetica* traditionally ascribed to Oppian) gives what may well have been then a common opinion about the lions of different countries : that those of Armenia and Mesopotamia—yellow, large-headed, bright-eyed, with high and prominent brows, and well-maned—were comparatively weakly ; that those of Arabia Felix (the Yemen) had large manes and were remarkably fine beasts, but there were not many of them ; that in thirsty Africa lions were very numerous and strong, " lording it over the lordly lions," and had scanty manes, and a sheen running over their bodies (this is correct), which were somewhat dusky in hue. The author of the poem had himself seen a well-maned black lion which had been brought to " Libya " (i.e. to some part of Roman Africa west of Egypt) from " the Ethiopians " (presumably some negro people), and had been sent to the Emperor. " Oppian," *Cyn.*, III, 20–47. The lions in the Troglodyte country on the African shore of the Red Sea had long been famous for their ferocity, if Strabo's remark that they were called μύρμηκες (XVI, 4, 15) means, as I think it does, that they had a grip like that of the ant which will lose its head rather than loose its hold.

The Indian rhinoceros is likely to have reached Rome by way of Egypt, where probably it would arrive by the overland route. Rhinoceroses, tigers and other rare beasts had been carried round with the Indian courts for show or fights from time immemorial.

Lastly, there were monkeys from Ethiopia, which Pliny, it seems, knew as cephoi (*quas vocant cephus*). He says that they had " hind feet like human feet and legs, and forefeet like hands," and that they had never been seen again at Rome. The cepos (κῆπος), says Strabo in one passage, is the size of a gazelle, with a leonine face and a body like that of the πάνθηρ (i.e., probably, of varied hues, like the genet's—see Appendix I) ; elsewhere he describes it as satyr-faced, something between a dog and a bear, and a native of Ethiopia. There is a much fuller description of the cepos in Ælian. " Pythagoras," he says, " writes in his book on the Red Sea that there is a land-animal on its shores appositely called cepos [κῆπος, a garden], because it is many-coloured. One full-grown is of the size of an Eretrian hound. . . . The head and back to the tail are of a bright fire colour, and golden hairs are scattered over the rest of the body. The face is white as far as the cheeks, whence to the neck descend golden bands ; the parts under the neck, to the breast and the front legs, are white. The two teats, the size of a fist, seem blue, the belly is white, the hind feet black. You can truly compare his muzzle to that of the dog-face." This description suits very well the nisnas guenon (*Cercopithecus pyrrhonotus*) found in North-East Africa, Kordofan, and Darfur, where it is known to this day as the keb. A fine engraving of the keb in the temple at Latopolis (near Esséne-Esneh) suggests sacred associations. Strabo says it was worshipped near Memphis.

No doubt the troop of these monkeys which was exhibited at Rome in 55 B.C. had been procured from Alexandria.

Between the shows of Pompey in the year 55 and those of Julius Cæsar at his quadruple triumph in 46 B.C., we have no record of any great exhibition of animals at Rome. How a Roman of this period would try to collect animals for the

Marginal notes:

Pliny, *N.H.*, VIII, 19(28), 70

Strabo, XVI, 4, 16 ; XVII, 1, 40 Ælian, *N.A.*, XVII, 8

Denon (D. V. Baron), *Égypte*, Paris, 1802, Plate 97 Strabo, XVII, 1, 40

ordinary *ludi* which he had to give as a magistrate, is illustrated
by the correspondence between Cicero and M. Cælius Rufus
in 51 B.C. ; it will be described in chapter IX. It has been

Plutarch,
Brutus, 8

already noticed (p. 53) that the outbreak of civil war in 49
prevented C. Cassius from giving a great show of Syrian or
Mesopotamian lions at Rome ; it appears that these lions were
appropriated by Cæsar for his own *ludi*.

Pliny, *N.H.*,
VIII, 16(21), 55
Plutarch,
Antonius, 9

Our first record of tamed and trained lions in Italy refers
to this time. Antony, when in charge of the country after
the Battle of Pharsalus, while Cæsar was in the East (48–47
B.C.), shocked respectable people by his extravagances, among
which was his appearance in public with the actress Cytheris
in a chariot drawn by lions.

Of the animal-shows given by Cæsar as Dictator, we know
that they included a *venatio* of 400 lions ; a combat, or combats, in which elephants and infantry, or horse, foot, and
elephants were engaged ; one or two torchlight parades of
elephants ; a display of bull-fighting by mounted Thessalians
—the first of its kind seen at Rome ; and the first appearance
at Rome of the giraffe.

A considerable number of Cæsar's lions were, no doubt, the
Syrian or Mesopotamian animals which, as we have seen, he
is said to have taken from Cassius. If more were required to

Pliny, *N.H.*,
VIII, 16(20), 53

bring the total up to 400, they may have been collected in
Africa, after Cæsar's victory over the Pompeians and Numidians

Beasts collected
for Caesar in
Africa before
the Civil War
had been des-
troyed there by
Pompeians. Cf.
Suetonius, *Div.
Iul.*, 75, 3

at Thapsus early in 46 B.C., or in Syria, on orders given by
Cæsar before he left the East in 47. It is just possible that
some of Cæsar's lions were survivors from Pompey's shows of
the year 55, or had been bred in Italy from animals captured
before the outbreak of the Civil War.

It is noticeable that leopards are not recorded as appearing
at Cæsar's shows. This may be due simply to an oversight
of Pliny's, in the passage (*N.H.*, VIII, 17(24), 64) where he
mentions large numbers of leopards exhibited by Scaurus,
Pompey, and Augustus respectively. Or leopards may have
been shown by Cæsar, but not in any very great number. Or
there may have been really none, because it was desired to

give these shows as much distinction as possible. Leopards were an ordinary exhibit at ordinary *ludi* ; Cæsar would show only lions, elephants, the exciting novelty of Thessalian bull-fighting, and the strange giraffe. Or again, if it be supposed that all Cæsar's lions had been either collected before the outbreak of the Civil War, or bred from animals in captivity, it may also be supposed that no leopards were available in these ways ; for leopards do not usually survive capture for so long as lions, and very rarely breed when captive.

Of the combat or combats in which elephants were engaged, mention is made in four writers.

Pliny's account seems to be confused. He appears to mean that 20 elephants engaged 500 foot, and that then the same number of elephants, with " castles " on their backs (*turriti*), and three fighting men on each elephant, encountered 500 foot and 20 (?) horse.[1]

Pliny, *N.H.*, VIII, 7(7), 22

Suetonius mentions a fight in the Circus between two mixed forces, each consisting of 20 elephants, 500 foot, and 30 horse. The conical pillars (*metæ*), which served for turning-post or goal, were removed, and where they had stood, at the two ends of the Circus, " camps " were made for the opposing forces.

Suetonius, *Div. Iul.*, 39, 3

Appian records combats of horse and foot, " and a fight of elephants, twenty a side."

Appian, *B.C.*, II, 102, 423

Dio, after mentioning combats of horse and foot in the Circus, adds, " And men fought from the backs of forty elephants."

Dio, XLIII, 23, 3

Nothing is said of the result of this fighting in the Circus. Possibly Cæsar was experimenting with elephants with a view to their use in the Parthian war which he was planning. A

---

[1] Pliny's words are : " Pugnavere [elephanti] et Cæsari dictatori tertio consulatu eius [46 B.C.] viginti contra pedites quingentos, iterumque totidem turriti cum sexagenis propugnatoribus eodem quo priore numero peditum et pari equitum ex adverso dimicante." Clearly he does not mean that there were sixty *propugnatores* to each elephant. And he can hardly have meant that the number of horse was equal to the number of foot (not to the number of elephants).

Cicero,
Philippics, V,
17, 46
Dio, XLV, 13, 4

few months after his death there was a body of war-elephants in Italy ; it is mentioned as part of the forces which went over from Antony to Octavian in the autumn of the year 44.

Suetonius,
Div. Iul., 37, 2
Dio, XLIII,
22, 1

Suetonius describes Cæsar as going up to the Capitol, on one of the days of his quadruple triumph in 46 B.C., with forty elephants bearing torches to left and right of him ; Dio says that on the last day he was escorted home by forty elephants

Coin of
Antiochus
shown as
frontispiece
of *Histoire
Militaire des
éléphants*,
Armandi

bearing torches. These torches were carried in the elephants' trunks ; an elephant thus holding a torch appears on Seleucid coinage. Only thoroughly trained animals could have been used for this torch-bearing, and we may therefore reject the idea that the elephants used for it at Cæsar's triumph had

Bell. Afr., 27, 2
Florus, II, 13 ;
(IV, 2), 67

been captured at the Battle of Thapsus. For the elephants which took part in that battle on the Pompeian side were only half-trained ; and the battle was fought only about six months before the triumph. But in the course of his African cam-

Dio, XLIII,
4, 1

paign, which was to be crowned by the victory of Thapsus, Cæsar had sent for some elephants from Italy. Of these animals Dio says that there were only a few, as Cæsar meant to use them, not on the field of battle, but for accustoming the horses of his cavalry to elephants. But it is possible that there were forty or more elephants in Italy at the time, and that Cæsar, not wishing to use them for battle in this cam- paign, sent only for the few that he needed for training his cavalry. And it is not unreasonable to suppose that at the end of the Republican period the Roman government owned in Italy a number of thoroughly trained elephants, which were used as torch-bearers in 46 B.C. Perhaps, when Syria was annexed in 63, some elephants of the Asiatic kind had been found in the stables formerly owned by the Seleucids and had

Polyænus,
VIII, 23, 5

been sent to Italy. If Polyænus is right in saying that Cæsar had an elephant with him in Britain (for the purpose, presum- ably, of terrifying the natives and their chariot-horses), it may

Dio, XLIX,
7, 6

have been one of the government's Italian herd. It was probably on one of the elephants which bore torches for Cæsar at his triumph that Cornificius was afterwards allowed to ride through the streets of Rome when returning from dining out, an honour conferred on him for distinguished services in Octavian's campaign of 36 B.C. against Sextus Pompeius in Sicily.

The display of bull-fighting by mounted Thessalians at Cæsar's *ludi* may have been due to the fact that Pharsalus, where Pompey had been defeated by Cæsar, was in Thessaly, and that after the Battle of Pharsalus Cæsar had granted privileges to the Thessalians. The latter may have voluntarily testified to their gratitude by sending a team of their bull-fighters to give a display at Cæsar's " Victory Games " ; or it may have been suggested to them that they should do so by Cæsar or one of his managers who had seen or heard of this sport. Pliny describes the Thessalian horseman galloping alongside of the bull, seizing it by the horns, and by a twist breaking its neck. Suetonius, in mentioning a display of this kind given under Claudius, says that the horsemen drive the wild bulls about the arena, leap on their backs when they are wearied, and bring them to the ground by their horns.

Lastly, Cæsar's giraffe was probably obtained in Alexandria. It was the first of its kind to appear at Rome. Others were seen there from time to time in the following century, but not till the reign of Commodus is there record of one killed in the arena.

On the whole, it would seem that there was a characteristic distinction about the animal-shows given by Cæsar as Dictator —a distinction which had been lacking in the *ludi* of Pompey.

Pliny, N.H., VIII, 45(70), 182

Plutarch, Cæsar, 48

Pliny, N.H., loc. cit.

Suetonius, Div. Claud., 21, 3

Pliny, N.H., VIII, 18(27), 69 Dio, XLIII, 23, 1–2

CHAPTER IV

SHOWS UNDER THE EARLY EMPIRE
(29 B.C.—A.D. 117)

THE Imperial age of the Roman animal-shows may
be taken as beginning in 29 B.C., when Octavian
(soon to be Augustus), having returned to Italy
from the East after overcoming Antony and annexing Egypt,
celebrated a triumph, and shortly afterwards, in the *ludi* which
accompanied the dedication of a temple to Julius Cæsar, gave
a *venatio* in which great numbers of animals were killed.   From
this time onwards, while shows were still given yearly by
annual magistrates at certain festivals, and wealthy private
individuals might occasionally give *ludi* at Rome, it was above
all the Emperors, with their great organized power and their
wealth, who could entertain the Roman public, if they chose,
by the magnificence, or the interest and variety, of their spectacles.   In particular, for collecting animals both from within
the Empire and from beyond its frontiers, the Emperors had
unrivalled opportunities and means.

In any attempts to draw general conclusions from our
evidence as to the *ludi* of the Early Empire, either about the
comparative numbers of different kinds of animals shown in the
arena, or about the ways in which the animals were exhibited,
certain things about that evidence must be borne in mind.
To begin with, it is throughout this period very scanty and
scrappy ; and in seeking to generalize about the first century
A.D. one may be often defeated by the fact that the evidence
for the two following centuries is even more scanty, besides
being in great part unreliable.   Secondly, the evidence for the

time from Augustus to the first years of Nero (29 B.C.–A.D. 60) differs in rather important ways from the evidence for the time from the later years of Nero to the death of Trajan (A.D. 60–117). For the former time we have much of the original narrative of Dio Cassius, but for the latter only an epitome of his History. Again, in the Lives of the Cæsars by Suetonius the accounts of the Flavian Emperors (A.D. 70–96) are on a slighter scale than those of the Emperors from Augustus to Nero. Yet again, the ' Natural History ' of Pliny, who died in A.D. 79, is, on the whole, an authority for the earlier time. For the Flavian age most of our evidence is to be found in some epigrams of Martial and an interesting poem by Statius.

The result is, that while for the time from Augustus to Nero something is known of exceptionally large numbers of bears, lions, leopards or " African beasts " appearing at particular *ludi*, for the time from Nero to Trajan information of this sort is almost wholly lacking : we hear of thousands of unspecified animals killed on two great occasions (the opening of the Colosseum and the Dacian triumph of Trajan), and we have three or four vague allusions in the poets to some large numbers of animals of one kind or another or from a particular region. On the other hand, what we know of the animals exhibited at Rome in Flavian times is mainly determined by Martial's choice of his subjects for his epigrams on them ; and usually he selected such details as tricks by performing animals, duels between single beasts, or the skill of a popular *venator* in dealing with this beast or that.

Our evidence being as it is, the fact (for example) that there is no indication in our records of any large number of leopards (whether described as " African beasts " or otherwise) being exhibited together at Rome from the middle of the first century A.D. till towards the end of the next century, allows us only to *guess* that during this time leopards did not appear in the arena at Rome in any great numbers. Again it is obviously possible to draw unjustified conclusions about the general character of the animal-shows under Domitian from the few epigrams which Martial wrote on particular incidents in them.

From the little that we know, a few generalizations about this period are perhaps allowable.

(1) As regards sources of supply, it seems that two regions were now drawn on far more than under the Republic—namely the region of the Nile, where Egypt was now a Roman province, and the central and northern parts of Europe, owing to the advance of the Roman Empire in that direction. North Africa (apart from Egypt) was still one of the main areas of supply ; but whether or how far the decrease in the number of dangerous animals in certain districts, owing to the spread of agriculture and the demand for wild beasts for the Roman Games, seriously increased the difficulty in collecting such animals from that region, we cannot tell. Nor is it known how much use was made in this way of Western Asia. India or North Persia, and perhaps the Caucasus, now and then sent a tiger or a number of tigers.

(2) The demand for animals for the Roman Games under the Early Empire was apparently on the whole much greater than under the Republic. It seems that, as the supply of lions and leopards did not suffice to meet the heavy demand for savage beasts (*bestiæ dentatæ*), and tigers were rarities, bears, which could be obtained from any part of Europe under Roman rule or influence, appeared in the Roman arena in larger numbers than before. Again, the proportion of exotic to Italian animals among the " grass-eating " beasts (*bestiæ herbariæ*) seems to have been greater under the Empire than under the Republic. Among the animals which in this period were certainly or probably exhibited in the Roman shows for the first time, were the tiger, camel, several kinds of antelope, wild ass, elk, and bison.

(3) While there was still in this period a great deal of killing of animals—9,000 were killed in the hundred days' shows at the opening of the Colosseum, and 11,000 when Trajan celebrated his Dacian triumph—novel and dramatic effects in the methods of killing them were devised. Moreover, the performances of trained and tamed beasts, which were not killed (though they might be set to kill other animals), became now

an important feature of the shows. Plutarch alludes to the great amount of animal-training done for the Roman Games, and there are signs that in the first century A.D. the skill of the trainers at Rome was very great. On the other hand, the public executions of criminals condemned to the beasts seem to have been more common under the Empire than under the Republic (the administration of criminal justice being now more " efficient "), and they appear to have been often deliberately so planned as to increase the agony of the sufferers ; and a horrible ingenuity was sometimes shown in dramatizing these executions by making them represent stories from Greek mythology and the like. On the whole, it would seem that under the Early Empire as compared with the Republic more striking appeals were made both to the capacity of the spectators for sympathizing with animals or for admiring exhibitions of skill, and also to their taste for the sight of agony. It would be misleading to say that the animal-shows were becoming more humane, though a humane element was now present, along with elaborations of, and refinements on, the old cruelty.[1]

Augustus was very lavish in providing spectacles for the Roman public. In the frequency, variety, and magnificence of the shows which he gave, he was, says Suetonius, unrivalled. The same author notes that he sometimes gave a *venatio* unaccompanied by any other kind of entertainment—evidently this was unusual. In the record which he left behind him of his achievements and honours, he claimed that in 26 *venationes* of " African beasts," which he gave in his own name, or in the names of his sons or grandsons, in the Circus or the Forum or in amphitheatres, about 3,500 animals were killed. These so-called " African beasts " were no doubt

Plutarch, de Sollertia Animal, 5

Suetonius, Div. Aug., 43, 1

Mon. Anc., XXII (IV) 39-42)

---

[1] One of the characters in Plutarch's dialogue on the intelligence of animals (*De Sollertia Animalium*, 7) protests against the killing of animals in the theatres or in hunting for sport—" forcing some to fight against their will, and destroying others that by nature are unable to defend themselves "—and he recalls the fable of the boy throwing stones at frogs—what was sport to him was no sport to them. But there is no sign that such feeling had as yet an appreciable influence in reducing the cruelty of the Roman shows.

mostly lions and leopards, and many of them probably came not from Africa but from Asia (see pp. 52–54 above).

Dio, LI, 22, 5
Pliny, N.H.,
VIII, 17(24), 64
Dio, LIV, 26,
1; LV, 10, 7-8;
LVI, 27, 5

A few occasions in the principate of Augustus when very large numbers of beasts were killed have been mentioned by other authorities. One of these occasions, at the *ludi* given in 29 B.C., has been already noticed (p. 60 above).[1] It is recorded in Pliny that 420 *variæ* (leopards or other large spotted cats) were once exhibited together by Augustus. Dio says that at the dedication of the Theatre of Marcellus (11 B.C.),[2] 600 " African beasts " were killed, and that in 2 B.C., at the dedication of the Temple of Mars Ultor, and in A.D. 12, at *ludi* given in the name of Germanicus, 260 and 200 lions, respectively, were killed in the Circus. At the games of 2 B.C., 36 crocodiles were killed in a pool which had been made in

Ibid., LIII, 27, 6

the Circus Flaminius.[3] Besides these shows, for which Augustus paid, P. Servilius, as prætor in 25 B.C., distinguished himself by giving a show of 300 bears and 300 " African beasts."

Strabo, VI, 2, 6

The elaborate execution at Rome of a brigand from Mt. Etna,

---

[1] Dio's phrase is θηρία καὶ βοτὰ παμπληθῆ. θηρία καὶ βοτά = feræ et pecudes (cf. Suetonius, Nero, 31, 1). Lions, leopards, and bears would be in the class of θηρία and feræ, cattle, deer and pigs in the class of βοτά and pecudes. Other general terms classifying the animals of the venatio were bestiæ dentatæ (lions, leopards, bears, and presumably boars), and bestiæ herbariæ (or herbaticæ or herbanæ). In the second century A.D. there was a præpositus herbariarum at Rome (Dessau, Inscr. Lat. Sel., 5159).

[2] Dio places the dedication of this theatre in 13 B.C. But the date given by Pliny (N.H., VIII, 17(25), 65), 11 B.C., seems more likely to be correct.

[3] These may have been the crocodiles which were accompanied to Rome by some men from Tentyra near Coptos (Strabo, XVII, 1, 44). The crocodile as a destroyer of garbage was appreciated and revered almost everywhere in Egypt, but the Tentyrites had a great reputation for pursuing it relentlessly and fearlessly. A number of these men, says Strabo, went with some crocodiles to Rome to give a display of their skill and courage, and there entered the beasts' pond and dragged them in nets to the platforms for the spectators to see, and drew them thence again into the water.

No animal is cheaper to obtain or more easily transported than the crocodile; the one difficulty is its refusal to eat when boxed in transit.

witnessed by Strabo in the Forum, where the man was put on a high stage with scenery suggesting the mountain, and was then dropped through the floor of the stage into a cage full of wild beasts, is an example from the time of Augustus of a form of public entertainment, of which dreadful variations were afterwards devised.

Performances of elephants in the arena seem to have been popular in the Augustan age. According to Pliny, at a time when elephants had not yet been shown walking the tight-rope, it was " common " (*volgare*) to make them throw weapons into the air (a trick probably suggested to trainers by the elephant in Pompey's shows that made a circle of shields round it ; see above, p. 52), and fight duels and go through a kind of " musical ride " (*lasciviente pyrrhice conludere*). As elephants on the tight-rope were exhibited at Rome in the reign of Tiberius, it would seem that in the time of Augustus these animals " commonly " appeared in other performances. At a gladiatorial show given by Germanicus, probably in A.D. 12, a dozen elephants danced and dined. That at this time elephants could be seen by the Roman public at close quarters elsewhere than in the arena, is shown by the story that Augustus, when presented with a petition by a timid suitor, genially told the man that he held it out " like a penny to an elephant."

According to Ælian, the twelve elephants which performed at the shows of Germanicus had been bred from the herd of large animals then at Rome, and had been bought when young by the trainer who taught them their tricks. No doubt under Augustus, as in the time of Julius Cæsar, a herd of elephants belonging to the State was kept permanently in Italy. Under the successors of Augustus there was a herd which was imperial property (or perhaps, more strictly, the property of the State under imperial management) established in the Campagna in the neighbourhood of Ardea and Laurentum. At Laurentum in the first century A.D. there was a *procurator ad elephantos*, and Juvenal speaks of the elephant-herd which pastured in the country about Ardea :

> Arboribus Rutulis et Turni pascitur agro
> Cæsaris armentum nulli servire paratum
> Privato.

Pliny, *N.H.*, VIII, 2(2), 5
Suetonius, *Galba*, 6, 1

Pliny, *N.H.*, VIII, 2(2), 4
Ælian, *N.A.*, II, 11

Suetonius, *Div. Aug.*, 53, 2

Ælian, *N.A.*, II, 11

Dessau, *Inscr. Lat. Sel.*, 1578
Juvenal, XII, 104-6

Pliny, *N.H.*,
VIII, 2(2), 5 ;
7(7), 22

Though elephants took part in fights in the arena (Pliny mentions not only elephant-duels, but also the appearance of " single elephants " in the finale of gladiatorial shows under Claudius and Nero—meaning perhaps that there would be one elephant on either side in a mêlée of gladiators), it is likely enough that these animals were not often killed in such displays. And the imperial government seems to have made little or no use of them for war. Though some elephants were taken to

Dio, LX, 21, 2

Britain in the Claudian invasion of the island (A.D. 43), it appears that they were not with the expeditionary force when it landed, but that they came later with the Emperor himself ; which suggests that they were brought rather to impress the natives in ceremonies than to be employed in military opera-

Dio (Epitome),
LXXIII, 16

tions. It is clear from a story in Dio that at the end of the second century A.D. the elephants kept in or near Rome were not trained for war.

Horace, *Epp.*,
II, 1, 196

A white elephant from Siam may have been sent to Augustus. Horace speaks of a giraffe or white elephant (*elephas albus*) attracting the attention of the public at *ludi*. It is possible that envoys from Siam are referred to in some vague phrases

Florus, II, 34 ;
(IV, 12), 62

of Florus, who mentions, among the foreign ambassadors received by Augustus, " Seres, and Indians living right under the sun, bringing elephants, as well as gems and pearls among their gifts," and having been four years on their journey.[1]

However that may be, a number of exotic animals which had rarely or never been seen before at Rome were exhibited there under Augustus. Some of these may have been spoils

Dio, LI, 22, 5

of war ; for example, the hippopotamus and the rhinoceros which were killed in the games of 29 B.C. may have been found at Alexandria when Augustus annexed Egypt. Others came as presents to Augustus from far countries. To the rulers of Eastern peoples beyond the limits of the Empire it would seem that a Great King had arisen in the West, to whom

---

[1] Seres etiam habitantesque sub ipso sole Indi cum gemmis et margaritis elephantos quoque inter munera trahentes nihil magis quam longinquitatem viae inputabant ⟨. . .⟩ quadriennium impleverant ; et iam (*mss.* et tamen) ipse hominum color ab alio venire sole fatebatur.

their ambassadors should bear gifts. The annexation of Egypt by Rome was followed by a development of trade between that country and Southern India, and in Augustus' own record of his achievements it is said that embassies were often sent to him by Indian Kings.

Mon. Anc., XXXI

Ambassadors from India on their way to Augustus were seen by Nicolaus of Damascus at Antioch ; and his account (as reported by Strabo) tallies in two points with the account given by Dio of an Indian embassy which found Augustus at Samos in the winter of 20–19 B.C.[1] Nicolaus wrote that among the gifts which the ambassadors were bringing to Augustus were some large venomous snakes (ἐχίδνας μεγάλας—hamadryad cobras ?), a snake of ten cubits (a length attained by the Python Molurus), a river tortoise measuring three cubits (which is quite possible), and " a partridge larger than a vulture "—probably the Argus pheasant, possibly the Lesser Bustard or the Tragopan pheasant. According to Dio, the Indian embassy received by Augustus at Samos brought some tigers. But Pliny says that the first tiger shown at Rome was a tame animal, exhibited in a cage at the dedication of the Temple of Marcellus in 11 B.C. And if tigers had been presented to Augustus at Samos in 19 B.C. it would surely not have been eight years before the Roman public saw this novelty, unless indeed the animals died before they could be brought to Rome from Samos. But in any case it is probably true that the first tiger seen at Rome was a gift to Augustus from some Indian king.

Strabo, XV, 1,73
Dio, LIV, 9, 8

Pliny, N.H., VIII, 17(25), 65

Suetonius says that a rarity brought to Rome would be put on view by Augustus somewhere in the city, and that in this way a rhinoceros was exhibited at the Sæpta, a tiger on the stage, and a snake fifty cubits long in front of the Comitium. Whether this rhinoceros was the one killed at the shows of 29 B.C., cannot be told. The tiger on the stage was no doubt the tame beast mentioned by Pliny as appearing at the dedica-

Suetonius, *Div. Aug.,* 43, 4

---

[1] According to both, one of the presents for Augustus was an armless boy, and one of the Indians accompanying the embassy voluntarily burnt himself to death at Athens.

F

tion of the Theatre of Marcellus. If the snake shown in front of the Comitium was really 75 feet long, it was much larger than any known in modern times ; probably it was not nearly so long. Most people grossly exaggerate the length of a snake, though it lies curled before them.

Augustus had the ordinary desire of the Roman noble to win popularity by the giving of shows, and to attain distinction by outdistancing others in this line. The Emperor Tiberius (A.D. 14–37) did not follow his predecessor's example in this respect, though at the beginning of his reign he was careful to appear at *spectacula* out of deference to public opinion. It seems that, probably from a mixture of reasonableness and morbid temper, he acted up to the disapproval, which he expressed, of lavish expenditure on *ludi*. The only record which we have of a notable animal-show in his time is the exhibition, already mentioned, of elephants on the tight-rope, given by the future Emperor Galba when prætor. It may be noticed that Tiberius shared the prevalent taste for animal-keeping so far as to own a large snake which he fed with his own hand.

Under Caligula (A.D. 37–41) the indulgence of public tastes which had been neglected by Tiberius may have been at first a matter of policy with the advisers of the young Emperor, and then have been continued by him, partly for his own extravagant amusement, and partly because his growing hatred and fear of the Senate made him court the favour of the masses. At the beginning of his reign the consecration of the Temple of Augustus was lavishly celebrated, and Dio notes among the entertainments then given a *venatio* of 400 bears and 400 " African beasts." Suetonius mentions—along with the gladiatorial shows, stage-plays, pageants, and races which the Emperor frequently gave—the exhibition of *venationes* in the Circus as interludes in the day-long series of chariot-races which were common in this reign. As will be noticed in chapter X, a day of mixed entertainment would usually begin with a *venatio* in the morning.

Under the Emperor Claudius (A.D. 41–54) a considerable number of magnificent shows were given at the Emperor's

Suetonius,
Tiberius, 34, 1

Ibid., *Galba*,
6, 1

Ibid., *Tiberius*,
72, 2

Dio, LIX, 7, 3

expense. To please the public by lavish spectacles was one of the ways in which it might be reconciled to the oddities of the Emperor. Claudius himself was fascinated by bloody sights ; he enjoyed seeing men fight for their lives against wild beasts or hacking one another. But when not under the influence of this attraction he could act humanely, and he was capable of ordering the destruction of a lion trained as a man-eater ; the lion's performances are said to have been very popular, but the Emperor decided that they were not fit for Romans to watch. *(Suetonius, Div. Claud., 21, 1; Suetonius, Div. Claud., 34, 2; Dio, LX, 13,)*

Dio records a great *venatio* of 300 bears and as many African beasts in the first few months of this reign. A feature of the shows which included this *venatio* was a race of chariots drawn by camels. Suetonius mentions that the exhibition of *venationes* as interludes in chariot-racing was continued under Claudius, and that on one occasion a troop of the cavalry of the Prætorian Guard, with some of the Guard's higher officers (*tribuni*), and even one of its commanders-in-chief (a *præfectus* —there were probably two prætorian prefects at the time) were pitted against a number of African beasts. On another occasion there was a display of bull-fighting by mounted Thessalians, such as had first been seen at Rome in the Victory Games of Julius Cæsar (p. 59 above). The appearance of elephants in mêlées of gladiators under Claudius has been already mentioned (p. 66). *(Dio, LX, 7, 3; Suetonius, Div. Claud., 21, 3)*

In contrast with the story of the man-eating lion, there is the incident, which probably happened under Claudius, of the slave Androclus, who had been condemned to the beasts, being recognized and affectionately greeted in the arena at Rome by a lion which he had relieved of a thorn in its foot when he was wandering as a fugitive in the desert.[1] It may have been under Claudius that Seneca saw a lion protect from other lions a beast-fighter who had been its keeper. *(Apion of Alexandria, quoted by Aulus Gellius, V, 14; Ælian, N.A., VII, 48; Seneca, De Benefic., II, 19)*

[1] The charming story is told in minute detail by Aulus Gellius, and by Ælian, who incorporates the interesting information, that the lion made short work of a leopard which had been subsequently released against Androclus.

Pliny, *N.H.*, VIII, 16(21), 54

Pliny tells a story that in the time of Claudius a lion in Africa was made dazed and helpless by having a shepherd's cloak thrown over its head, and that this method of dealing with lions was then exhibited in the arena.

Ibid., 17(25), 65

Four tigers were shown together by Claudius. These may have been the first animals of the kind to be seen by the public at Rome since the tiger which Augustus put on the stage at the dedication of the Theatre of Marcellus. It seems from Pliny's notice of them that four tigers together were an unprecedented sight at Rome.

Nero (A.D. 54–68) had a liking for the extravagant, the novel, and the fantastic. Moreover, he, like Caligula, may have felt in the later part of his reign that to gratify the masses by spectacles was to do something to counterbalance the hatred of him in the minds of the senatorial aristocracy. He had the taste for keeping exotic animals; in the grounds of his

Suetonius, *Nero*, 31, 1; 11, 2

Golden House at Rome were animals of all kinds [1]; and wild beasts which had been tamed (*mansuetæ feræ*), as well as birds and draught animals, were among the prizes which he offered in free public lotteries.

Ibid., 11, 1

The spectacles which he gave were of many different kinds. But we have very few details of animal-shows which can quite certainly be dated to his reign. He repeated some of the more remarkable displays given under his predecessor. For example, there were races of camel-drawn chariots, four camels

Dio, LXI, 9, 1

being harnessed to a car; cavalry of the Prætorian Guard had to engage 400 bears and 300 lions; there was an exhibition of bull-fighting (though, if Dio's account is exact, the fighters were on foot, not on horseback as under Claudius); and

Pliny, *N.H.*, VIII, 7(7), 22

elephants still took part in the final mêlées of gladiatorial shows. But a fight between (apparently) men in boats and sea-beasts in an artificial lake filled with salt water seems to have been

Suetonius, *Nero*, 12, 1

a novelty. Suetonius notes that at Nero's shows senators and knights appeared in the arena to kill wild beasts.

Calpurnius, *Ecl.* VII, 57–69

The poem known as the Seventh Eclogue of Calpurnius

---

[1] Cum multitudine omnis generis pecudum ac ferarum. On *pecudes ac feræ*, see p. 64, n. 1.

describes an animal-show at Rome. If, as is generally, but, as I think, wrongly supposed, it was written under Nero, we should infer that in this reign Rome saw the polar bear, probably for the first and perhaps for the only time. For it is most likely that the bears which the poet describes as (apparently) fighting over seals were of this kind. It would be interesting to know just how polar bears reached Italy in the time of the Roman Empire. Other animals mentioned in the poem as exhibited at the *ludi* there described are the variable hare (*niveos lepores*), " the horned boar " (*non sine cornibus apros*), perhaps the warthog from the sources of the Nile, the elk (from Germany), humped oxen (zebu cattle from Cyprus ?), oxen maned and bearded, and with bristles about the throat (probably the gnu now found in Uganda), and a hippopotamus from the Nile. Animals were made to emerge into the arena from underground. The question whether the poem is of the Neronian age or later is discussed in an Appendix (pp. 188–189). If polar bears were seen at Rome under Nero, it is somewhat remarkable, though not, of course, wholly unaccountable, that they are not mentioned in Pliny's *Natural History*.

It may have been under Nero that Pliny saw the performing bulls, which he describes as fighting and rolling over at the word of command, letting themselves be caught and lifted by the horns, and even standing like charioteers in cars going at a gallop. [Pliny, *N.H.*, VIII, 45(70), 182]

Seneca mentions as an ordinary morning item in a show, a fight between a bull and a bear tied together, the winner being afterwards killed by a *confector*, one of the attendants who despatched wounded beasts or men. [Seneca, *De Ira*, III, 43, 2]

In Seneca's Letters, which were written in this reign, we have an allusion to the feats of tamers and trainers of animals —to the tamer who puts his hand into the lion's mouth, to the keeper who kisses the tiger, to the negro dwarf (*minimus Æthiops*) who orders an elephant to kneel or walk the tightrope. [Seneca, *Epp.*, 85, 41]

Another passage in these Letters shows that tamed lions [Ibid., 41, 6] sometimes had their manes gilded. " The lion with gilded mane, what with being trained and forced by weariness to endure the decoration, is sent into the arena in a state quite different from that of the wild lion whose spirit is unbroken ; of course the latter, bold in his attack, as nature wished him to be, impressive in his wild appearance, and whose glory it is that he cannot be looked at without fear, is thought a finer animal than the other in his languor and gold leaf (*præfertur illi languido et bratteato*)."

Petronius,
Satyricon,
119, 14

Petronius, Nero's *arbiter elegantiarūm*, gives a grim picture of ghastly magnificence in the public execution of criminals condemned to the beasts. " Wild beasts are hunted in forests for gold, and Hammon deep in Africa is searched to supply the monster whose teeth make him precious for giving men their deaths ; strange ravening creatures freight the fleets, and the padding tiger is carried in a gilded palace, to drink human blood while the crowd applauds." [1]

The death of Nero was followed by eighteen months of insecurity and civil war, and the three Emperors, Galba, Otho and Vitellius, who reigned and fell in this period, did not particularly distinguish themselves, while they ruled, as givers of shows. Vespasian (A.D. 69–79) found a public deficit of about £320,000,000, and set about the work of restoration in a businesslike way. This may partly account for our knowing only one detail about the exhibition of animals at Rome that can be dated to this reign with certainty—namely that the Emperor and others were much struck by a clever per-

Plutarch, *de
Sollertia Anim.,*
19

forming dog, which took part in a dramatic entertainment at the Theatre of Marcellus. Yet it was Vespasian who began the building of the great Flavian Amphitheatre, the Colosseum, which was opened under his successor, Titus.

Titus (A.D. 79–81) enjoyed spending money in ways that made him popular, and the dedication of the Colosseum, in the year 80, was celebrated by shows lasting for a hundred days. Besides the gladiatorial fights and chariot-races there

---

[1] Tigris et aurata gradiens vectatur in aula,
Ut bibat humanum populo plaudente cruorem.

were *venationes* in which 9,000 animals were killed, 5,000 being exhibited in one day, no doubt in a procession or parade (*pompa*).[1] In the Epitome of Dio there are a few details about the animals shown ; and it will be assumed here that all the epigrams on animals which Martial published in his *Liber de Spectaculis* refer to these *ludi*—if these verses or some of them were in fact written on incidents that occurred at shows early in the reign of Domitian, that matters little for our purpose.[2] Dio (Epitome), LXVI, 25
Suetonius, *Div. Tit.*, 7, 3

Of the *lions*, a trained animal that bit its trainer's hand was destroyed. A lion was killed by a woman, and at least one lion was among the twenty beasts killed by the young " Star " *venator* Carpophorus, whose skill seems to have been one of the most admired things in these *ludi*. Note the curious observation, " The lion would not face him but sprang on the spears." Yet another lion was fought and defeated by a tame tiger, though whether this fight was according to programme is not clear. This is the only mention of a *tiger* at these shows, and the *leopard* appears only as one of the beasts that fell to the hand of Carpophorus. Of course it is likely that among the 9,000 animals killed there were hundreds of leopards and lions. Martial, *de Spectac.*, 10 ;
6 b ; 15 (cf. 23 and 27) ; 18

Ibid., 23
Cf. p. 178
below

Bears were used for the execution of criminals. One of these men had to play the part of the robber Laureolus in a mime of that name, and as Laureolus he was bound to a cross for a bear to devour. A Caledonian bear, Martial calls it : the advance of Agricola into the northern part of Britain was bringing Caledonia to the notice of the Roman public. A bear tore another condemned man who was made (apparently) first to appear to be flying and then to fall where the bear was. Martial's epithet for this animal is " Lucanian "— Lucania in South Italy was a noted bear-country. Again, a *Ibid.*, 7 ; 8   21

---

[1] Dio, or his epitomator, says that the 9,000 were καὶ βοτὰ καὶ θηρία ; Suetonius, that 5,000 of all sorts of *feræ* were shown on one day. But if βοτά here means *bestiæ herbariæ*, and θηρία *bestiæ dentatæ*, one cannot be sure that the *feræ* of Suetonius were only the θηρία and did not include also wild " grass-eating " animals.

[2] The references to Martial in this book follows the numbering of the epigrams in W. M. Lindsay's edition (Oxford Classical Texts).

stage, on which rocks and a forest were represented, was made to rise from out of the crypts below the arena with Orpheus on it among beasts and birds ; but the Orpheus was a criminal and the scene ended with a bear killing him.

Ibid., 15 ; 11, 22

A bear died by the hunting-spear of Carpophorus, and another, in flight from a *venator*, was caught in bird-lime. Lastly a bear was tossed by a two-horned rhinoceros.

Ibid., 22 ; 9

This two-horned (African) *rhinoceros—cornu gemino—*was of a kind which appears to have been rarely brought to Rome ; it was the one-horned (Indian) variety which had " often "

Pliny, *N.H.*, VIII, 20(29), 71

been seen there by Pliny's time. This two-horned beast that Martial saw was sluggish, and its keepers had difficulty in making it show fight ; but when roused at last it threw the bear into the air like a bull tossing a dummy figure. It also killed a bull.

Dio (Epitome), LXVI, 25
Martial, *de Spectac.*, 19 ; 17

Four *elephants*, according to the Epitome of Dio, fought in these shows—perhaps in a gladiatorial mêlée. Martial describes the goading of a *bull* by flaming darts, and the irritating of it by dummy figures, till it was brought to attack an elephant, which killed it, and then kneeled before the Emperor—entirely of its own accord, says Martial : " You may be sure that it too recognizes our god."

Dio (Epitome), LXVI, 25
Martial, *de Spectac.*, 28

Trained *bulls* and *horses* appeared in a water-show—the arena being suddenly flooded, and the animals swimming in the water and drawing boats shaped as cars ; at least something of the sort is suggested by Martial's description. The

Ibid., 16; 16b ; 5 ; 23

bull that was lifted in the air by a machine, as carrying Hercules up to heaven, may have been a real bull ; that in a representation of the story of Pasiphæ was probably a wooden figure, as in a performance in Nero's time. Carpophorus killed an *aurochs* and a *bison*, probably from Germany. Martial

Pliny, *N.H.*, VIII, 15(15), 38

calls the former *bubalus* ; but Pliny had written that this name, which was properly that of an African antelope, was wrongly applied by the vulgar to the *urus*. The maned bison and the very strong and swift *urus* Pliny mentions as two kinds of wild

Cæsar, *B.G.*, VI, 28

ox native to Germany ; and Cæsar had heard tales of *urus*-hunting among the Germans.

A great *boar* was killed by Carpophorus. And in a representation of Diana hunting wild animals, a pregnant wild sow was killed, which in its death gave birth to its young—a reference to Diana's function as Lucina, the goddess of birth. Martial, *de Spectac.*, 15; 12–14

A deer or antelope of some kind (*damma*), chased by hounds in the arena, fled to where the Emperor sat, and seemed to implore his protection, while the hounds refrained from attacking it. On how this was managed, Martial's reference to the Emperor's divinity throws no light. *Ibid.*, 30

Lastly, the Epitome of Dio records a fight of *cranes*. Possibly the birds were exhibited performing their curious mating-dance—a " turn " that would be much to the credit of the skill of its producer. Dio (Epitome), LXVI, 25

Domitian (A.D. 81–96), the brother and successor of Titus, was not genial, but was ambitious of using his power in an imposing way. " He frequently gave magnificent and expensive shows," says Suetonius. He was interested in archery, and had an arena at his Alban villa, where the *venationes* were " very fine " (*eximiæ*), and where he admitted spectators to exhibitions of his own skill with the bow, often killing a hundred beasts at a single shoot, and practising the trick of making two successive arrows stick in an animal's head as if they were horns. It seems that some privileged persons were allowed to shoot with him. And when one of them, M.' Acilius Glabrio (whom the Emperor afterwards put to death), was holding the consulship, he was compelled, says the Epitomator of Dio, to fight a large lion ; but it may have been a voluntary action, for Glabrio was apparently a noted amateur *venator*. Suetonius, *Dom.*, 4 *Ibid.*, 4, 4; 19 Dio (Epitome), LXVII, 14 Juvenal, IV, 94–101

Under Domitian Martial occasionally wrote verses on particular incidents in the animal-shows given by the Emperor at Rome, but his references to the subject under this reign (if those in his *Liber de Spectaculis* belong to the reign of Titus) are not many, and about half of them are concerned with a single trick—that of lions trained to " retrieve " hares without harming them. The following points in his allusions may be noticed.

(*a*) In A.D. 93, at the fêtes which celebrated the return of Martial, VIII, 26

the Emperor from the Sarmatian War on the Danube, a
number of tigers were exhibited—a number large enough to
make it possible for Martial to say that Rome had now seen
more new tigers than the tiger-hunter by the Ganges had to
fear, and that she could not count her treasures. But that
only means that this lot of tigers was considerably larger than
any lot of these animals previously brought to Rome ; and that
may mean very little. Pliny had thought it worth recording that
four tigers were exhibited together by Claudius. And the only
definite assertion as to their number that is made in Martial's
epigram is to the effect (ll. 7, 8) that it was more than two.

The fact that these tigers were exhibited at the end of a
Sarmatian War, and the further fact, that a tiger is among the
animals which appear on a diptych of Constantine the Great
connected with the festivals that followed a pacification of the
Sarmatians, have caused it to be suggested that the tiger was
still to be found west of the Volga, and that those brought to
Rome in A.D. 93 came from that region. This argument has
some weak points, which may be noticed.

(1) Constantine, at the festivals mentioned above, was
receiving embassies from Persia and India, and the animals
on the diptych in question include an elephant.

(2) The Sarmatian people with whom there was *certainly*
war in Domitian's time was the tribe of the Iazyges, who lived
as far west as the Hungarian plain, in the country between the
Theiss and the Danube. We do not *know* that this war spread
to the Sarmatian peoples east of the Carpathians, though it
may have done so.

(3) At any rate, the war did not end in any great success
for Rome, for Domitian did not celebrate a triumph at its close.
And though one might imagine some Sarmatian chiefs trying
to gain their ends in negotiation by offering the Emperor a
present of tigers (if they had any in their country), yet surely,
if the tigers had been acquired in that way, the fact would
have been impressed on the public as showing the submissive-
ness of the barbarians, and Martial would have made a compli-
ment to the Emperor out of it. But he only says that Cæsar's

show outdoes the triumph of Bacchus who, when he led India captive at his chariot-wheels, was content with a pair of tigers.[1]

Probably, therefore, these tigers were a purchase or a diplomatic present from India or Persia. That these were the countries from which tigers were expected to come is oddly brought out by Martial, who mounts the tiger-hunter by the Ganges on a Hyrcanian (North-Persian) horse.

On the whole, the tiger, which had to be sought beyond the boundaries of the Empire and at such a great distance from Italy, continued to be a rarity at Rome. No doubt, after the time of Claudius there were nearly always a few specimens in Italy ; but apart from these tigers of Domitian's, and the 51 tigers exhibited by Elagabalus (p. 91), and, perhaps one should add, the unnamed number shown by Antoninus Pius (p. 84), it seems that we have no indication of a large number of these animals being exhibited in Imperial Rome.

(b) Martial had seen the wild ass—*pulcher onager*. He refers to its whiteness, which is also mentioned by " Oppian." Wild asses were to be found in Africa, in Asia Minor (those of Phrygia and Lycaonia, says Pliny, are the finest—*præcipui*), and in Syria. *(Martial, XIII, 100; "Oppian," Cyn., III, 186-8; Pliny, N.H., VIII, 44(69), 174)*

(c) Martial seems to allude to the crowd in the amphitheatre amusing itself by waving its togas to startle a gazelle (*dorcas*). He mentions a gazelle of this kind as a pet for a little boy, and no doubt the animal meant is the little creature 24 inches high (*Gazella dorcas*), very common in Egyptian deserts. *(Martial, XIII, 99)*

(d) Apparently he saw the *oryx* (beisa antelope)—the *sævus oryx*—killing hounds in the arena. " Oppian " celebrates the fierce courage of the *oryx* ; Pliny knew of it as coming from African deserts. It had long been domesticated in Egypt. *(Ibid., 95; "Oppian," Cyn., III, 445 foll.; Pliny, N.H., X, 71(94), 201 ; XI, 46(106), 25)*

[1] Non tot in Eois timuit Gangeticus arvis
    Raptor, in Hyrcano qui fugit albus equo,
  Quot tua Roma novas vidit, Germanice, tigres ;
    Delicias potuit nec numerare suas.
  Vincit Erythræos tua, Cæsar, harena triumphos,
    Et victoris opes divitiasque dei :
  Nam cum captivos ageret sub curribus Indos
    Contentus gemina tigride Bacchus erat.

Aristotle, *H.A.*, II, 499b, 20

Aristotle, copied by Pliny, calls it one-horned. This was probably the result of a simple breeder's trick, by which the

Cf. Pliny, *N.H.*, XI, 37(45), 127

two horns of the oryx were bound together tightly as soon as they appeared on the young animal ; in a year they would touch, grow alongside, and form a single sutured horn.[1] The writer has seen a ram on which the trick had been worked.

Martial, IV, 74 ; cf. 35

The small *dammæ* (animals of the deer kind) which surprised the spectators by butting each other fiercely *parvis frontibus*, may have been antelopes of some sort ; for these animals are more ferocious than lions.

Martial, V. 31 ; I, 104, ll. 9–10, ll. 1–8

(e) The other interesting references in Martial (outside his *Liber de Spectaculis*) to the animals of the arena are concerned with the performances of tamed and trained beasts. Boys dancing on bulls are the subject of one epigram. An elephant dancing to the orders of a negro is mentioned in another, where also a number of wild animals are described as going in harness —the list includes the leopard, tigers, stags, bears, the wild boar, and the bison ; the greatest marvel of all here is the success of the trainer with stags.

Martial, I, 6 ; 14 ; 22 ; 44 ; 48 ; 51 ; 60 ; 104, ll. 12–22 (on the bulls, see 48 ; 51 ; 60 ; 104)

It has been mentioned already that Martial seems to have been extraordinarily impressed by the lions trained to catch hares alive and hold them in their mouths without harming them. It was certainly a wonderful manifestation of the trainer's skill. Apparently the producer of the trick made his lions kill bulls in the arena before they were set to play with the hares.

Ibid., IX, 71 ; II, 75

Martial had seen a lion and a ram living and feeding peacefully together in one cage. On the other hand, he records a tamed lion that suddenly turned savage in the arena, and killed two of the boys who were raking over the blood-stained sand.

Ibid., VIII, 53 ; V, 65

Of lions killed in *venationes* in this reign, Martial mentions only, besides one exceptionally fine beast, a vaguely indicated

---

[1] Pliny (*N.H.*, XI, 37(45), 127), in his notes on the horns of animals, says : " Adeoque sequax natura est ut in ipsis viventium corporibus ferventi cera flectantur." Horns are so pliable that even on the bodies of living animals they can be bent with hot wax.

large number, which, with many boars and " beasts from the Nile," were killed, probably, at the Games accompanying the triumph of the Emperor over Dacians and Chatti in A.D. 89.

The poet Statius, who wrote under Domitian, gives an interesting picture of the death of a trained lion in the arena. Statius, *Silvæ* II, 5

" What has it availed you to turn mild after your shows of anger [1] ; to unlearn your wicked instinct for man's blood ; to endure commands, and to obey a master weaker than you ; to be taught to leave your cage and return to it and quit your prey of your own accord ; to release the hand which you had held loosely in your jaws ? You have fallen, you well-trained ravager of tall beasts, not compassed about by a band of Massylian hunters, nor caught in winding toils, nor with terrible spring overleaping the spears, nor duped by the masked mouth of the pit, but conquered by a beast in flight. Your cage stands with open door, a cage of mourning. All round, by their locked gates, the lions that were lying quiet [2] bristled [3] with anger that this wrong was permitted. Then they all drooped their manes, and were ashamed to watch your body carried back, and drew their grim [4] foreheads over their eyes. But not at one blow, when you were smitten down, did that strange dishonour overwhelm you. Your spirit remained, and as you were sinking, your valour returned to you even in the jaws of death, and all your menaces did not give way at once. As a soldier that knows how deep is his wound moves dying against the enemy before him, and raises his hand, threatening with failing sword ; so did this lion, moving with slow steps, and stripped of his wonted pride, open his jaws and harden his eyes, and pant for breath and for his enemy.

" Yet for your sudden death, defeated lion, much consolation will it be to take with you, that People and Senate mourn you and lament for your death, as though you were a famous gladiator falling on the sorrowful sand—that among so many

---

[1] Reading : *Quid tibi monstrata mansuescere profuit ira ?* To teach a beast to make a show of anger is common with trainers.

[2] Reading *placidi*.   [3] Reading *intumuere*.   [4] Reading *torvas*.

beasts whose death is of no account, from Scythia and from Libya,[1] and the banks of the Rhine and the land of Egypt. Cæsar's countenance was changed only for one lion lost."

The description of the dying lion is admirably true. Apparently the *fera* which had been fleeing from it had rounded on it, and had caught it a blow or nipped it on the backbone just above the loins—a fatal spot in lions. The place is so weak that I have known two lions killed unintentionally by a blow there from a broomstick. To the lion in Statius death comes slowly ; the hindquarters, paralysed, drop on the sand, while the beast, panting, snarling, open-mouthed, eyes blazing, wild with impotent rage, drags his useless body towards his foe.

What was the *fera* that had the luck to bring the lion down ? I can imagine but three, a bear, a leopard or another lion—the first is ruled out at once, it would not have run away ; the leopard, recognizing, as all wild creatures do, its master, would have fled at all speed, and nothing but the bounds of the arena would have stopped it there ; of course it might have made a snap as does a cornered rat. Probably it was another lion, however inferior. The whole point of the fight was to show that, tamed though it was, this magnificent lion need fear no foe. The weaker beast would certainly fight, and flee after the first exchanges went against him, and then, when his strong adversary joined him once again, would turn and strike or snap, and, as it chanced, by a lucky stroke achieve a victory.

Nor need we wonder that the other lions were angry that such a *nefas*—such a breach of the due order of things— should have happened. Lions fight often, but between them such an accident is almost, if not quite, unknown, though a man could so easily destroy a lion in this way.

The last lines of the poem are interesting. If they are not to be taken as exactly informing us where the animals killed in these shows came from, they may indicate what regions would naturally be thought of at this time as sources of supply for

---

[1] Reading *Scythicas Libycasque.* See note on l. 28 in Phillimore's edition (Oxford Classical Texts).

the Roman animal-shows. " Scythia," presumably, stands for the countries on and beyond the eastern part of the northern frontier of the Empire, as the Rhine for the countries on and beyond the western part. The reading *Libycasque* not being quite certain, North Africa may or may not have been mentioned here by Statius.

Enough evidence has perhaps been given to make what was said at the beginning of the chapter, about the performances of trained animals at the Roman Games under the Early Empire, seem permissible. Plutarch says that it would be easy to draw from the imperial theatres at Rome innumerable examples of the teachableness and intelligence of animals. A mention of the staff of trainers for the amphitheatre is to be found in Martial's epigram on the bitch Lydia, " brought up among the *amphitheatrales magistri*," and owned by Dexter, who used her for hunting till she was killed by a boar. This suggests that these *magistri* made a business of training animals for private owners, just as gamekeepers do to-day. [Plutarch, *de Sollertia Animal.*, 5] [Martial, XI, 69]

On the animals exhibited at Rome in the reigns of Nerva and Trajan (A.D. 96–117) there is only the statement in the Epitome of Dio, that when Trajan celebrated his Dacian triumph (A.D. 107), Games were held for 120 days, in the course of which 10,000 gladiators fought, and 11,000 animals ($\theta\eta\rho\iota\alpha$ $\varkappa\alpha\iota$ $\beta\sigma\tau\dot{\alpha}$) were killed. But we have a reference, in the Letters of the Younger Pliny, to an entertainment given by a friend of his (about A.D. 106) in the amphitheatre at Verona, for which, says Pliny, " very many African beasts " had been purchased, though they were prevented by bad weather from arriving in time. And this may serve as an excuse for noting some of the little evidence which we have about the animals exhibited at shows in the municipalities of Italy and Sicily under the Empire. [Dio (Epitome), LXVIII, 15] [Pliny, *Epp.*, VI, 34, 3]

What can be gathered on this point from the inscriptions in Dessau's Selection may be set out here.

(1) Pompeii. (*a*) Bulls (with bull-fighters), boars, bears, and other animals not specified. (From the time of Augustus.) [Dessau, *Inscr. Lat., Sel.* 5053] [*Ibid.*, 5147]

(*b*) From a notice on a wall : " This *venatio* will be fought on August 28th. Bear-fighting by Felix." (*Hec venatio pugnabet V k. Septembres, et Felix pugnabet ad ursos.*)

Ibid., 5054   (2) Probably in Campania. A mixed *venatio* (*venatio passiva*), 10 *bestiæ* (*herbariæ* ?), 4 *feræ dentatæ*.

Ibid., 5055   (3) Panormus (Palermo). " Every kind " of *bestiæ herbariæ*, many " eastern beasts " (*orientales bestiæ*).

Ibid., 5059   (4) Allifæ. African beasts (*bestiæ Africanæ*).

Ibid., 5060   (5) Telesia in Samnium. African beasts (*feræ Libycæ*).

Ibid., 5061   (6) Salernum. African beasts (*feræ Libycæ*).

Ibid., 5062   (7) Minturnæ (A.D. 249). (*a*) At one show, bears, and *bestiæ herbanæ* (i.e. *herbariæ*).

             (*b*) At another show lasting 4 days, 10 fierce bears (*ursi crudeles*), and on each day 4 *herbanæ* (*herban. univers. in dies sing. occidit quaternos.*).

Iibd., 5063a   (8) Beneventum. 4 *feræ* (*Africanæ* ?), 16 bears, 4 criminals condemned to the beasts (*noxii*), and *herbariæ*.

It will be noticed, that where the numbers of animals at these local shows are given, they are small.

THE SHIP OF CARACALLA (*see p.* 90)

CHAPTER V

SHOWS FROM HADRIAN TO HONORIUS
(A.D. 117–410)

OUR information about animals exhibited at Rome in the three centuries from Hadrian to Honorius is very fragmentary (indeed, it contains one gap of over a hundred years), and in so far as it comes from the Augustan History it is unreliable. But perhaps one or two general impressions which it gives are not mistaken.

In the second and third centuries A.D. there seems to have been on the whole a decline in the number of lions and leopards in the Roman arena, while the proportion of herbivorous animals increased. This is not to say that it is incredible that 400 lions and leopards were assembled at Rome for an imperial show in 281. But taking it by and large one may believe that a change of this sort did come about.

On the other hand, most or all of the animals that had been rarities at Rome in the first century A.D. continue to appear there from time to time, and perhaps on the whole more frequently, while some kinds (the zebra, for example) may now have made their first appearance. While the Empire was failing in elasticity, its influence on, and commerce with, some distant countries such as Ethiopia may have been on the increase.

Lastly, there is a blank in our information from the time of Carinus (284 A.D.) till the last years of the fourth century. It was now, as a rule, no longer the master of the Roman world, or even one of its masters, that gathered beasts from all quarters for the amusement of the City of Rome. And at the latter end of this gap we find the Roman noble Symmachus, in his long and expensive preparations for *ludi*, reduced to Irish wolfhounds and crocodiles for his rarities, doing his best to obtain lions, leopards, antelopes and above all bears, but suffering cruel disappointment in the failure of beasts to arrive in good condition, or even to arrive at all.

Dio (Epitome), LXIX, 10, 2
Hist. Aug., Hadrian, 19, 2-4

Hadrian (A.D. 117–38) spent about half of his reign away from Rome and Italy. But he was interested in animals and hunting, and was ready enough to gratify the public taste for shows. And though he gave *ludi* in provincial cities when staying in them—a *venatio* of 1000 wild beasts was given by him at Athens on one of his visits there (A.D. 125–6 or 128–9) —yet, according to the *Historia Augusta*, he never deprived Rome of a single *venator* or actor. However, the only information which we have about the animals exhibited at Rome in his time is in the vague statement of his biographer, that " he had many wild beasts killed in the Circus, and often a hundred lions." A curious incident which has some bearing on the question, where lions could be found in the Roman Empire, is that of his killing a lion, which had done much damage, in Libya, near Alexandria.

Ibid., 19, 7

Athenæus, XV, 677d, e, f

In the quiet reign of the respectable Antoninus Pius (A.D. 138–61) one set of *ludi* seems to have been particularly notable for the collection of animals exhibited at it. Coins issued in A.D. 149, bearing the word *munificentia*, and the figures of a lion and an elephant, may have recorded some shows of the previous year, celebrating the tenth anniversary of the Emperor's accession. And these, again, may have been the shows at which, according to the evidence of the *Historia Augusta*, there were exhibited elephants, hyenas, lions and tigers, rhinoceroses, crocodiles, and hippopotami.

Hist. Aug., Antoninus Pius, 10, 9

Here the hyena is the new feature, and there are some difficulties about its appearance. In the passage of the *Historia Augusta* referred to above, it is called *corocotta*, which Diodorus gives as the Ethiopian name of an animal that, from his description, is clearly the hyena. Now the Greeks and Romans knew the striped hyena, very common in Asia and North

Diodorus, III, 35, 10

Aristotle, H.A., VI, 579b, 16–30 ; VIII, 594a, 31–b, 5

Africa, under the name ὕαινα, *hyæna*. Pliny's account of the *hyæna* includes an inaccurate notion of that similarity between the sexes in this kind of animal which baffles naturalists, and he shows that the hyena was the object of much strange superstition. But he also mentions the *corocotta* (or *crocotta*) as an Ethiopian animal, and describes it in one passage as the offspring of hyena and lioness, in another as looking like a cross between dog and wolf, and as able to crack anything (*omnia*) in its jaws and swallow and digest it. This last detail seems to refer to the bone-swallowing powers of the hyena, which are astonishing and are noticed by Diodorus. Again, Dio says that the *corocotta* (κοροκότας) was brought to Rome (" for the first time, so far as I know ") in A.D. 202. He calls it an Indian animal, but he may be using " Indian " in the vaguest sense. He describes it as having a skin that was a mixture of those of lioness and tiger, and as being in its form a singular blend of lion, tiger, dog and fox. This certainly represents the striped hyena. The skin which made this impression on Dio (he was at Rome at the time, and evidently had seen the animal himself) is dirty grey in its ground colour, with tawny or blackish stripes. He would be reminded of a fox by the ears, of a dog by the nose, and of a lion by the mouth.[1]

Possibly the explanation is that hyenas from countries within the Empire had not been exhibited at the Roman shows, because this animal, though easy to capture and even to tame, is cowardly and would be unsuited to a *venatio*, but that in the reign of Antoninus Pius, and again in that of Septimius Severus, hyenas were sent as a present to the Roman Emperor from Ethiopia, and that these specimens were shown to the Roman public.

Pliny, N.H., VIII, 30(44), 105 seq.; XXVIII, 8(27), 92 seq.

Ibid., VIII, 30(45), 107; 21(30), 72

Dio, LXXVI, 1, 4

---

[1] Both Pliny and Diodorus knew of the other and larger hyena from North Africa, the spotted hyena (*Hyena crocuta*), often called the Laughing-hyena from its demoniacal vociferations under excitement, which were perhaps near enough to the yells of African natives, in their midnight orgies, to mislead bewildered men, as the story says, to their doom. Diodorus does not believe that the beast can imitate the human voice, Pliny is more credulous.

Pausanias, IX, 21, 1–2 ; VIII, 17, 3

Pausanias in the Antonine age saw giraffes, two-horned Ethiopian rhinoceroses, Pæonian bulls,[1] and white deer in the shows or in a garden (see pp. 131, 132).

Hist. Aug., M. Antoninus, 4, 8 Marcus Aurelius, Meditations, III, 2 ; IV, 16; X, 8

It need hardly be said that Marcus Aurelius (A.D. 161–80) did not care for the public entertainments of his age. It is mentioned as an instance of his reasonable conformity to social demands, that when he was young he let himself be taken to hunts, or the theatre, or spectacles. And he could admire the beauty of the lion's scowl, or of the foam that dripped from the wild boar's mouth. But the cruelty of the Roman shows repelled him. Yet once, when the spectators demanded a performance by a lion trained as a man-eater, Marcus Aurelius apparently showed less firmness than Claudius (see p. 69 above). He yielded so far as to allow the performance, but turned his back on the spectacle, and refused to give way to a clamorous request by the public that he should free the slave who trained the beast.

" Mémoire sur les animaux promenés ou tués dans les cirques," Mongez, Mém. A. des inscriptions et Belles Lettres, 2e Serie, 1833

This story suggests the remark that there would often be difficulties about getting untrained animals to attack men in the arena. The strange scene and the noisy multitude would scare wild beasts, and make them reluctant to attack even a victim bound to a stake. Men condemned to the beasts were forced, as we shall see in Appendix IV, to move their hands so as to irritate the animals.[2]

---

[1] These have been thought to be bison, but Pliny says that neither the bison nor the *urus* was used in Greek medicine (*N.H.*, XXVIII, 10 (45), 159) ; and he seems to distinguish bison from the *bonasus* of Pæonia, an animal " equina iuba cetera tauro similem, cornibus ita in se flexis ut non sint utilia pugnæ " (*ibid.*, VIII, 15 (16), 40). This βόνασος is also described in Ps.-Aristotle, *H.A.*, IX, 630a, 19 ff., and mentioned by Aristotle (*H.A.*, II, 500a, 1). I think that the Pæonian bulls of Pausanias, though in X, 13, 1–2, he calls them βίσωνες, were *bonasi*, and that these may be identified with the musk-ox (*Ovibos moschus*).

[2] Plutarch, *De Sollertia Animalium*, 25. After telling tales of fishes (*scari* and *anthiæ*) coming to the assistance of members of their kind that were in danger, one of the characters in the Dialogue goes on : " And yet we do not know of any land-animal—bear or boar or lioness or leopard—that will help another of its kind in danger. Animals of

The son and successor of Marcus Aurelius, the Emperor Commodus (A.D. 180–92), was incapable and uninterested in the serious work of government, but was passionately fond of the sports of the amphitheatre. He was himself an ardent *venator* in the sense of a killer of wild animals in public or private arenas, and, as a slayer of beasts, he took the title of the Roman Hercules. He collected rare animals for slaughter at Rome, and Dio, who witnessed his performances, describes him as killing elephants (3 are mentioned altogether), hippo-potami (6 are mentioned altogether, 5 on one occasion), rhino-ceroses, a giraffe, a tiger, and, on one day, 100 bears. Herodian, a contemporary, adds lions and leopards to the list, and mentions the emergence of a hundred lions into the arena from below ground. (Nearly two centuries later, Ammianus Marcellinus wrote that Commodus killed, with different kinds of weapons, a hundred lions let loose at once in the arena, without needing to give any of them a second shot or blow.) According to Herodian, the Emperor shot ostriches with crescent-shaped arrows meant to decapitate the birds, the headless bodies continuing to run as though nothing had happened. This last detail is correct ; the same phenomenon may be observed in ducks and geese in like circumstances. Dio tells how the Emperor, having decapitated an ostrich with a sword, came to where the senators (Dio among them) were sitting in the amphitheatre, and held up the head of the bird in his left hand, and his blood-stained sword in his right, saying nothing, but smiling and nodding, to make them feel that this was what he would do to them.

Pertinax, the successor of the murdered Commodus, was himself murdered, after reigning for less than three months, by the Prætorian Guard, who sold the imperial authority to a senator, Didius Julianus, and he in his turn fell, after reigning sixty-six days, before the governor of Pannonia, Septimius

Hist. Aug., Commodus, 8, 5 ; Dio (Epit.), LXXII, 15, 5 ; Dessau, *Inscr. Lat. Sel.,* 400
Dio (Epitome), LXXII, 10, 3 ; 18, 1 ; 19, 1 Herodian, I, 15 3–6 Ammianus Marcellinus, XXXI, 10, 19

one kind will *get together in the arena and will move round it together* ; yet one animal will not think of helping another—rather, they bound away in flight as far as they can from one that is wounded and dying." My experience leads me to think that such action denotes abject fear.

Dio (Epitome), LXXIII, 16, 3
Severus (A.D 193). Julianus thought of using against Severus the elephants which were kept in or near Rome ; but the animals (or some of them) found the " towers " or armoured howdahs which were put on them irksome, and objected to carrying the armed men who were to fight from the " towers." These elephants had therefore not been trained for war.

Septimius Severus (A.D. 193–211) was inclined, in his hard, vehement way, to conform to the ideal of magnificence and munificence in the exercise of the imperial power. Of the animals exhibited in this reign to the Roman public, we learn a few details from Dio. We hear of sixty boars (the property Dio (Epitome), LXXVI, 1 ; 7 (ad fin.) of Plautianus, the Emperor's chief minister) fighting each other at their trainers' orders (ὑπὸ παραγγέλματος), of an elephant killed on a special occasion, of ten tigers killed at another time, and of the hyena which Dio (apparently wrongly) believed to be the first of its kind brought to Rome (see p. 84 Ibid., LXXV, 16, 5 ; LXXVI, 1, 5 above). A new device was adopted for making an effective display of a large number of animals. A whale having been found stranded on the Italian coast, a model of it was constructed, and brought, with fifty bears inside, into the arena, where the animals were (it seems) released from it. This idea was afterwards modified and elaborated. At the Games with which Severus celebrated the tenth year of his reign, a mock ship was " wrecked " in the arena, and from it emerged 400 animals : lions, lionesses, leopards and similar beasts,[1] bears, ostriches, wild asses, and bison. The quarters for the animals in the " whale " or the " ship " may seem rather confined, but an aperture in the base communicating with a trap would remove any difficulty in this respect.

The most interesting reference to exotic animals brought to Rome in this reign is to be found in the story of Dio, that Dio (Epitome), LXXV, 14, 3 ; LXXVII, 6, 2 Plautianus, the Emperor's minister, " despatched centurions and carried off from the islands in the Red Sea the Horses of the Sun which resemble tigers." Plautianus was put to death in

[1] This is probably the sense in which Dio uses the word πάνθηρες in the passage referred to. But it may mean cheetahs here ; see Appendix I.

A.D. 205, when no doubt these animals became imperial property ; one of them (Dio calls it a hippotigris) was killed at some show early in the reign of Caracalla. Evidently these Horses of the Sun, resembling tigers, were zebras. The Abyssinian zebra (*Equus grevii*) would be nearest to the Red Sea, but its stripes are too narrow to resemble closely those of a tiger. Possibly these zebras were of some kind living nearer to the equator—the Chapman kind, for example. Zebras are found only on the mainland of Africa, but there are small islands at the southern end of the Red Sea to which the animals could be brought in dhows, and on which they could be kept till forwarded to Persia.

It was probably towards the end of the reign of Severus that the wealthy noble, Gordian, afterwards to be the Emperor Gordian I, gave in his ædileship the shows of which we have an account in the *Historia Augusta*. There it is said that Gordian exhibited 100 " African beasts " (probably leopards and lions), and 1,000 bears. But it is noticeable how large a proportion of the total number of animals alleged to have been shown were not carnivora. There were, according to the list in the *Augustan History* (professedly taken from a painting in the house which Gordian had owned), 200 stags of the fallow deer (*cervi palmati*) including some from Britain, 200 *dammæ* (gazelles ?), 30 wild horses (perhaps from the Danubian plains or from Spain or Britain), 10 elk (from the forests of Germany ?), 200 ibex (from the Alps or Spain ?), 100 wild sheep (from some mountainous country of the western Mediterranean area ?), 300 Moorish ostriches with reddened feathers (*miniati*), 30 wild asses (from Asia Minor, Syria, Arabia or North Africa), 150 wild boars, and 100 zebus (from Cyprus ?). It is possible that many of the foreign animals belonged to herds long kept in Italy, and had been bred there.

Hist. Aug.
Gordiani Tres, 3

Caracalla (A.D. 211–17) affected a martial pose, and had an enthusiasm for Alexander the Great. He was accompanied on journeys by an escort of elephants, and owned many lions, some of which he had always with him, particularly a tame

Dio (Epitome),
LXXVII 7 ;
LXXVIII, 7,
2–3

lion named Acinaces (Scimetar), which (so says Dio) was
his table-companion and slept in his room. The greater part
of his short reign was spent away from Italy. He made senators
pay for *venationes* and chariot-races in the cities where he
stayed, and was himself a keen *venator*. But there is little
evidence as to the animals exhibited at Rome in this reign. It
has already been noticed that Dio mentions a zebra among the
animals killed in the amphitheatre early in Caracalla's time ;
the others there recorded are an elephant, a rhinoceros, and
a tiger. On a medal struck by this Emperor is represented the
device of the wrecked ship, with animals engraved below—
elk, one-horned rhinoceros, elephant, lion, ostrich, an antelope,
and what appears to be a fox (see p. 82).

Elagabalus (A.D. 218–22), a fantastic, effeminate, and vicious
youth, is represented in the *Historia Augusta* as having a taste
for keeping animals and employing them in childish amusements and very disagreeable practical jokes. On this more
will be said in chapter VIII below. Here it may be noticed
that some of the statements in the account of this Emperor in
the *Historia Augusta* would, if trustworthy, do great credit to
the animal-trainers of the time. Elagabalus is said to have
driven in harness lions, tigers, and even stags. Breaking stags
to harness (which had been done under Domitian : see p. 78
above) is particularly difficult. Again, if the Emperor used
really to play the practical joke of turning his tame lions,
leopards, and bears at night into the rooms of drunken sleeping guests, this would be a still more remarkable proof of the
skill of his trainers (*mansuetudinarii*). For though the animals
had been deprived of teeth and claws (*exarmati*), that would
not have prevented them from doing harm if they had not
been perfectly trained. Another point which may be noticed
here is, that the Emperor's zoological collection is represented
in the *Historia Augusta* as being largely drawn from the region
of the Nile. After a mention of the Emperor's Egyptian
snakes, his hippopotami, his crocodiles, and his rhinoceros,
it is added that he had all Egyptian things suitable for exhibition. If the rhinoceros was really of African origin (and not

Ibid., LXXVII, 9–10

Ibid., LXXVII, 6, 2

Coins,
Morellius,
Leipsic, 1695

Hist. Aug.,
Elagabalus,
28, 2

Ibid., 25, 1 ;
cf. 21, 1

Ibid., 28, 3

an Indian animal imported through Egypt), it was of the two-horned variety.

As regards the exhibition of animals at public shows in the time of Elagabalus, we learn from Dio that at the Games which celebrated the Emperor's marriage, among the many beasts killed, were an elephant and 51 tigers. Whether the elephant fell in a fight against three or four tigers our authority does not say. Such a struggle would, however, suggest itself to any Persian but the 51 tigers must have met other deaths. This is by far the greatest number of tigers of which we have definite record as appearing at the Roman shows (see p. 77 above), and Dio believed it to be unprecedented. Possibly the Eastern campaigns of Septimius Severus (who, it will be remembered, exhibited 10 tigers on one occasion) had somehow made it easier for the Romans to obtain this animal from the Persian plateau. Dio, LXXIX, 9, 2

Alexander Severus (A.D. 222–35) was a most respectable young man, who did his best to be a model Emperor. He was regular in attending the public spectacles, and (so it is said) had a plan, which was not carried out, for distributing the Roman Games throughout the year at regular monthly intervals. Perhaps the intention was to effect an economy with as little offence as possible to public opinion. The Emperor is said to have disapproved of showing much favour to actors, or charioteers, or *venatores*. His own interest in animals was, it is recorded, chiefly an interest in the birds which he kept in his aviaries (see p. 101, *n*. 1). The document given in the *Historia Augusta*, containing a statement that the Emperor in his Persian war captured 30 elephants from the enemy and led 18 of them in his triumph at Rome (A.D. 233), is probably spurious. But it is likely that some elephants of the Indian kind reached Rome in this way. In the Life of Gordian III in the *Historia Augusta*, it is implied that 10 elephants which Alexander Severus had sent to Rome were there in 248. *Hist. Aug., Severus Alexander*, 37, 1 ; 43, 4

Ibid., 41, 6–7

Ibid., 56, 3

Hist. Aug., Gordiani Tres, 33, 1, 2

After the death of Alexander Severus, the Empire sank into a troubled half-century of civil war and barbarian invasion,

from which it emerged under Diocletian. How far the disturb-
ances of the time interfered with the supply of animals for the
Roman shows, cannot be told. A few scraps of very doubtful
information on our subject may be mentioned.

*Historia
Augusta, loc. cit.*

In a list of animals said to have been intended for Gordian
III's Persian triumph (a triumph that was never celebrated)
and to have been exhibited by Gordian's murderer and successor, Philip the Arabian, at the Secular Games of A.D. 248
the items are : 32 elephants (of which, it is said, Gordian III
had sent 12—that is, had sent them from the East as spoils
of his Persian war—and Alexander Severus had sent 10), 10
elk, 10 tigers, 60 tame lions, 30 tame *leopardi* (maneless lions :
App. I, pp. 186–7), 10 hyenas (*belbi, id est hyænæ*), 6
hippopotami, a rhinoceros, 10 *argoleontes* (wild lions ; or
perhaps *archileontes*, " lions of exceptional size," should be

Loisel, Vol. I,
f. p. 108

read). A medal of Gordian's seems to show an impalla
antelope.

*Hist. Aug.,
Gallieni,* 12,
3–5

Passing by an anecdote of bull-fighting under Gallienus
(the Emperor crowning a *venator* for the remarkable feat of
failing ten times to strike a bull), and a story of the same
Emperor letting off with a fright a man whom he had condemned to the beasts for selling his wife sham jewellery (from

*Hist. Aug.,
Aurelian,* 33, 4

the lion's den emerged, not the lion, but a capon), we may
come to the list, perhaps fictitious, of the animals said to have
formed part of the triumphal procession of Aurelian, the
conqueror of Zenobia of Palmyra, in A.D. 274. The list includes 20 elephants, 200 tamed animals of different sorts from
Africa and " Palestine " (distributed after the triumph to
private citizens in order to save the Treasury the cost of
their keep), 4 tigers, giraffes, elk, and " other such animals "
(*cetera talia*), which may have been added to the imperial
collection.

Ibid., 33, 3

The author of the Life of Aurelian in the *Historia Augusta*
asserts it as well attested (*ut multi memoriæ tradiderunt*), that
in this triumph the Emperor rode to the Capitol in a chariot
which had once belonged to a King of the Goths (whom he
had defeated), and that the chariot was drawn by four " stags "

(*cervi*), which had been taken along with the chariot. These stags were sacrificed to Jupiter Optimus Maximus. The Goths lived at this time in the country to the north-west of the Black Sea, and a trade-route to the Baltic ran through their land. It has been suggested that these *cervi* were reindeer which the King of the Goths had obtained from the North, but they are more likely to have been Red deer stags, which are very difficult to train.

It is related in the *Historia Augusta* that Aurelian, before he was Emperor, and when he was serving on an embassy to the Persian king, was given an elephant by the Persians, and thus became the only Roman citizen, below imperial rank, to own an animal of this kind, though even he surrendered his elephant to the Emperor then reigning. This story illustrates the fact that the elephant continued to be regarded as an imperial animal (*nulli servire paratum privato*, as Juvenal had written). *Hist. Aug., Aurelian, 5, 6*

In A.D. 281 the Emperor Probus celebrated a triumph and gave *ludi* at which *herbatica animalia* and *bestiæ dentatæ* were shown. The information in the *Historia Augusta* about the animals exhibited on this occasion may be given for what it is worth. On one day, there were turned into the Circus Maximus (which had been planted to look like a forest) 1,000 (?) ostriches, 1,000 (?) stags, and 1,000 (?) boars, and then *dammæ* (gazelles or fallow deer ?), ibexes, wild sheep, and other grass-eating beasts. Those spectators who wished to appropriate any of these animals were allowed to do so. On another day, 100 maned lions (*iubati leones*) were let loose in the amphitheatre, and after them 100 African *leopardi* (not leopards but maneless lions ; see Appendix I, pp. 186–7), and 100 *leopardi* from Syria, and then 100 lionesses with 300 bears. *Hist. Aug., Probus, 19*

It is added that the show of maned lions was not a great success, because they were killed as they came out of *postica*, from which they did not emerge with the dash (*impetus*) of beasts coming out of *caveæ*. Many of them would not charge at all and had to be shot with arrows.

This might be interpreted in one or other of two ways.

First, the *postica* [1] might be taken to mean the doors giving on to the arena from the backs of dens in the amphitheatre, the animals preferring to remain ensconced in these dens, and coming out only with reluctance.

Secondly, the *postica* might be taken to be the removable ends of narrow " travelling boxes " in which the animals had been brought to Rome. An animal having been induced to enter such a box, it would be closed behind him, and an end would be knocked away in order to release him. But the animal, when released, would be stiff from confinement, and would lack dash. On this it may be observed, that a phrase of Symmachus seems to imply that such beasts as leopards or lions were brought to Rome in iron-barred *caveæ*. For he says that his Irish hounds excited so much interest at Rome, that one would think they had been brought there in iron cages (*ut ferreis caveis putaret advectos*). More will be said about this in connection with Capture and Transport (see pp. 148–9 below).

It has been suggested that the animal-show described in the poem known as the Seventh Eclogue of Calpurnius was given in the reign of Carinus (A.D. 283–85), for there is evidence that the *ludi theatrales* and *circenses*, with which the government of Carus (A.D. 282–83) and of his son Carinus entertained the public, were very popular. In the seventeenth century the new discoveries concerning the animals would have constituted confirmatory evidence to date the poem, but it has been already noticed that according to the view now prevalent this poem was written under Nero (see p. 71 above, and Appendix, pp. 188–189). It is said that in the years when Carus and Carinus were reigning, an acrobat at Rome gave an exhibition of wall-climbing with a bear in pursuit, and tame bears acted in a farce.

From the time of the accession of Diocletian (A.D. 285), Rome ceased to be a place of regular imperial residence, except

Cf. the remark about " pickled beasts " τεταριχευμένοις. Libanius, Or., XVIII, 170 Symmachus, *Epp.*, II, 77

Hist. Aug., Carus, Carinus, Numerian, 19, and 20, 2

Ibid., 19, 2 See Gorius, Thesaurus veterum diptychorum, Florence, 1759, for this and similar feats

---

[1] *Posticum* is the word for a back door. For the *postica* from which beasts might emerge into the arena see Ammianus, XXVIII, 1, 10 : amphitheatrales feræ diffractis tandem solutæ posticis.

for six years, under Maxentius (A.D. 306–12). In the fourth century, Emperors visited it occasionally, and their visits might be celebrated with *ludi*; and shows were still regularly given at Rome by the wealthy and eminent, when they or their relations were filling the titular positions of the old urban magistracies.

The residence of holders of imperial authority elsewhere than at Rome no doubt had the effect, that those provincial cities which they made their administrative capitals enjoyed more elaborate *venationes* than had previously been given there. But—whatever may have happened at Constantinople, the New Rome—it seems very doubtful whether even now shows at places like Milan and Trèves came to surpass those given at Rome itself. The rulers of the Western part of the Empire had a heavy and harassing task to keep together and defend the territories in their charge, and for this task they had none too much money. On the other hand, at Rome there was the force of an ancient tradition that the City, which was still accounted the Mistress or Mother of the World, should enjoy spectacles on a great scale, and there was an aristocracy of very wealthy landowners, who would take it in turn to maintain that tradition as well as they could in the circumstances of the time.

The Letters of Symmachus throw an interesting light on the preparations which he made for two sets of *ludi* which were given in the name of his son, the first when the latter was quæstor (A.D. 393), the second when he was prætor (A.D. 401). Expecting that his son would be prætor in 400, Symmachus began in 398 to make arrangements for the prætorian games of the year after next, and he took advantage of a year's delay to increase the scale of his preparations. We find him sending his agents to collect animals in provinces or in Italy; writing to friends who have offered him animals as gifts, or whose aid he requires in the choosing of animals or their transport; writing to officials to obtain the imperial permission required for purchasing *Libycæ feræ*; writing to officials asking them to assist his agents in their work of collection and trans-

Symmachus, Epp., VI, 35,

Ibid., IV, 63

Ibid., II, 46. 77; IV, 7, 8, 12, 58–60; V, 56, 62, 82; VI, 33; VII, 48, 59, 82, 97, 105, 106, 122; IX, 15, 16, 20, 27, 117, 135, 144

Ibid., IV, 8 ;
VI, 33

Ibid., V, 62

port ; writing about getting leave to produce his shows in the Flavian amphitheatre ; writing to point out that although quæstors had the right not to pay customs duty on animals for their shows—an exemption which he had enjoyed when preparing for his son's Games in 393—another relation of his, who was to give quæstorian Games, had been unfairly charged with a duty of two per cent, to which only professional dealers in bears (*ursorum negotiatores*) were properly liable.

Ibid. (e.g.), IV,
58, 60 ; VII, 48

Ibid. V, 82

Ibid., IX, 20

Ibid., V, 56

Symmachus apparently got nearly all the *horses* for the chariot-races of the prætorian *ludi* from Spain, which was evidently then famous for its studs. He seems to have been given a few from near at hand (*de proximo*)—presumably from Italy—and he hoped that he might get some through a friend at Arles. It is noteworthy that of 16 horses given him by a friend in Spain, 5 were lost on the way to Rome, and some of the others died at Rome before the Games (see further on transport, pp. 151–152 below.)

Ibid., II, 76

For the quæstorian Games of 393, Symmachus hoped to get some *lions*—probably, though not certainly, from Africa, for he refers to the *venatio* in which he hoped to exhibit them as a *Libyca congressio*—the epithet being perhaps conventional.

*Ammianus
Marcellinus,*
XVIII, 7, 5

(Some forty years previously, Ammianus Marcellinus had found that the reed-beds of the rivers in Roman Mesopotamia contained " innumerable " lions ; but the distance of that country from Italy would be a reason against collecting in Mesopotamia for the Roman Games.) Symmachus professed

*Symmachus,
Epp.*, II, 46

himself " philosophic " about the suicide of twenty-nine Saxon prisoners who were to have fought as gladiators in the quæstorian *ludi* ; he would apply to the Emperor for leave to compensate the public by a special show of *Libycæ*. But some of

Ibid., IX, 117

the animals which he was expecting in 393 were apparently lost by shipwreck. For the prætorian Games, we hear nothing

Ibid., IV, 12 ;
VII, 59 ; 122

of lions *eo nomine*, but there is a permission to obtain *leopardi* (maneless lions ; see Appendix I) and an application for leave to buy a supplementary lot of *Libycæ feræ*.

Ibid , II, 76

For both the quæstorian and the prætorian Games Symmachus collected *bears*. On the eve of the Games in 393 hardly any bears had arrived ; Symmachus had received only a few starving and weary cubs (*paucos catulos maceratos inedia et labore*). For the Games of 401, he obtained plenty of bears from Italy, and some from Dalmatia, and perhaps from other countries to the east and north of the Italian peninsula. He was expecting some bears to be brought from overseas to Apulia—probably from the Balkan peninsula—and he mentions that his people whom he employed in the purchase of *feræ* had been passing by Aquileia. *Ibid.*, VII, 121 ; IX, 132 ; 142 *Ibid.*, IX, 135 *Ibid.*, IX, 27

Symmachus wanted *antelopes* for the prætorian Games— *addaces* (topi antelopes), and *pygargi* (impalla antelopes)— from some province (in Africa) where they were to be found on the frontier. *Ibid.*, IX, 144

Crocodiles, for the prætorian Games, he obtained, no doubt, from Egypt. After a first exhibition of them, Symmachus had meant to keep them, till some relations of his, absent from Rome, could return and see them. But as they had refused to eat for fifty days on end, they were reduced to such a condition that it was thought best to kill nearly all of them at *secundi ludi*. Two had been left alive, for the correspondents of Symmachus to see, if they came in time ; for the animals were not expected to live long. It may be noticed that Symmachus thought crocodiles specially needed for his shows, and in writing to the Emperor he says that his ambition is to exhibit to his fellow-citizens " crocodiles and other things from abroad." *Ibid.*, IX, 141 ; VI, 43 *Ibid.*, IX, 141, 151

Lastly, for the Games of 393, Symmachus got 7 *Scottici canes*—apparently Irish wolfhounds (the Scotti then lived in Ireland), and these animals, as we have already seen, aroused great interest in Rome. *Ibid.*, II, 77

So far, then, as can be told, Symmachus obtained his animals from Spain (horses), the British Isles (hounds), Italy (especially bears), the countries east and north of the Adriatic (bears), Africa (probably lions and *leopardi* and antelopes ; he writes to two high officials in Africa asking for their aid in his collection of animals from that region), and Egypt (crocodiles). *Ibid*, IX, 15, 16

Claudian,
*Paneg. Manlio
Theodoro dictus*,
291–310
*De cons.
Stilichonis*, III,
237 foll.
*De sexto cons.
Honorii*, 619–20
In the poems of Claudian, which were written in the years
A.D. 394–404, there are a few references to animal shows given
by, or expected from, great men enjoying the honours of a
consulship, or an Emperor celebrating a triumph.   Claudian
is sure that Stilicho, the great military chief of the time and
father-in-law of the Emperor Honorius, has taken pains to
procure " noble beasts " for the spectacles at Rome that would
*De cons.
Stilichonis*,
III, 302 foll.
celebrate his consulship.   The poet gives some general indications of trapping and transport (see pp. 144, 150 below),
and of sources of supply.   The coverts of Gaul are drawn,
and the great boar of the Rhine marshes is taken.   Alps and
Apennines are searched, and the Apulian mountain of Gar-
ganus.   Bears are roused from their caverns by Tagus' side
and in Pyrenean oakwoods.   Stags and other creatures that
are not savage are to come from Corsica and Sicily.   Africa
is scoured for lions and leopards, and if not for elephants, at
any rate for ivory—ivory for the tablets that are to bear the
name of Stilicho as consul.   Stilicho's agents, it may be re-
Ibid., 357–8
marked, are Diana and her nymphs.   And there is a pleasant
picture of a great lion in a ship on the voyage from Africa to
Italy.

> Caudamque in puppe retorquens
> Ad proram iacet usque leo.

" His tail curled on the poop, he stretches to the prow." [1]

---

[1] That *venationes* were being given in the Colosseum in the later years
of Theodoric, who reigned in Italy from 493 to 526, we know from
Cassiodorus, *Var.* V, 42 ; see p. 180 below.

MARBLE RELIEF WITH CIRCULAR ORNAMENTATIONS FROM SOFIA

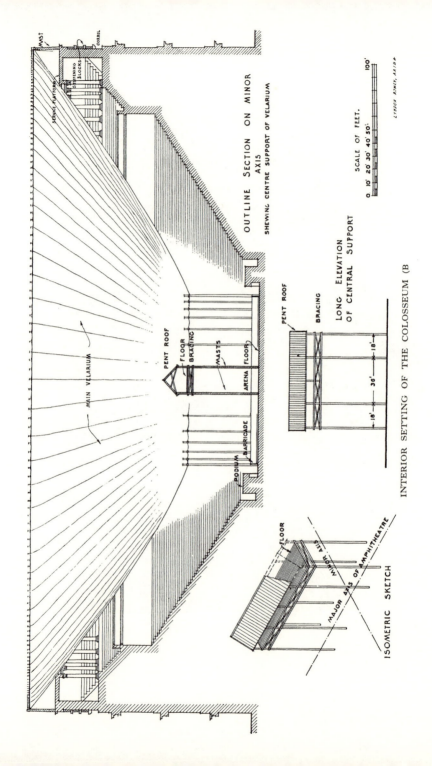

MAST

CORBEL

SERVICE PLATFORM

STIFFENING BLOCKS

OUTLINE SECTION ON MINOR AXIS

SHEWING CENTRE SUPPORT OF VELARIUM

MAIN VELARIUM

PENT ROOF

FLOOR

BRACING

MASTS

ARENA FLOOR

PODIUM

BARRICADE

PENT ROOF

BRACING

LONG ELEVATION OF CENTRAL SUPPORT

18'   30'   18'

LYNDON RONGY, SA18+

SCALE OF FEET.

0 10' 20' 30' 40' 50'   100'

FLOOR

MINOR AXIS

MAJOR AXIS OF AMPHITHEATRE

ISOMETRIC SKETCH

INTERIOR SETTING OF THE COLOSSEUM (B

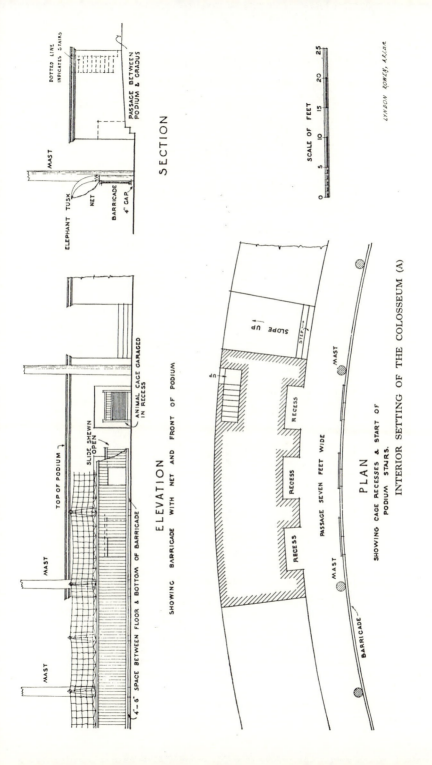

SECTION

DOTTED LINE
INDICATES STAIRS

PASSAGE BETWEEN
PODIUM & GRADUS

MAST

ELEPHANT TUSK

NET

BARRICADE

4" CAP

ELEVATION

SHOWING BARRICADE WITH NET AND FRONT OF PODIUM

MAST

TOP OF PODIUM

SLIDE SHEWN OPEN

ANIMAL CAGE GARAGED IN RECESS

MAST

MAST

4'—6" SPACE BETWEEN FLOOR & BOTTOM OF BARRICADE

SCALE OF FEET

0   5   10   15   20   25

LYNDON ROWLEY, A.R.I.B.A.

SLOPE UP

STEP

UP

RECESS

RECESS

RECESS

RECESS

MAST

PASSAGE SEVEN FEET WIDE

MAST

BARRICADE

PLAN

SHOWING CAGE RECESSES & START OF PODIUM STAIRS.

INTERIOR SETTING OF THE COLOSSEUM (A)

AN AFRICAN DRIVE FOR THE ARENA

DENS AND BOUNDARY WALLS OF ARENA

FROM A MARBLE TABLET SHOWING SCENES FROM A
MENAGERIE OF PERFORMING BEARS

THE WART-HOG

A MALE SHOT IN THE KATANGA DISTRICT, SOUTH-EAST CONGO, SHOWING THE LONG TUSHES,
THE LONG MANE AND BLACK FACE WARTS, ETC.

CHAPTER VI

THE AMATEUR'S MENAGERIE

BIRDS

THERE were three main ways in which animals might be kept for pleasure in Roman Italy, apart from the keeping and training of them for public shows.

They might, of course, be kept as single pets, as were, for example, birds (especially songsters, and such as could be trained to talk), lapdogs, monkeys, and harmless snakes.

Secondly, they might be kept in some numbers, not for profit, or to supply the household with food, or not for those purposes only, but wholly or partly in the way of a hobby, for the interest which the owner took in breeding them, or in observing their habits, or for the pleasure which they gave his eye or ear. Several forms of this kind of animal-keeping were introduced into Italy in the last age of the Republic, a great time of discovery by wealthy Romans of new ways of spending or investing the fortunes which they had made, directly or indirectly, out of their Empire. In this age, for example, large and varied collections of birds were first kept for pleasure ; the keeping of sea-fish in salt-water ponds, for the pleasure which they gave the eye, became a fashionable and expensive hobby among the rich who had sea-side villas ; and it also became the fashion to keep beasts of the chase in a park or warren attached to one's villa, largely, it would seem, for the pleasure of watching them.

Thirdly, animals might be kept for sport, as beasts of the

chase might be preserved for shooting or spearing, or hounds
might be kept for hunting, or cocks for fighting. We shall
see that there is some evidence that the largest hunting
parks belonging to wealthy Romans of the imperial age were
to be found in the provinces, and that Gaul was particularly
noted for them. It is, again, from the last years of the Republic
that we have the first recorded instance of a large provincial
hunting-park owned by a Roman; it was in Transalpine Gaul,
and is mentioned by Varro as if it were a novelty in the Roman
use of land (see p. 136 below).

BIRDS

Among the birds mentioned as pets by Latin writers are
the dove and pigeon, nightingale, blackbird, starling, goldfinch,
thrush, raven, crow, pie and parrot. The most famous of
all pet birds in literature is the *passer*, which belonged
to the Lesbia of Catullus; reasons will be given on p. 117
for thinking that it may have been a bullfinch. Birds were
often sent as presents (either to be kept as pets or to be
eaten) on birthdays and festivals. Talking birds were very
popular; and in this connection are mentioned the parrot,
starling, raven, crow, pie, nightingale, and (as a singularity) a
thrush.

Martial, IX,
54; 55; XIV,
73-6

Flocks of pigeons, poultry, geese and ducks, had been
kept in Italy from time immemorial, and foreign breeds
of these birds were imported from Greece, Egypt, or Asia.[1]
Several kinds of exotic birds were first bred in Italy in the last
age of the Republic or under the early Empire—guineafowl
and peafowl, for example, in the life-time of Varro (116–27 B.C.),
flamingoes perhaps in the Augustan age, and pheasants before
the end of the first century A.D.

---

[1] The debt of the Roman bird-farmer in Varro's day to Greek
experience and skill is suggested by Varro's use of Greek terms in
his account of bird-farming: ὀρνιθών (*aviarium*), ὀρνιθοβοσκεῖον,
περιστεροτροφεῖον, χηνοβοσκεῖον, νησσοτροφεῖον. Columella has *cheno-
boscium, nessotrophium*.

The first notable collection of " birds of all sorts " to be made in Italy for the owner's amusement is said to have been that of M. Lænius Strabo, a knight who lived at Brundisium in the earlier half of the first century B.C. This kind of aviary soon became the fashion—*amatores invenit multos*, says Varro· It was perhaps for such a collection of birds that Q. Cicero, the brother of the orator, was having an *aviarium* made in 54 B.C., among the amenities which were being added to one of his villas. Varro himself made an aviary of this kind in the grounds of his villa at Casinum. It was a high-walled enclosure, where he kept behind netting " birds of all sorts, especially songsters, such as nightingales and blackbirds " ; it contained a duck-pond and fish-ponds, and was planted with trees and shrubs, and beneath a rotunda by the duck-pond was a place in which to dine[1] (see page 125).

As regards the keeping of birds for sport, it may be noticed that cock-fighting, very popular in Greece, and mentioned by Columella as a Greek sport, seems to have been a Roman amusement by the time of Lucilius, towards the end of the second century B.C. ; " When the victor cock proudly struts and rises on his toes." Columella, writing in the middle of the first century A.D., refers to it as the subject of heavy betting. Rock-partridges were kept for fighting in the imperial age, and probably also quails. There seems to be no trace of hawking with horse and hound in ancient Italy, though this sport (probably introduced into the Roman Empire from Persia) was common among the Gallic nobles of the fifth century A.D. A

Varro, R.R., III, 5
Pliny, N.H., X, 50(72), 141

Cicero, Ad. Q Fr., III, 1, 1

Varro, loc. cit.

Lucilius, 300 Marx

Columella, VIII, 2

Pliny, N.H., XXII, 21(30), 65 ; XI, 51(112), 268 Hist. Aug., Alex. Sev., 41, 5 Keller, A.T., II, 25

---

[1] The aviary of Lucullus at Tusculum was maintained partly (as one would have expected) for the owner's table, but in it was a dining-room, where birds were allowed to fly about as a pretty sight at meal-times ; but their smell was found unpleasant by guests. Varro, R.R., III, 4.

In later imperial times, the favourite hobby of the Emperor Alexander Severus (A.D. 221–35) was the keeping of pea-fowl, pheasants, poultry, ducks, partridges, and above all pigeons, in aviaries on the Palatine (*Hist. Aug., Alexander Severus*, 41, 6–7). The Emperor Honorius (A.D. 395–423) was an amateur of poultry : Gibbon, *Decline and Fall*, XXXI, note 153, referring to Procopius, *Bell. Vandal.*, I, 2.

Martial, XIV,
217(216)
Pliny, N.H., X,
37(52), 109
passage in Martial shows that the hawk in his time might be used to " drive " birds for the fowler [1]; and kestrels were flown with flocks of pigeons as a protection against wild hawks.

Pigeons and doves (*columbæ*, pigeons ; *palumbes*, ring-doves ; *turtures*, turtle-doves).[2] These birds, and especially pigeons, were very commonly kept, not only on farms and at country-houses, but also in towns. Varro counts the breeding of pigeons, and that of hens (*gallinæ*), as ancient elements of Italian farming in contrast to forms of bird-breeding that were modern in his day ; and he refers to the fitting of pigeon-lofts in the roofs of houses at Rome as if it were a common practice. A pigeon-house, he says, will often contain as many as 5,000 birds. Such houses were erected in the country, where possible on high ground ; the birds were semi-wild and only valuable as food or as producers of manure.

Varro, R.R.,
III, 3

Ibid., III, 7,
ad fin.
Plautus, Mil.
Glor., 163
Juvenal, III,
200-2

Pigeons and doves were bred largely, of course, for sale in the market as food,[3] but also no doubt to supply the demands of those who made a hobby of breeding the fancy varieties of pigeons. " Many people," says Pliny, " have a craze for pigeons, building turrets for them on house-roofs, and tracing the distinguished pedigrees of single birds ; precedent for this can be quoted from long ago." He then gives, on the authority of Varro, the high price asked for a pair of pigeons by a fancier, L. Axius, in the last years of the Republic. Columella refers to those who spend large sums in buying pigeons " for the sake of owning what delights and amuses them." Single doves and pigeons were no doubt often treated as pets : Varro mentions that people often brought pigeons with them to the theatre and let them loose there, knowing that the birds would return

Pliny, N.H.,
X, 37(53), 110

Varro, R.R.,
III, 7

Columella,
VIII, 8

Varro, loc. cit.

---

[1] Martial's couplet on the hawk is as follows :
" Prædo fuit volucrum : famulus nunc aucupis idem
Decipit et captas non sibi mæret aves."

[2] The Greeks and Romans knew the tame pigeons perfectly and intimately—there are full and detailed references for Greece and Rome under the heading περιστερά in *Glossary of Greek Birds* (D'Arcy W. Thompson).

[3] They were often crammed, the birds so treated usually having their legs broken. Varro, *R.R.*, III, 7 ; Columella, VIII, 8 *ad fin.*

to them (or, we may suppose, to their home with the results of certain events in the arena). Ovid's Corinna had a dove who made friends with her parrot ; and Martial compares the pet pigeon of his friend Stella (*Stellæ delicium mei columba*) to the *passer* of Catullus ; probably Stella had written a poem on his bird. It seems that the only known case of pigeons being used by the Romans for communication elsewhere than in Egypt is that in 43 B.C., when Decimus Brutus was besieged in Mutina by Antony, pigeons (according to Frontinus) took messages to Brutus from the consul Hirtius, who was preparing to relieve the town ; Pliny says that they were sent by Brutus to the consular camp.

Completing this from the detailed account in Frontinus we are enabled to see clearly the perfecting of a brilliant idea under very difficult circumstances.

Frontinus says, " Hirtius also shut up pigeons in the dark, starved them, fastened letters to their necks by a hair, and then released them as near to the city walls as he could. The birds, eager for light and food, sought the highest buildings, and were trapped by Brutus, who in that way was informed of everything, especially *after* he set food *in certain spots* and *taught the pigeons* to alight there."

Probably therefore (in spite of Pliny's statement to the contrary) the idea originated with Hirtius, who used pigeons accustomed to stone-built dovecots on high ground. That he was intending to communicate by pigeon was equally probably told by Hirtius in the letters conveyed on thin slabs of lead strapped to the arms of soldiers who swam across the river Scultenna. The birds were kept without food, but not without water, as thirst would have caused them to alight at the river and defeated his purpose.

Brutus no doubt had some difficulty in catching the first messengers—but once caught he accustomed them to a cote and regular feeding. The river was too well watched for many of them to be sent back to Hirtius for a second journey. But it was not necessary—those retained in Mutina, if made to fly around, when other strange pigeons appeared, would quickly

Ovid, *Amor*, II, 6, 12–16

Martial, I, 7

Frontinus, *Strat.*, III, 13, 7–8

Pliny, *N.H.*, X, 37(53), 110 *loc. cit.*

Frontinus *loc. cit.*

absorb them in the flock and so attract them into the cote.

Wrapping the message round a hair, which was passed over the bird's head and hidden in the neck feathers, is in accordance with the age-long practice in the East and (except that rubber rings were used) our own in the late war. The easier but more clumsy method of attaching the message to the leg has little to recommend it. Enclosing the message in a tube which was fastened along the tail-feathers was used in Roman Egypt, where there were pigeons, black or dark-grey in colour, that were called *columbæ tabellariæ*. In the Ptolemaic days the message was tied, as in Assyria, round the neck.[1]

There appears to be no record of pigeon-racing—and no wonder, as an hour's race would have entailed a two-days' journey each way for the convoyeur.

Varro distinguishes the shy rock pigeons (*agrestes, saxatiles*), not white, but of varied colour,[2] that fly out from their lofts or turrets to seek their food in the countryside, and the tamer white house pigeons that are fed at home, *intra limina ianuæ*. A third sort, he adds, is a cross between the first two kinds and is bred for sale. Columella says that if pigeons are kept in the depths of the country, they may be allowed to fly out as they will to feed in the neighbourhood, their owner not having to supply them with food for more than two or three months in the year ; but that pigeons kept near towns are so liable to be caught by fowlers, if they are permitted to fly abroad, that it is necessary to keep and feed them at home in a netted enclosure. It has been mentioned that tamed kestrels often were flown with them as a protection against other hawks. Columella mentions two breeds, the Campanian and the Alexandrian ; and according to Pliny the Campanian kind produced the largest birds. Columella reckons on pigeons breeding eight times a year, if the mother bird is a good breeder ; Pliny reports them as breeding in Egypt ten or eleven times annually.

In Varro's day an ordinary price for a good pair of pigeons

---

[1] On homing pigeons among the Greeks see p. 13 above.

[2] The lines of Lucretius on the sheen of pigeons' necks and peacocks tails will be recalled (II, 801–07).

Keller,
*Antike
Tierwelt*, II,
128, 129

Denon, D.V.,
Égypte ; Paris,
1802 ; Plate 114

Varro, III, 7

Columella,
VIII, 8

Pliny, *N.H.*, X,
37(52), 109

Pliny, *N.H.*, X,
37(53), 110

Pliny, *N.H.*,
X, 53(79), 147

Varro, *loc. cit.*

for breeding was 200 sesterces, or rather less than £2, but a particularly fine pair might be sold for 1,000 sesterces, or about £8 17s, and the price demanded by L. Axius for a pair was 1,600 sesterces—about £14 3s.[1] Some owners of pigeon-lofts on the roofs of Rome had each a stock that was worth, says Varro, more than 100,000 sesterces, or over £880. In Columella's day, when the value of the sesterce was somewhat lower than in Varro's age, the maximum price for a pair of pigeons was 4,000 sesterces, or about £31.[2] Columella is shocked at it, though he admits that it is better to spend large sums on the pleasures of pigeon-fancying than on the purchase of foreign game for the table. The highest price in England before the war was £120 for a single bird and £200 for three ; and in 1923 Mr. S. M. Joel gave £300 for a pair of homing pigeons, £225 for the hen winner of the San Sebastian race, and £75 for her mate.

Columella, loc. cit.

Poultry (galli, gallinacei, gallinæ).—The common farmyard fowl (*gallina villatica, cohortalis*) was ordinarily bred for profit. Chickens, capons, and eggs were, of course, much sold for food, and the cramming of hens was a usual practice in the times of the elder Cato, of Varro, of Columella and of Pliny, though from the middle of the second century B.C. the sumptuary laws of the Republic had repeatedly forbidden the serving of crammed hens at banquets or dinner-parties. Eggs were also much used in the sick-room ; as now, they supplied, with vinegar, the basis of most of the liniments in common use. Albumen mixed with quicklime was used as a cement for mending glass.

Cato, R.R., 89 Varro, R.R., III, 9 Columella, VIII, 7 Pliny, N.H., X, 50(71), 139–40 Pliny, N.H., XXIX, 3(11), 39–51

But cocks of foreign breeds (Tanagran and others) might be kept also for fighting. And that poultry might be bred for " show points," may be inferred from Columella's allusion

Columella, VIII, 2

[1] £2 would be dear for an ordinary pair of fancy birds in England, £9, on the other hand, would be ludicrously low for a particularly fine pair. Probably there were no pigeon-shows with big prize money.

[2] The pay of a legionary when Columella wrote was 900 sesterces a year, or about £6 15s. Under Domitian it was increased to 1,200 sesterces, or about £9.

to the breeding of Rhodian and Median fowls for their beauty (*propter corporum speciem*). Moreover, his remark that he does not think much of bantams (*pumiliones aves*) as regards any profit to be made out of them apart from the pleasure which may be taken in their smallness (*nisi quem humilitas earum delectat*), seems to show that bantams were sometimes kept as pets or for the pleasure which they gave the eye. Probably they were also set to fight.

Besides " native " Italian barndoor fowl (" native " in the sense that memory of the breed being imported was lost by the first century B.C.) the foreign Tanagran, Chalcidian, and Median breeds were being kept in Italy in Varro's time—the last, says Varro, being often mistakenly called Melian. Columella mentions these imported breeds, and also the Rhodian. These kinds were bred for fighting or for their beauty ; but they were thought considerably less prolific than the Italian, though good results were obtained by breeding from cocks of foreign varieties and from native hens.[1] Pliny specially commends the Hadrian bantam for its fertility. But here he is copying Aristotle, who notices that this bird often kills its chicks—a remark which Pliny, in another passage, seems to take as meaning that it did not incubate well.[2] Columella expresses a low opinion of the fertility of bantams, without mentioning any exceptions (*pumiliones aves . . . nec propter fecunditatem nec propter alium reditum nimium probo*). The criticism is still justifiable.

The quality of poultry in Roman Italy was distinctly below that of the well-established strains of to-day. The best hens laid about 60 eggs. That eggs were smaller than to-day, may be inferred from the fact that Varro and Pliny give 25 as a suitable maximum for a setting ; Columella's figure is 21.

Varro *R.R.*, III, 9, Columella, *loc. cit.*

Pliny, *N.H.*, X, 53(74), 146 ; 56(77), 156 Aristotle, *H.A.*, VI, 558b

Columella, *loc. cit.*

Pliny, *N.H.*, X, 53(74), 146

Varro, *R.R.*, III, 9

Pliny, *N.H.*, X, 53(74), 150 Columella, VIII, 5

[1] Varro condemns the Tanagran, Median, and Chalcidian breeds for a low degree of fertility, Columella the Rhodian and Median. But the latter says that the Tanagran and Chalcidian birds were not much different in their breeding qualities from those of the Italian kind.

[2] Aristotle says : εἰσὶ δὲ χαλεπαὶ καὶ κτείνουσι τοὺς νεοττοὺς πολλάκις. Pliny says *incubatio ovis noxia*.

The construction of hen-coops, and indeed the general management of the poultry yard, differed little from modern practice, but there were rather more silly superstitions about the days for setting hens and the causes of failure in hatching. Italian poultry-farmers may have learnt much from the skilled poultry-breeders of Greece and particularly of Delos. The Delian breeders, says Varro, made large profits by their knowledge and skill ; and according to Pliny they were the inventors of the art of cramming poultry. It is interesting to note that the Romans probably introduced the open-fronted rearing-coop (*cavea*) to Scotland, where the chicken cavy is still in use.

Varro, loc. cit. Columella, VIII, 2

Pliny, N.H., X, 50(71), 139

Burns, " The Jolly Beggars "

Besides farmyard poultry (*gallinæ villaticæ*, " tame villatic fowl "), there was a wild kind called *rusticæ*. Birds of this sort did not breed in captivity, but were caught by fowlers to be fattened for the table, or to be kept in cages. Varro says that they were sometimes exhibited at public shows, along with parrots, white blackbirds, and other curiosities. He describes them as resembling guinea-fowl, but Columella says that they were not unlike domestic poultry. It was believed that the island of Gallinaria, off the Ligurian coast, was so called from these birds. It seems that one idea about them was that they were farmyard poultry gone wild.[1]

Columella, VIII, 12

Varro, loc. cit.

Columella, VIII, 2, 2 ; 6

Varro R.R. 3, 9, 17

Guinea-fowl (*gallinæ Africanæ, Numidicæ*) were rare enough in Italy, when Varro wrote, to be expensive, and the taste for them as food had been only recently acquired. In the time of Caligula (A.D. 37–41) they were still deemed sufficiently valuable and " exotic " to be among the birds which were regularly sacrificed to the Emperor's godhead—the others being flamingoes, peacocks, capercailzie, and pheasants. Columella says that the method of keeping and breeding them is much the same as for peafowl. They appear among the birds on the farm of Martial's friend Faustinus at Baiæ.

Varro, loc. cit. Pliny, N.H., X, 26(38), 74 Cf. Horace Epod., 2, 53 Suetonius, Caligula, 22, 3

Columella, VIII, 12 Martial, III, 58, 15

Columella describes the guinea-fowl ordinarily bred in Italy as red-wattled. And while Varro simply identifies *gallinæ Africanæ* with the birds called in Greek μελεαγρίδες, Columella

Columella, VIII, 2 Varro, loc. cit.

---

[1] Varro's words are, *Ab his [sc. rusticis] gallinis dicitur insula Gallinaria . . . Alii ab his villaticis invectis a nautis, ibi feris factis procreatis.*

would restrict the latter name to the blue-wattled variety (the Turkey guinea-fowl of Liberia Gabun). Whether Suetonius meant to distinguish *Numidicæ* from *meleagrides* in his list of birds sacrificed to Caligula, is not certain, but he probably did.[1]

Pliny, *N.H.*, X, 26(38), 74; 47(67), 132

Pliny takes *meleagris* to be the word for some African guinea-fowl, but also mentions *Numidicæ* in another passage, without suggesting that they were the birds which he knew as *meleagrides*.

Peafowl (*pavones*) were much bred in Italy from the first century B.C. They were probably received from Greece.[2]

Varro, *R.R.*, III, 6

It was in Varro's lifetime that the breeding of flocks of these birds was introduced into Italy.[3] They were kept mainly for their beauty, or for the profit to be made by supplying the taste for it; Varro distinguishes between those who kept peafowl for profit, and those who kept them for pleasure (*ad delecta-tionem*)—the latter would want more male birds than females.

Columella, VIII, 11

Columella reckoned the breeding of peafowl rather as a hobby for the cultivated gentleman than as an occupation for the serious farmer (*magis urbani patris familiæ quam tetrici rustici*); but, he adds, it is a way of increasing even the farmer's pleasure in a country life.

In the last years of the Republic there was a demand for pea-fowl as a luxury of the table. Q. Hortensius, the orator, whom we shall meet again as an amateur of fish, first served these birds at an augural banquet. In 46 B.C. they were a feature of the dinners given by Cæsarian *nouveaux riches*, who had made fortunes out of the conquest of Gaul or the Roman civil war. But perhaps when the novelty had worn off, the fashion waned, though it did not disappear. Peacocks' brains were among the more fantastic dishes served to the Emperor Vitellius, who enjoyed dining extravagantly as well as heavily. Juvenal refers

Varro, *loc. cit.*

Cicero, *Ad. Fam.*, IX, 18, 3

Suetonius, *Vitell.*, 13, 2

Juvenal, I, 143

---

[1] His list runs: *phœnicopteri pavones tetraones numidicæ meleagrides phasianæ*.

[2] On peafowl in Greece, see pp. 15–16.

[3] *Nostra memoria*, says Merula, a character in the dialogue of Varro's third Book on Farming; and Merula could hardly have been much older than Varro.

to peacock as the rich glutton's food, and Martial to the waste of beauty in giving this bird to the cook. Fly-flaps were made of peacocks' tails. Martial, XIII, 70 ; XIV, 67

It would seem that the peacocks of Roman Italy were all of one kind (*Pavo cristatus*) ; and there appears to be no trace of sports, such as the black-shouldered peafowl common in England, or the white-pied birds that are rarer and are sacred in India.

Peafowl were allowed their freedom on small islands off the Italian coast, where they were safe from thieves or predatory animals. Under such conditions their keeper had little to do but to call them to be fed once a day on barley. On the mainland they had to be kept in enclosures. Columella advises enclosing with a wall some grassy and treed land for the flock, which should be in the proportion of one cock to five hens. Each separate group should be taught to come to feed in its own pen of upright reeds, a very wise precaution against fighting and damage. The peahens were tested, and when ready to lay were enclosed apart. The eggs were set under barndoor hens. The poults were placed in the common sleeping shed when 7 months old. Varro, *loc. cit.* Columella, *loc. cit.*

Varro was much impressed by the prices obtained for peafowl in his day ; but their commercial value probably declined, as their numbers in Italy increased ; Columella does not note any very high prices for them as he does for pigeons. In Varro's time peahens' eggs were sold for 20 sesterces each (about 3s. 6d.) ; an ordinary price for a bird was 160 sesterces (£1 8s.), and M. Seius, who expected his flock to produce yearly thrice its number of birds for sale, could get 200 sesterces (£1 15s.) for each. One owner made on his flock over 60,000 sesterces, or more than £530. And it was thought that the annual net profit on a flock of 100 birds might be 40,000 sesterces (about £355).

Pheasants (*phasianæ*), imported from Colchis, the land of the River Phasis, at the south-eastern corner of the Black Sea, had been known as rarities in Greece since the fifth century, and also in Ptolemaic Egypt where they had been bred for the table and for their beauty in the royal gardens (see pp. 16, 33 *n*.1). When they were first brought to Italy is not known ; but it seems that they became fashionable as an expensive food about the middle of the first century A.D. Neither Varro nor Columella alludes to the breeding of pheasants in Italy, but the latter speaks of extravagant expenditure on foreign game from the Phasis and elsewhere. They were among the exotic birds sacrificed to Caligula—perhaps the victims were supplied from stock which was imperial property—and pheasants' brains were served to Vitellius. Pliny notes that they were " by this time in Italy " ; Statius mentions them among the birds given to the spectators at a festival in the time of the Flavian dynasty ; and as in Martial they appear among the birds on the farm of Faustinus at Baiæ, one may suppose that they were well established in the country by the end of the first century A.D. Later, it seems, pheasant-breeding was widely spread in the Empire. In the Edict of Diocletian fixing prices (A.D. 301), the pheasant is priced little higher than the goose ; *phasianus pastus*, 250 denarii ; *anser pastus*, 200 denarii. The bird is represented on a relief from the Rhineland and on a mosaic from North Africa. Palladius, who wrote on agriculture in the fourth century A.D., has a chapter on the keeping of pheasants. He recommends a proportion of two hen-pheasants to one cock,[1] and advises that their eggs be set under barndoor hens. He gives instructions for cramming birds of this kind. But in the second and third centuries frugal emperors still rarely had pheasants served to them ; and when Julian was governing Gaul (A.D. 356), his anxiety that his table should be a model of plain living led him to exclude the pheasant from it. There is evidence of the pheasant in the Frankish kingdom of the early Middle Ages.

The bird shown in Rome in A.D. 47 or 48 as a " phœnix " may have been a golden pheasant from the Far East.

Geese (anseres) and *ducks (anates).* Geese were kept for profit, and as sacred birds in temple precincts, as on the Roman

Marginal references:
Columella, VIII, 8
Suetonius, Caligula, 22, 3 ; Vitellius, 13, 2
Pliny, N.H., X, 47(67), 132 Statius, Silvæ, I, 6, 77 Martial, III, 58, 16
C.I.L., III, p. 806 Keller, Antike Tierwelt, II, 146
Palladius, I, 29
Hist. Aug., Pert., 12, 6 ; Alex. Sev., 37, 6 ; Tac., 11, 5. Contrast Elag., 32, 4 Ammianus Marcellinus, XVI, 5, 3
Keller, loc. cit. Loisel, Vol. I, 240 Oath on the pheasant, 1453
Pliny, N.H., X, 2(2), 5
Petronius, 136

---

[1] In modern times very rare pheasants are mated in the proportion of two hens to one cock, well established varieties ten to one.

Capitol and elsewhere.   An instance of ducks being kept partly, at least, *ad delectationem* is to be found in Varro's description of his aviary at Casinum, where there was a duckpond.   Even at this early date the Britons kept geese for show.

Varro, *R.R.*, III, 5
Cæsar, *De Bell Gall.*, V, 12, 6

Large white geese were recommended to the farmer by Varro and Columella ; the grey goose had been domesticated, but was found not so prolific and did not fetch so good a price. Pliny reports that geese from the country of the Morini (Picardy) were driven on foot all the way to Rome ; why this was worth the trouble, he does not explain.[1]   The best goosedown was thought to be that of the small wild geese (*gantæ*) of Germany[2]; and Pliny says that commanders of auxiliary cohorts on that frontier had been charged with sending their men away from their proper duties to go fowling for these birds.   Geese in Italy were fattened for the table on pearl-barley and flour, and *foie gras* was known to the Romans from the last years of the Republic, whether introduced by Metellus Scipio, the father of Pompey's last wife, or by M. Seius, a knight who is celebrated by Varro as an expert in different kinds of bird-keeping, and other special lines in farming.   Horace alludes to the cramming of geese on figs, a method invented by the famous epicure Apicius ; dried figs were given to the birds, and then mead.

Varro, *R.R.*, III, 10
Columella, VIII, 14
Pliny, *N.H.*, X, 22(27), 53

Cato, *R.R.*, 89
Varro, *loc. cit.*
Columella, *loc. cit.*
Pliny, *N.H.*, X, 22(27), 52

Varro, *R.R.*, III, 2

Horace, *Sat.*, II, 8, 88
Pliny, *N.H.*, VIII, 51(77), 209

Among the imported breeds of duck the *phalaris* or *phaleris*, mentioned by Varro and Columella, was perhaps the most valued.   Pliny calls it the most admired of waterfowl in Mesopotamia (*in Seleucia Parthorum*, near the site of the modern Baghdad), and in Asia—presumably the Roman province of that name.   But it seems to have been common enough in Greece in the time of Aristophanes, and Aristotle mentions it as found by rivers and lakes, as though it were native in Greece. Perhaps it was the coot (*Fulica atra*).

Varro, *R.R.*, III, 11
Columella, VIII, 15
Pliny, *N.H.*, X, 48(67), 132

Aristophanes, *Birds*, 565
Aristotle, *H.A.*, VIII, 593b, 19

---

[1] The cheapest method of transport.   A flock of geese will march daily thirteen miles as against the usual eighteen miles of infantry. Cf. Goose-step.

[2] The Gray-lag goose (*Anser ferus*) " Candidi ibi, verum minores gantæ vocantur," Pliny, *N.H.*, X, 22 (27), 54.

The *querquedula* (from the Greek κερκεθαλίς) may have been the pintail (*Dafila acuta*).   Columella also mentions the *boscis* or *boscas* which was presumably the Greek βόσκας described by Aristotle as like the common duck, νῆττα, but smaller.   The νῆττα was the mallard (*Anas boscas*) and the βόσκας was probably the teal (*Querquedula crecca*).   Columella advises the farmer who wishes to start duck-keeping to collect the eggs of wild duck and set them under hens.

Columella, VIII, 14

For geese, says Columella, an enclosure should be provided, surrounded by a nine foot wall, and containing separate pens for breeding birds.   The geese would be turned out to feed in the meadows, and would have their pond near the farm.

Columella VIII, 15

Ducks should be protected by a fifteen-foot wall, smoothed to keep out vermin, and the space enclosed by it should be netted over as a protection from hawks and eagles.   Under the wall on its inner side, and hidden by shrubs, there should be receptacles, a foot square, where birds would breed.   The pond in the middle of the enclosure should have twenty feet of grass round it.   Its sides should be sloping, and its bottom hard, except in the centre, which should be of earth to encourage the growth of water plants and reeds.   Columella understood the birds and their need of privacy in the mating season ; his pond and enclosure cannot be bettered, but they would be expensive to construct to-day.[1]

Cranes (*grues*) and *storks* (*ciconiæ*).   An enclosure such as that recommended by Columella for ducks would suit these birds as well.   Cranes of the ordinary kinds and storks could be trapped in Italy.   Varro, in one of his Satires, gave a list

Aulus Gellius, VI, 16, 5

of delicacies with the countries or places where they were to be found at their best ; and among them were the cranes of Melos.   The demoiselle crane (*vipio*) is mentioned by Pliny as

Pliny, N.H., X, 49(69), 135

found in the Balearic Islands ; whether it had been brought

---

[1] It is perhaps worth noticing that in his directions for making enclosures for peafowl and geese, he mentions in each case the quarters to be built in the enclosure for the *custos*, who would be a slave. Poultry, he says, could be watched by an old woman (*anus sedula*) or a boy.

to Italy he does not say. He describes the antics of tamed cranes ; and he notices that a writer who died under Augustus had said that storks were preferred to cranes as food, though in Pliny's day cranes were highly esteemed in this respect,[1] and no one would touch stork. The " pious " stork was known as a destroyer of snakes, and was probably welcomed as such in Italy ; in Thessaly the killing of it was once a punishable crime.

Flamingoes (*phœnicopteri*) may have been imported from Egypt, where they were very common, or from elsewhere in North Africa, by the time of Augustus. It is probable, at least, that it was in Italy that Apicius, the epicure of the Augustan age, tasted the flamingoes' tongues which he thought so excellent—a dish served later to the Emperor Vitellius, and mentioned by Martial as a delicacy for *gourmands*, while Juvenal includes a whole flamingo in a fantastic menu. But no doubt the birds were ordinarily admired and kept for their beauty. They were among the exotic birds regularly sacrificed to Caligula at his temple in Rome ; and (according to Suetonius) flamingo's blood spurting over the Emperor at a sacrifice a few hours before his death was thought afterwards to have been ominous.[2] There were flamingoes on the farm of Faustinus, the friend of Martial, at Baiæ. The birds would need a pond or stream with a muddy bottom.

Purple galinules (*porphyriones*) seem to have been fairly common at Rome in the imperial age. In Ælian's time (about A.D. 200) they were kept for their beauty as ornaments of the

Ibid., 23(30), 59–60

Juvenal, XIV, 74 Pliny, *N.H.*, 23(31), 62

Pliny, *N.H.*, X, 48(68), 133

Suetonius, *Vitell.*, 13, 2 Martial, XIII, 71 Juvenal, XI, 139

Suetonius, *Caligula*, 22, 3 ; 57, 4 Josephus, *Ant.*, XIX, 87 Martial, III, 58, 14

Ælian, *N.A.* III, 42

---

[1] Cranes are eaten in Japan to ensure longevity—their life is long as food they have a very poor reputation.

Crane and goose farming were common in Thessaly in the fourth century B.C. Plato, *Pol.*, 264c.

[2] According to Josephus (whose account is preferred by Balsdon, *The Emperor Gaius*, p. 168, n. 1) the blood spurted over one who was present at a sacrifice offered by Caligula to Augustus. Elagabalus' dishes of flamingoes' *brains* and peacocks' *tongues* may be an invention of the writer of his life in the *Historia Augusta* (Chapter 20).

palaces of the wealthy, or in temples. They were not used as food.

Pliny, *N.H.*, X, 46(63), 129

Pliny, who says that the finest purple galinules were those of Commagene (the country at the northern extremity of Syria, between the Taurus and the Euphrates), describes their peculiar habit of holding a morsel in one foot while feeding. Ælian draws attention to their ways of dusting (like fowls), and bathing like pigeons. On the keeping of these birds by the Greeks, see p. 17.

Ibid., 49(69), 135

Pliny notices another *porphyrio* " better known even than that already mentioned " (*nobiliorem etiam supra dicto*), and found in the Balearic Islands, whence it was brought to Italy ;

Ibid., 47(64), 130

probably it was the water-rail (*Rallus aquaticus*). The *himantopus* from Egypt, much smaller than the purple galinule, but with legs as long as that bird's, would be the red-legged courser (*Cursorius*) found on the Nile ; it had been brought to Italy, but never lived many days. It is closely related to the Black-backed courser or plover (*Pluvianus ægyptius*),

> The bird that dared with ceaseless hum
> Within the crocodile's jaws to come.

Ibid., 47(66) 131

The *pelican* (*onocrotalus*) is well described by Pliny, who says that it came to Italy from the northernmost coast of Gaul (*Gallia hos septentrionali proxima oceano mittit*)—that is, from Flanders or Picardy, a strange place for pelicans, but not impossible, for even in this century a naturalist, the late Abel Chapman, saw a flock of these birds in Jutland, and was in-

Martial, XI, 21, 10

formed that they were regular visitors. Apparently " Ravenna pelican " was a phrase used to stigmatize the inhabitants of Ravenna as gluttons.

Capercailzie (*tetraones*) from the Alps and the North, were

Pliny, *N.H.*, X, 22(29), 56

among the exotic birds sacrificed to Caligula. But Pliny records (and his statement is confirmed by modern experience) that birds of this kind moped quickly to death in captivity.

Keller, *Antike Tierwelt*, II, 156–7 Pliny, *N.H.*, XI, 51(112), 268 ; copying Aristotle, *H.A.*, V, 536a, 26–8 ; XXII, 21(30), 65

Partridges (*perdices*). The common partridge of Northern Europe was probably not a native of Italy, where to-day, it seems, there are only the rock partridge and the red partridge. The rock partridge, which is easier to tame than the common sort, was probably the bird which the Romans kept for fight-

ing. Statius includes the partridge among the " talking "
birds summoned to mourn for a dead parrot—*quique refert
iungens iterata vocabula perdix*—referring perhaps to the sad
sound of its natural cry, not to its learning to imitate words.[1]

Quails (*coturnices*) were kept for fighting in Italy as well as
in Greece. Ovid contrasts the fate of a parrot prematurely
dead, though so peaceful a bird, with that of quails, who live
through their fights to reach old age. Fattened quails and
ortolans fetched a good price as food in Varro's time, but Pliny
says that quails were little esteemed as food, for it was believed
that they fed on poisonous plants.

Ostriches (*struthocameli, struthiones*). There seems to be no
definite evidence that ostriches were kept permanently in
Italian aviaries, though they probably were, as the climate is
suitable and the cost of an enclosure is almost negligible ; they
had been imported for the Roman Shows as early as the time
of Plautus, and are mentioned as appearing in the Roman arena
under Commodus and later Emperors.[2] Even at the begin-

Hist. Aug.,
Alex. Severus,
41, 5
Statius, Silvæ,
II, 4, 20

Ovid, Amor, II,
6, 27–8
Pliny, N.H.,
XI, 51(112),
268
Varro, R.R.,
III, 5
Pliny, N.H.,
X, 23(33), 69

Plautus,
Persa, 198

---

[1] What were the " new birds " brought to Italy in A.D. 69, and
still so called when Pliny wrote of them some years later (*N.H.*, X,
49(69), 135) ? They were like thrushes, a little smaller than dove-
cot pigeons, and good eating. They came, says Pliny, in the campaigns of Bedriacum, the two short civil wars which were both decided
in that year at Bedriacum near Cremona. In those campaigns armies
from the Rhine and the Danube entered Italy, and perhaps these
new birds were Hungarian partridges.

" As for the Pegasi headed like horses," Pliny continues (§ 136),
" and the gryphons with an ear-shaped hooked beak, the former in
Scythia, the latter in Ethiopia, I regarded them as fabulous." But
perhaps the Pegasus was the Loon, or Great Northern Diver, and the
gryphon the Curassow.

[2] Seneca records that he had seen Cornelius Fidus, the son-in-law
of Ovid, weeping in the Senate at having been called a " plucked
ostrich " by Corbulo (*Ad Serenum, Nec Iniuriam*, etc., 17, 1). But
this shaft may have been from the quiver of Corbulo's provincial
experience ; or a plucked ostrich may have been occasionally shown
in the arena to make the spectators laugh. It is not definite evidence
of ostrich-farming in Italy, but six hundred ostrich-heads at a banquet
under Elagabalus and a thousand ostriches in the arena under Probus
leave little doubt in the matter.

Synesius,
Ep., 134
Hist. Aug.,
Elagabalus,
22, 1 ; 28, 4 ;
30, 2

ning of the fifth century A.D. ostriches were being shipped from Cyrene to Rome. If the Life of Elagabalus in the *Historia Augusta* is to be believed, that Emperor sometimes made " ten ostriches " a prize in a lottery for his guests ; which would point to their being kept in imperial aviaries in Italy. In this same Life of Elagabalus occurs the first mention of serving ostriches at an Italian banquet ; the Emperor, it is said, often dined on them, and on one occasion his guests were given ostrich heads from which they were to eat the brains.

The singing or " talking " birds that were kept as single pets or in aviaries may now be noticed. They were all natives of Italy except the parrot.

Nightingales (*lusciniæ, luscinii, lusciniolæ*). A passage in

Pliny, N.H.,
X, 29(43),
81-5

Pliny describing the nightingale's song shows the interest and delight which it caused. He adds that the prices paid for these birds might be as great as those given for slaves, and that to his knowledge a white nightingale was sold as a rarity for 6,000 sesterces (about £46), the purchaser wishing to present it to the Empress Agrippina, the mother of Nero. Nightingales were sometimes trained to take their part in concerts of musical

Ibid., 42(59),
120
Martial, VII,
87, 8
Horace, Sat.,
II, 3, 245
Hist. Aug.,
Elagabalus,
20, 5

instruments. When Pliny wrote, the princes of the Flavian dynasty had nightingales that were taught to imitate Greek and Latin words and sentences. A lady who put up a monument over her dead nightingale is mentioned (or invented) by Martial. These birds were occasionally eaten, as an extravagance.

Varro, R.R.,
III, 5
Pliny the
Younger, Epp.,
IV, 2, 3
Philostratus,
Apollonius
of Tyana,
VI, 36
Horace, Sat.,
II, 8, 91 ;
Ars Poet, 458
Varro, loc. cit.
Pliny, N.H.,
X, 30(45), 87
Cf. Pausanias,
VIII, 17, 3

Blackbirds (*merulæ*) were probably often kept in aviaries or as pets. Varro says that in his aviary at Casinum he kept " mostly singing birds, such as nightingales and blackbirds." A boy who died in Trajan's reign, the son of a rich man, had " nightingales, parrots, and blackbirds " among his playthings, and they, with his ponies and dogs, were killed by his father at the funeral pyre. Blackbirds were also snared to be sold as food ; sometimes before sale they were fattened in captivity. White blackbirds, which, says Pliny,[1] were to be found on Mt. Cyllene in Arcadia, and " nowhere else "—of course a

[1] Copying Pseudo-Aristotle, *Historia Animalium*, IX, 617a, 12-14.

mistake—, were occasionally exhibited as rarities at the public Varro, *R.R.*,
III, 9 shows in Varro's time.

Lesbia's *passer* was small and desirable, eminently tame Catullus, 2,
1–4 ; 3, 1–10 and loving, and piped to his mistress (*ad solam dominam usque pipilabat*). This should be the beautiful piping bullfinch. *Passer* may mean bullfinch in *meus pullus passer*, a term of endearment in Plautus ; one of the meanings of *pullus* is Plautus,
Casina, 138 dusky. Martial says he will give the *Passer* of Catullus in Martial XI,
6, 14–16 return for thousands of kisses ; which may refer to the affectionate ways and kisses of the bullfinch. *Passeres* seem Apuleius,
Metam., VIII,
15 (Teubner
text, 1913) to be mentioned in Apuleius as domestic pets.

The *goldfinch* (*carduelis*) appears as a boy's pet in Petronius. Petronius, 46 A father who says that his son is crazy about birds (*morbosus in aves*) speaks of having already killed three goldfinches belonging to the boy, and of having said that the *mustela* had eaten them.

Thrushes (*turdi*).—These birds were sometimes kept as Pliny, *N.H.*,
X, 42(59), 120 pets. The Empress Agrippina owned a thrush that could " talk," but such a thing had never been known before, says Pliny.

But thrushes were in demand chiefly for the table, and were kept in great numbers to be fattened. The fattening of thrushes was introduced in the last years of the Republic. Pliny, *N.H.*,
X, 23(30), 60 Lucullus took it up, and it annoyed Pompey to hear that Plutarch,
Lucullus, 40 ; the thrushes which a doctor had ordered him in summertime *Pompeius*, 2 could hardly be got except from Lucullus, with whom he had quarrelled. Varro knew of a farm in the Sabine country from which 5,000 thrushes were sold in a year at 12 sesterces (about Varro, *R.R.*,
III, 2 ; 5 2*s*. 3*d*.) each. He gives directions for making such an aviary as will be suitable to the keeping and fattening of thousands of thrushes and blackbirds, and of quails and ortolans too. The thrush is mentioned by Horace and Martial as excellent Horace, *Epp* ,
I, 15, 40–1 eating—the best of birds, says the latter. It is still renowned Martial,
XIII, 92 —" *Faute de grives on mange des merles* " says the French proverb. *Les merles de Corse*, however, are famous. Martial means, perhaps, the fieldfare (*T. pilaris*).

The *Starling* (*sturnus*) was trained to talk. Statius describes

Statius, *Silvæ*,
II, 4, 18–19

Pliny, *N.H.*,
X, 42(59), 120

Ibid., 42(59),
118

Petronius, 28

Martial, VII,
87, 6; XIV, 76

Macrobius,
Sat., II, 4,
29–30

it as storing up in its memory words which it had heard [1];
and when Pliny wrote, the young Cæsars had a starling which
(like their nightingales mentioned above) was taught Greek
and Latin words and sentences.

Pies (*picæ*) were favourite talking birds. Pliny says that
they enjoy their talking, and make visible efforts in practising
it. Pies have been known, he says, to be killed by their difficulties with words ; they forget what they have learnt unless
it is now and then repeated to them, and they are wonderfully
delighted at hearing again a word which they have been trying
to recall.[2] Trimalchio had a pie (*pica varia*) in a golden cage
over his door to greet visitors. So in Martial " the pie that
utters its greeting " has a place in a list of animal pets, and
in another epigram the bird is made to say, " A talking pie,
I greet my master distinctly, and if you do not see me, you
will think that I cannot be a bird." Pliny thought that pies
talked more distinctly than parrots ; but the best talking
parrots were unknown to the Romans.

Ravens (*corvi*) and *crows* (*cornices*) were kept as talking pets,
especially, perhaps, by the poor. When Octavian returned to
Rome after the defeat of Antony, an artisan produced a raven
which he had taught to say, *Ave, Cæsar victor imperator*.
Octavian bought the bird for 20,000 sesterces (about £155) ;
but a treacherous friend of the seller demanded that the latter
should be made to show another raven which he had trained ;
and what that bird said was *Ave, victor imperator Antoni*. The
man was made to pay for his prudence by dividing the money
given him with the informer. Octavian also bought a parrot

---

[1] This may remind the reader of what Hotspur says in *Henry IV*,
Pt. I, I, iii, 224–6.
> " I'll have a starling shall be taught to speak
> Nothing but ' Mortimer,' and give it him,
> To keep his anger still in motion."

[2] Plutarch (*De Sollertia Animalium*, 19) tells a story of a talking
pie at Rome, which, after hearing trumpets at a funeral, fell into a
prolonged silence, puzzling and alarming its master, a barber in the
Forum. But this silence it suddenly broke, to imitate nothing but
trumpet music.

and a pie which had been taught to greet him. Whereupon a cobbler, hoping to make money in this way, purchased a raven and tried to teach it how to salute the Emperor. But the bird not being an apt pupil, its teacher exclaimed more than once, *Opera et impensa periit* (" Labour and money wasted ! ") At last the bird could say the greeting, and was placed where the Emperor would pass. It duly repeated its lesson ; but the Emperor only said that he had enough birds already to salute him. And then, fortunately, *Opera et impensa periit*, said the raven. The Emperor laughed and bought the bird.

Pliny tells of a raven which, when young, flew from its parents' nest, on the roof of the Temple of Castor, into a cobbler's stall opposite the temple, and was given a home by the cobbler, partly out of piety. It soon learnt to talk, and then every morning it flew into the Forum, and perching on the speakers' platform, the Rostra, it saluted by name first Tiberius (the reigning Emperor), then Germanicus and Drusus (the adopted son and the son of Tiberius), and then the Roman People passing below it (*transeuntem populum Romanum*) ; and after that it flew back to its master's shop. This courteous habit it kept up for years, till at last it was killed by the owner of another cobbler's stall, either out of commercial jealousy, or (as the man afterwards protested) in a fit of temper because the bird had dirtied the shoes in his shop. The neighbourhood was so shocked at the atrocity that the destroyer of the bird had to leave that part of Rome and was soon afterwards murdered. On 28 March, A.D. 35, the raven was given a funeral which was attended by a great crowd. A flute player went in front of the bier, which was carried by two negroes, and was covered with garlands. And so the bird was borne in state to a funeral pyre at the second milestone on the Appian Way.

Pliny, N.H., X, 43(60), 121–3

In Pliny's day a knight at Rome had a Spanish crow, of a wonderful glossy black, which was a very quick learner. And a few months before the tyrannical Domitian was assassinated, a talking crow settled on the Capitol, and uttered the words, *Ἔσται πάντα καλῶς*—" All will be well."

Ibid., 43(60), 124

Suetonius, *Domitianus,* 23, 2

Witherby,
*Early Annals
of Ornithology,*
16

It is said that in Britain the bones of ravens, probably soldiers' pets, are among the commonest finds in a Roman camp.

Varro, R.R.,
III, 9

Parrots (psittaci).—Varro mentions them among rare birds exhibited at public shows. The increase of trade between Egypt and India in the time of Augustus probably helped to make the parrot a common pet in Italy under the Empire. For it was chiefly, at least, the green Indian parrot that the

Pliny, N.H.,
X, 42(58), 117

Romans knew. " India sends us this bird," says Pliny ; and he adds that its whole body is green, except for a red band on the neck. Of the grey West African parrot, a far better talker than the Indian, there is no trace in the Roman Empire.

Pliny, N.H.,
VI, 29(35), 184
Persius *Prol.* 8
Pliny, X,
42(58),117
Statius, *Silvæ*
II, 4, 29–30
Martial,
XIV, 73

But green African parrots may have found their way to Italy.[1]

It was the loyal and correct thing to teach one's parrot to say *Ave, Cæsar*. The birds were taught the conventional greeting χαῖρε, " How d'you do," and little tricks such as pulling a chariot. A parrot that would not learn its lesson was punished by being beaten on the head with an iron rod—its head, says Pliny, is as hard as its beak. It seems to have been a common amusement to give one's parrot wine and watch the effects.

Ovid, *Amor.*,
II, 6
Statius, *Silvæ*,
II, 4

Two Roman poets composed elegies on dead parrots—Ovid on one that had belonged to his mistress, Corinna, and Statius on the bird of his friend Melior. Melior's parrot had a cage with silver bars and with decorations in tortoise-shell and ivory. It had seemed to be quite well on the evening before its death,

---

[1] On p. 143 of *Commerce between the Roman Empire and India*, by E. H. Warmington (Cambridge Univ. Press, 1928), there is reproduced a silver dish, found at Lampsacus, with representations of six animals, which seem to be African, not Indian. The parrot might possibly be Indian, but with its stout build and broad round head it looks more like a bird of the green African sort. The next animal is surely an African guinea fowl. The two monkeys with long pendant tails resemble African white-lipped monkeys more than langurs of India ; for the latter always carry their tails curved over along their backs. The two carnivorous animals supposed to be a tiger and a leopard are badly drawn and doubtful, but the tufted tail suggests that they are a lion and a lioness.

flitting about the room where its master was dining with guests, taking morsels offered to it and answering when spoken to. Probably it was given something at dinner which mortally disagreed with it—parsley, perhaps. No doubt parrots in the Roman Empire, as in modern Europe, often suffered from people's ignorance of how to feed and treat them. Corinna's parrot seems to have lived on nuts and poppy seed.

Elagabalus is said to have amused himself by giving parrots and pheasants to his lions, and even to have eaten parrots' heads—presumably their brains. *Hist. Aug., Elagabalus, 20, 6; 21, 2*

CHAPTER VII

THE AMATEUR'S MENAGERIE
FISHPONDS

VARRO draws a distinction between the fresh-water fish ponds which are to be found on the properties of ordinary people (*apud plebem*), and yield some profit,[1] and the sea-water ponds, stocked with sea-fish, a plaything for the nobility. The latter are expensive to make, the cost of feeding the fish in them is high and yields no return save the æsthetic pleasure of the mind and eye. Q. Hortensius, when living at his villa at Bauli (near Baiæ), where he had famous salt-water ponds, always sent to Puteoli for fish to eat. It is probable that most of those who kept ponds of this sort were not quite so disinterested as Hortensius, and were occasional sellers of stock or used it for their own tables. That is suggested in what is said about these ponds by Columella, Seneca, and Martial. But it seems clear that sea-fish were kept chiefly as a hobby; and it may have been not unusual to keep certain of one's fish as sacred from the cook as were the murenas and red mullet of Hortensius.[2] Small ornamental fishponds, like those in Varro's aviary at Casinum, were no doubt common.

Columella,
VIII, 16; 17
Seneca, Epp.,
90, 7
Martial, X,
30, 19–24

[1] Plato mentions the keeping of " tame " fish (τιθασεῖαι τῶν ἰχθύων in Egypt and Greece in his day (*Politicus*, 264c).

[2] In Seneca's time there was a fish in the ponds at the imperial villa of Pausilypum (Pausilipo), near Naples, which was sixty years old or more. (Pliny, *N.H.*, IX, 53(78), 167.) Among the carp at Fontainebleau there are, I was told, some over one hundred years old. I am very sceptical of these records,

The fashion of keeping sea-fish had begun about the end of the second century B.C., and the Licinius who started it acquired thereby the name of Murena for himself and his descendants. In the last years of the Republic it was something of a craze among Roman nobles. In 60 B.C. Cicero was using the nickname *piscinarii* (fish-pond keepers) for the influential conservative set whom he disliked, and he wrote bitterly of " our leading statesmen, who think themselves in heaven if they have bearded mullet in their ponds ready to come and feed out of their hands (*qui ad manum accedant*), and who care for nothing else." Lucullus was believed to have spent enormous sums on cutting a tunnel through a hill in order to bring sea-water to his fishponds near Naples, and on connecting his ponds at Baiæ with the sea by an underground channel. The fish in his ponds were sold after his death for four hundred thousand sesterces (about £3,600). From Columella's advice on how to make ponds for sea-fish, it would appear that such ponds were common enough on seaside properties in the first century A.D.

The fish most often mentioned as kept by way of a hobby was the snake-like murena—the Sicilian kind being thought the finest. A certain C. Hirrius *lent* some six thousand murenas from his ponds to Julius Cæsar for the banquets at the Dictator's triumphs ; he refused to *sell* them. Single fishes of this kind were sometimes treated as pets. There were stories (probably inventions) of Q. Hortensius and M. Crassus (the associate of Cæsar and Pompey) weeping over the deaths of favourite murenas. That of Crassus is said to have come at its master's call to take food from his hand, and to have been adorned with ear-rings and a jewelled necklace. Pliny records that Antonia, the grandmother of Caligula, and the owner of the fishponds at Bauli which had once belonged to Hortensius, had earrings put on the murena which was her favourite. But murenas were known as fiercely biting fish. Columella says that they were liable to a form of rabies, so that it was better not to keep them in the same pond with fish of other kinds. It was told of Vedius Pollio that he threw to his murenas the

Pliny, *N.H.*, IX, 54(80), 170

Cicero, *Ad. Att.*, I, 19, 6 ; 20, 3 ; II, 1, 7

Varro, *R.R.* III, 17

Columella, VIII, 16

Pliny, *N.H.*, IX, 54(79), 169
Varro, *R.R.*, III, 17
Pliny, *N.H.*, IX, 55(81), 171
Ibid., 172

Keller, *Antike Tierwelt*, II, pp. 361–2 ; also Loisel, Vol. I, 88

Columella, VIII, 17

Pliny, *N.H.*, IX, 23(39), 77

slaves whom he chose to punish with death, because only so could he see a whole human body torn to pieces at once. This Vedius Pollio was the son of a freedman, and had probably made his fortune in the Civil Wars that destroyed the Republic ; for he died in 15 B.C. The story is well known, how he was prevented by Augustus from throwing to the murenas a slave who had broken a crystal goblet.

That Red mullet (*mulli barbati*) were sometimes kept as pets, is shown by Cicero's allusion, quoted above, to nobles who had bearded mullets that would come to feed from their hands. Of the reasons which might be given for thinking that Cicero had Q. Hortensius particularly in mind, the only one which

need be mentioned here is that Varro says of Hortensius that it would have been easier to persuade him to give away a team of carriage mules from his stables than a bearded mullet from his ponds. The pride of Hortensius in his mullets may be

accounted for in the light of Columella's remark that it is very difficult to get fish of this kind to live and thrive in captivity.

Other fish that the Romans kept in their salt-water ponds were the Gray mullet (*mugil*), the sea-pike (*lupus*), the turbot (*rhombus*), sole (*solea*), and gilt-bream (*aurata*). The last-named was thought to be best for eating when it had been fed on Lucrine oysters. C. Sergius Orata (for *Aurata*, as

Clodius for *Claudius*) was the first Roman to lay down oyster-beds, not long before 90 B.C. ; and he was the first to proclaim the superiority of the Lucrine oyster to the other kinds which were then available in Italy.[1]

Varro remarks that amateurs of fish kept different kinds in different ponds ; Columella distinguishes between the pond suitable to flat fish, and the pond needed for fish of other sorts. It has been noticed that there was a special reason for keeping murenas in a pond by themselves.

Lastly, it may be observed that some lakes in Italy had been stocked with seafish that would thrive in fresh water, such as pike and gilt-bream, and that in the reign of Claudius the

commander of the fleet at Misenum had introduced the Parrot

[1] He has another claim to fame as the inventor of shower-baths.

wrasse (*scarus*), which was highly esteemed as food, but till then had been found only in the Eastern Mediterranean, into the sea off the Italian coast from Ostia to Campania. The wrasse were given five years' protection in their new home, and after that, says Pliny, they were found in considerable numbers off Italy. Columella notices that this fish had not reached the sea off Liguria or Gaul or Spain.

Columella, VIII, 16

A CONCEPTION OF VARRO'S AVIARY (*see p.* 101)

CHAPTER VIII

THE AMATEUR'S MENAGERIE
QUADRUPEDS AND REPTILES

O N dogs, which were of course kept in ancient Italy for hunting, for guarding houses, for protecting and driving flocks and herds, and as pets, only a few general remarks will be made here ; the subject is a very large one.[1]

Virgil, *Æn.*,
XII, 753
Gratius, 171–3
Varro, *R.R.*,
II, 9

Three Italian breeds are mentioned by our authorities : the Umbrian, which was used for hunting and shepherding, was lively and keen (*vividus Umber* is Virgil's phrase), and had a good nose for a scent, but was not very courageous ; the

Varro, *loc. cit.*
Nemesianus,
231–6
" Oppian,"
Cyn., I, 396
Keller, *Antike
Tierwelt*, I, 95

Sallentine (i.e. Calabrian) is mentioned by Varro among kinds of sheepdog ; and the Etruscan, though not built for speed (it was apparently something like the modern Pomeranian), was a good scenting dog, and might be crossed with the Laconian for the hunter's purposes.

Dogs and hounds of many foreign kinds were imported into Roman Italy, and no doubt there was much crossing of foreign and Italian strains. From Epirus came the large dogs of the heavily built Molossian kind, which were highly esteemed as houseguards and for shepherd's work. From Greece came the light-built Laconian and Cretan hounds, which had a great reputation for their hunting qualities (Laconians are also men-

Varro, *loc. cit.*
Horace, *Epod.*,
6, 5–6

tioned as sheepdogs by Varro and Horace), and the heavier hounds of Thessaly, and the Acarnanians that stalked their

Gratius, 183–4

quarry silently (*clandestinus Acarnan*). From Gaul came dogs

[1] Reference may be made to Keller's *Antike Tierwelt*, I, 91–151.

of the greyhound type called *vertragi* (or *vertrahæ* or *veltrahi*) famed for their speed and used especially for coursing the hare. A rather small rough-haired hound from Britain had a great reputation as a tracker.[1]

Lastly, the small pet-dogs (*catelli*, *catellæ*) which were common in Imperial Italy, were probably often of the Maltese kind, which for centuries had been popular in Egypt and Greece ; it had a long-haired, silky coat and a curly feather tail. Such may have been the white pet-dog of the Emperor Claudius.[2]

Monkeys (*simii*, *simiæ*) were household pets at Rome (as appears from allusions in Plautus) by the end of the third century B.C. ; a man caught on a neighbour's roof might account for his being there by saying that he was after a monkey (*se sectari simiam*). The tailless barbary ape and the tailed *cercopithecus* (Barbary ape, *Macacus inuus*, and the many varieties of Cercopithecus) seem to have been the kinds usually imported into Italy ; they are mentioned together by Martial and appear in frescoes and reliefs. Martial works in the joke already age-old against all monkey keepers :

> Si Cronius similem cercopithecon amat
> (If Cronius loves a monkey ugly as himself—).

There seems to be no definite evidence of dog-faced monkeys or baboons (*cynocephali*) being kept in Italy, though no doubt they were occasionally brought there. Cicero, writing to Atticus from Cilicia in 50 B.C., tells how he had come across a Roman named Vedius, who had met him at Laodicea with two chariots, a horse-drawn litter, a large train of slaves, and a *cynocephalus* in one of the chariots, not to mention some wild asses ; the cortège did not impress Cicero favourably.

Side notes:
Gratius, 203
Martial,
XIV, 200
Gratius,
174–85
"Oppian,"
Cyn., I, 468–80
Cf. Strabo,
IV, 5, 2

Keller, *Antike Tierwelt*, I,
92–4
Athenæus, XII,
518f
Seneca, *Ludus de Morte Claudii*, 13, 2

Plautus, *Mil. Glor.*, 162 ; 179
Cf. *Mercator*,
229–33

Martial, XIV,
202
194–5
Martial, VII,
87, 4

Cicero, *Ad. Att.*, VI, 1, 25

---

[1] Gratius, an author of the Augustan age, who wrote a poem on hunting, also mentions hounds of Ukrainian (" Gelonian "), Anatolian (" Lycaonian "), Median, and Persian breeds, and also a fierce " Seric " kind, which may have been of Tibetan origin (155–60).

[2] The famous pet-dog of Latin literature is the Issa of Martial's friend Publius (Martial, I, 109). Epitaphs in verse on pet-dogs are in Bücheler's *Carmina Latina Epigraphica*, Nos. 1175, 1176, 1512.

Pliny, *N.H.*,
VI, 29(35), 184;
VIII, 54(80),
216; XXXVII,
9(40), 124
Aristotle, *H.A.*,
II, 502a, 19–22
Juvenal, X,
194–5

But Pliny, apart from a few references to *cynocephali* in Ethiopia, and to the use of their hairs in Eastern magic, only copies Aristotle's remark that they are wilder than other monkeys. Juvenal's allusion to the wrinkled face of a mother-ape may have been suggested by the sight of a baboon. The ape which the Greeks called *tityrus* (probably the orang outan) is apparently not recorded as seen in Italy. The *cebi* which were exhibited at Rome by Pompey (see above, p. 55) had not appeared there again by the time when Pliny wrote of them. There seems to be no trace of common Indian monkeys in Roman Italy ; they are hardy and very intelligent, and apt at all kinds of tricks ; but probably the food and water which they would have needed on the voyage from India to Egypt made them an unprofitable freight.[1]

Pliny, *oc. cit.*

Pliny speaks of domesticated monkeys (*simiæ mansuefactæ*) breeding in the houses where they were kept ; and he does not seem to regard this as exceptional, though to-day the breeding of monkeys in captivity is extremely rare. He may have been copying a Greek author, and his statement may not refer to monkeys in Italy ; but the description which he gives of the behaviour of these domesticated monkeys with their young is like that of an eye-witness. He notes that the young ones were often killed by the mother holding them too tightly— as he thinks, from affection, but really from fear.

Ælian, *N.A.*,
VI, 10

Gusman,
*Pompeii
Mosaics*, p. 2,
85
Zahn, *Schönste
Gemälde aus
Pompeii*, II, 50

Ælian says that in Ptolemaic Egypt baboons (κυνοκέφαλοι) were taught to distinguish letters,[2] to dance, and to play the flute or lyre ; and probably trained monkeys were brought by showmen to Italy in early days. Performing monkeys are represented in Pompeian frescos. Pliny had heard of monkeys taught to play at draughts [3] ; Juvenal mentions an ape that

---

[1] See p. 120 above, footnote.

[2] I tried our chimpanzee Consul I with the letters B (banana), L (lemonade) : he noted the shapes and the association of idea.

Furthermore the chimpanzee Consul II stamped with disgust and rage whenever he was shown a picture of a monkey.

[3] Charles V is said to have had a mona (probably a North African cercopithecus) that played chess.

was to be seen on a boulevard at Rome armed with a helmet and target, and taught to ride a goat and throw javelins ; and Ælian had seen a monkey (πίθηκος), the Barbary ape, performing as a charioteer.

Pliny, N.H., VIII, 54(80), 215
Juvenal, V, 153–5
Ælian, N.A., V, 26

Though Apulian vase-paintings, and coins of Tarentum and Rhegium seem to show that the *house-cat* was introduced into the Greek parts of South Italy towards the end of the fifth century B.C., it appears that the animal was not ordinarily to be found in Roman houses till the imperial age was well advanced. Seneca and the elder Pliny are the first Latin authors who mention the cat in such a way as to suggest that it was being kept in Italy in their time. Seneca, in arguing that there is such a thing as instinctive understanding, asks why chickens should fear a cat and not a dog. Pliny seems to appeal to his readers' acquaintance with cats : " How silently, with what light steps, they creep up to birds ! How covertly they watch before jumping out on mice ! " Yet it is said that in Herculaneum and Pompeii, which were destroyed in A.D. 79, no remains of cats have been found. A cat in mosaic at Pompeii may have been the work of an Alexandrian artist. But a house-cat figures on a Roman tombstone of the Early Empire, and a relief in the Capitoline Museum at Rome shows a cat being trained (apparently) to dance on its hind legs to music, a couple of birds being hung above its head to encourage it. Palladius, in his treatise on agriculture (of the fourth century A.D.) advises keeping cats in artichoke beds (*in carduetis*) for destroying moles. Palladius uses the word *catus* for the earlier *felis*. On *catus* or *cattus*, a word for which a North African origin has been suggested, see Keller, *Antike Tierwelt*, I, 74.[1] It must be remembered that, the cat being sacred in Egypt, exportation was prohibited and in addition commissioners were sent out periodically to buy and repatriate such cats as had been smuggled abroad.

Keller, Antike Tierwelt, I, 67–81

Seneca, Epp., 121, 19
Pliny, N.H., X, 73(94), 202

Keller, Antike Tierwelt, I, 79

Ibid., 72, 76, 80

Palladius, IV, 9

Salomon Reinach, Orpheus, p. 45

Weasels or polecats (*mustelæ*) were kept in Roman as in Greek houses to destroy mice, before cats were common there. They

Keller, Antike Tierwelt, I, 169

---

[1] Martial mentions Pannonian *cattæ* (XIII, 69), which were probably birds. Cata in Turkish is the hazel hen (*Tetrastes bonasia*).

Petronius, 46

are represented in Etruscan wall-paintings ; and in Petronius, " The *mustela* has eaten them," is offered as a plausible excuse

Palladius, IV, 9

for the disappearance of pet-birds. Palladius says that some people use tame *mustelæ* for keeping down moles. As I never heard of a tame weasel, I think the polecat (*Mustela putorius*),

Pliny, *N.H.*, VIII, 55(81), 218 ; cf.Strabo, III, 2, 6

the ancestor of our ferret, is the more likely animal. Pliny notices the use of ferrets (under the name *viverræ*) for catching rabbits.

Non-poisonous *snakes*, which might be kept as in Egypt for destroying vermin (their use for this purpose is mentioned

Palladius, *loc. cit.*

by Palladius), were not uncommon as pets. Seneca, Martial, and Suetonius refer to pet-snakes as *dracones*, which implies

Suetonius, *Tiberius*, 72

that they were fairly large. Tiberius had a *draco*, which he fed with his own hand ; it was eventually destroyed by ants, being no doubt too ill and debilitated to struggle against them.

Seneca, *De Ira*, II, 31, 5 Martial, VII, 87, 7

Seneca mentions *dracones* gliding harmlessly about cups and bosoms at dinner-parties ; and a Roman lady in Martial has a *draco* which she allows to coil round her neck. These *dracones* may have been Æsculapius snakes or Four-lined snakes. The yellow Æsculapius snake had been brought to Rome from Epidaurus, apparently because it was thought to

Pliny, *N.H.*, XXIX, 4(22), 72 *Hist. Aug.*, *Elagabalus*, 28, 3 ; 23, 2

have a healing or health-preserving influence, and Pliny says of it, *Volgo pascitur*. Elagabalus is said to have kept some Egyptian snakes of the kind known as *agathodæmones*, " good spirits." They are described in the *Historia Augusta* as *dracunculi*, which suggests that, though small, they somehow resembled snakes of a larger kind ; perhaps they were Grass snakes (*Tropidonotus natrix*.) It is also told of Elagabalus that he had a collection of snakes (apparently poisonous) made for him by Marsic priests, who were well known as snake-charmers.

Martial, VII, 87, 1, 5

Two quadrupeds which may have been rarely kept as pets, but are mentioned as such by Martial, are the *lagalopex* (a long-eared fox, perhaps the fennec from Egypt), and the Egyptian *ichneumon.*

It is perhaps worth noticing here that while there seems to be no mention of dormice (*glires*) as pets in Roman Italy, the *edible dormouse* (*Myoxus glis*) was a favourite delicacy of the

Romans. Allusions to it occur in Latin literature from the "swarms of dormice" in a fragment of Plautus to the satirical description by Ammianus Marcellinus of how boring were the Roman nobles of the fourth century A.D. with their interest in the weight of the fishes and birds, and their talk of the size of the dormice, which were served at their dinners. Dormice might be served in honey with a sprinkling of poppy. The censors of the later Republic vainly forbad this animal to the Roman diner. Q. Fulvius Lippinus, towards the middle of the first century B.C., introduced the breeding of dormice in a special enclosure, and the fattening of them in jars ; the process is described by Varro. They were fed on acorns, walnuts, chestnuts and beechnuts.

Plautus ap. Nonium, 119, 26 Ammianus Marcellinus, XXVIII, 4, 13

Petronius, 31 Pliny, N.H., VIII, 57(82), 223-4

Varro, R.R., III, 15 Pliny, N.H., XVI, 6(7), 18

Native or imported animals of the deer or wild-goat class might be preserved in parks and gardens, and might be treated also as pets, like the pet stag of the family of Tyrrhus in the *Æneid*. It is noticed in the Institutes of Justinian that some people keep tame stags which are accustomed to go into the woodland and return to the house. Small gazelles (so Martial seems to imply) might be kept as children's playthings ; and gazelles or antelopes (*dorcalides*) might be used as foster-mothers to dogs that were to be trained for hunting, on the principle that the milk of a speedy animal makes for speed.

Virgil, Æn.,VII, 483-92 Institutes, II, 1, 15

Martial, XIII, 99 "Oppian," Cyn., I, 440-1

Pliny mentions the following animals of this class as " sent " to Italy : *caprea* (roe), *rupicapra* (chamois), *ibex*, *oryx*, *damma* (probably here the common gazelle), *pygargus* (impalla antelope), and *strepsiceros* (Lesser koodoo, *Strepsiceros imberbis*). He remarks that the earlier items on his list (probably the *caprea*, *rupicapra*, and *ibex*) come from the Alps, the others from overseas. Animals of these latter kinds would come mostly from Africa and Egypt. In Egypt, antelopes of different sorts had been kept in a semi-domesticated state for thousands of years, just as similar races are kept to-day by the Boers of South Africa on their immense farms.[1] Pausanias saw white

Pliny, N.H., VIII, 53(79), 214

Pausanias, VIII, 17, 3

[1] Columella, writing under Nero, and apparently referring to Italy, mentions the oryx antelope among the animals which a landowner might ordinarily keep in his park (IX, 1).

deer at Rome, probably in a garden ; he forgot to ask where they came from. Albinos of the Red deer (*Cervus elaphus*) and of the Fallow deer (*Dama vulgaris*) are fairly common in England, and no doubt over most of Northern Europe, but would be unusual at Rome.

Probably the giraffe was sometimes to be seen in a zoological collection in Italy. This gentle animal was not well suited for a *venatio* ; the actual killing of it in the arena is not mentioned before Commodus. But it was seen from time to time at Rome, and Pliny calls it more remarkable for its appearance than for its wildness (*adspectu magis quam feritate conspicua*). In a wall-painting at Pompeii there is a picture of a giraffe haltered and led by a keeper. That would be impossible except with a giraffe accustomed to captivity.

Bestiæ dentatæ (lions, leopards, and bears) might be kept in cages or pits in the houses of the wealthy or in imperial palaces ; or even, if sufficiently tamed and trained they might be allowed into the living-rooms. Seneca speaks of tame lions and bears " in the house " (*intra domum*).[1] " Some people," says Epictetus, " keep tame lions in cages and feed them, and take them about with them." The Emperor Caracalla, as has been noticed elsewhere (p. 89), kept a number of lions which he took with him on his journeys, and one of them, called Scimetar, ate and slept in the same room with him. The tame lions, *leopardi* (maneless lions : see pages 186–7) and bears of Elagabalus had been deprived of teeth and claws (*exarmati*) ; but even so they must have been very well trained, if, as is related, they could be turned at night into the bedrooms of the Emperor's guests without doing harm except by the fright which they caused. They were sometimes brought to meals to make the diners uncomfortable.

A tiger of which Plutarch tells an interesting story may have

Pliny, *N.H.,* VIII, 18(27), 69
O. Jahn, *Die Wandgemälde des Columbariums in der Villa Pamfili*

Seneca, *De Ira*, II, 31, 5
Epictetus, IV, 1, 25
Cf. Juvenal, VII, 76–7

Dio, LXXVIII, 7, 2–3

Hist. Aug., Elagabalus, 25, 1 ; cf. 21, 1

Plutarch, *De Sollertia Animal.*, 20

---

[1] Accidents of course happened. *Feras cum labore periculoque venamur*, says Seneca (*De Vita Beata*, 14, 3), *et captarum quoque illarum sollicita possessio, sæpe enim laniant dominos.* On the law about damage done by captive wild animals to others besides their owners, see p. 153.

been in an imperial collection in Italy. A live kid was put into its cage, but the tiger would not touch it, going without food for two whole days, and on the third breaking its cage in its search for something else to eat. Plutarch attributes its behaviour to a fast, at first, for health's sake, and then a feeling that the kid had become its cage-mate. It was probably a whim.

The two savage bears of Valentinian I to which criminals, or the corpses of criminals, were thrown to be devoured, had their cages near the Emperor's bedroom ; their names were Innocence (*Innocentia*), and Grain of Gold (*Mica Aurea*). In Justinian's time there was a bearward among the officials of the imperial household. *Ammianus Marcellinus, XXIX, 3, 9*

Animals of this class that were trained to perform in public might be imperial property, or belong to private persons, who might give exhibitions under their own management, or contract with the organizers of shows in Rome or in the municipalities. The tame bear in Apuleius, that was dressed like a matron and carried on a chair in the procession in honour of Isis at Corinth, had probably been provided by a showman. *Apuleius, Metam., XI, 8*

Vivaria for Quadrupeds

An enclosure or park in which wild animals were kept might serve (as Columella said) for magnificence (*lautitiæ*), for pleasure, or for profit. It might gratify the owner's pride and impress other people ; it might provide him with sport or with the pleasure of watching the animals in it ; or it might contribute to the supply of his table, or yield live animals and meat for sale. *Columella, IX, 1*

It was an ancient fashion in Italy to have a *leporarium* (enclosure for hares) near one's country house. And it is likely enough that deer or wild goats were sometimes kept there.[1] Aulus Gellius quotes from a speech of Scipio Æmilianus the phrase, *roborarium atque piscinam*, and says that some scholars *Varro, R.R., III, 3* *Columella, IX, Præfatio* *Aulus Gellius, II, 20*

[1] But Varro seems to think of the change from keeping hares in a *iugerum* or two to keeping *cervi aut capreæ in iugeribus multis* as quite modern (*R.R.*, III, 12).

interpreted *roborarium* to mean an enclosure for wild animals, from the oaken paling used for fencing such ground.

At any rate, towards the middle of the first century B.C. the old Italian *leporarium* or *roborarium* was developed into something larger and more variously stocked. " I would have you understand by *leporaria*," says Varro, " not only what were so called by our remote ancestors (*tritavi*)—places where hares were to be found—but any enclosures attached to a country-house (*villæ afficta*), and containing animals that are to feed or be fed there (*animalia quæ pascantur*)." The orator Hortensius in Varro's time preferred to call his park at Laurentum a θηριοτροφεῖον. Later the word *vivarium* was usual for this kind of park.[1]

Varro, *R.R.*, III, 3

Ibid., III, 13

This development of the *leporarium* was probably suggested by what Romans had seen or read of enclosures and parks that were owned by Kings and nobles in the East, or were attached to Eastern temples. Such enclosures probably differed greatly in size, from some that included large tracts of country, to others that were only spaces in which beasts could be shot down without trouble, or from which they might be taken to be hunted in the neighbourhood, or where they might be easily watched for the pleasure of watching them. At Cabeira in Pontus were the *vivaria* (ζωγρεῖα) of Mithradates, and his neighbouring hunting grounds (αἱ πλησίον θῆραι). An example of a temple where animals of many kinds could be seen by visitors was at Hierapolis in Northern Syria. And it may be noticed here that when the army of Julian was invading Babylonia in A.D. 363, it came across " an extensive circular space, enclosed with a friezed wall (*lorica*), and containing wild animals reserved for the King's sport, maned lions

Strabo, XII, 3, 30

Lucian, *De Dea Syria*, 41

Ammianus Marcellinus, XXIV, 5, 2

---

[1] It should be noticed that the word *vivarium* seems to have been also used for the place where animals were kept before being shown in an amphitheatre. Thus the *custos vivarii* of the prætorian and urban cohorts, who appears in an inscription of the third century A.D. together with some soldiers described as *venatores immunes*, i.e. with special duties in the arena, was probably the keeper of a *vivarium* connected with the military amphitheatre (*amphitheatrum castrense*) at Rome. Dessau, *Inscr. Sel. Lat.*, 2091.

and bristling boars, and bears that were extraordinarily fierce, as Persian bears are, and a choice collection of other great beasts ; and our cavalrymen, breaking open the gates, killed them all with hunting spears and missiles." Ammianus Marcellinus, who is here quoted, was an officer in the invading army. Probably kings who ruled in the Mesopotamian region had owned such preserves since Assyrian times.

The Roman who led the way in the development of the *leporarium* during the last years of the Republic was Q. Fulvius Lippinus—that same Fulvius who first bred and fattened dormice (and snails too) for the table. Not many years before 50 B.C. he established a *vivarium* of about 27 acres (40 *iugera*), on his estate at Tarquinii in Etruria, for boars, stags, roes, and wild sheep. Q. Hortensius, L. Lucullus, and others followed his example, and larger *vivaria* than the one at Tarquinii were made, though it seems that in Italy no very large parks were established ; that of Hortensius at Laurentum was about 34 acres (50 *iugera*) in extent. On Varro's estate at Tusculum (which he had bought from M. Pupius Piso who had served under Pompey in the East) guests were entertained with the sight of boars and roedeer, coming to be fed at the summons of a horn. At Laurentum, while the guests of Hortensius dined at a spot overlooking the park, a servant dressed as Orpheus blew the horn that drew together a large and varied collection of wild animals.

It has been noticed already that Columella seems to think of the oryx antelope as one of the animals of the deer kind which, with boars and hares, one might expect to find in an Italian park of Nero's time. And it will be remembered that Nero's Golden House at Rome had grounds in which were " a multitude of all kinds of *pecudes et feræ*."

It would seem that Domitian's " shoots " at his Alban Villa (see above, p. 75) were in a private amphitheatre ; *Albana arena* is Juvenal's phrase, and Suetonius implies that the Emperor there gave " shows " of the kind called *venationes*. But there was probably a *vivarium* attached to the villa.

It was apparently in the provinces that wealthy Romans

Varro, *R.R.*, III, 12
Pliny, *N.H.*, VIII, 52(78), 211 ; IX, 56(82), 173

Varro, *R.R.*, III, 13

Columella, IX, 1

Suetonius, *Nero*, 31, 1

Juvenal, IV, 100
Suetonius, *Domitianus*, 4, 4

Varro, *R.R.*,
III, 12
owned hunting parks of the largest size. In Varro's day a certain T. Pompeius had enclosed for sport some 14 or 15 English square miles in Transalpine Gaul ; and Varro implies that there was no park in Italy to compare with it for size.

Columella,
loc. cit.
Columella says that by a method of rail fencing, which he describes, it is possible to enclose " wide regions and mountainous tracts, as the abundance of waste land (*locorum vastitas*) permits in Gaul and some other provinces." He seems to assume that animals kept for sport in an Italian *vivarium* would always have their food and water brought to them.[1] The wild cattle at Chillingham in Northumberland have access to water and support themselves except for a certain amount of hay supplied in winter.

Imperial hunting parks, or enclosures for shooting big game, are occasionally mentioned in the history of the later Empire. About the middle of the fourth century A.D. there was a hunting park on the imperial estate of Macellum in Cappadocia, where Constantius placed his young nephews Gallus and Ammianus
Marcellinus,
XXXI, 10, 19 Julian. And some thirty years later the young Emperor Gratian, residing in Gaul, was devoted to the sport of shooting *bestiæ dentatæ* " in the enclosures which are called *vivaria*."

---

[1] *Qui venationem voluptati suæ claudunt, contenti sunt, utcumque competit proximus ædificio loci situs, munire vivarium, semperque de manu cibos et aquam præbere.* In a *vivarium* established for profit, on the other hand, some woodland, he says, would be needed, and a supply of water (natural or artificial) within the enclosure. This suggests that a *vivarium* for " sport " was often only a place where animals were kept to be shot down easily, or at least with comfort to the shooter.

CHAPTER IX
CAPTURE AND TRANSPORT

A S regards the obtaining of wild animals for transport
to Rome or Italy in the days of the Roman Republic,
there seems to be no illustration of the methods of
animal-traders, in their dealings with natives or professional
hunters. But, in the correspondence of Cicero, there is an
example of how a Roman magistrate might set about collecting
animals from the provinces, for the shows which he had to
give at Rome.

Cicero left Italy in June 51 B.C. on his way to take up the
governorship of the province of Cilicia in Southern Asia Minor.
His friend, M. Cælius Rufus, hoped to be elected that summer
to the curule ædileship of the year 50, and as ædile he would
have to give some of the official *ludi*. Before Cicero was well *Ad, Fam.,*
out of Italy Cælius was writing to him, " As soon as you hear *VIII, 2, 2*
that I am elected, please attend to that business of the leopards
(*ut tibi curæ sit quod ad pantheras attinet, rogo*) "—from which
it would seem that he had already spoken to Cicero on the
subject. On 1 August Cælius (not yet elected ædile) was *Ibid., 4, 5*
reminding Cicero " about the leopards—to set the people of
Cibyra [1] to work, and to see about their transport for me."
On 2 September, soon after his election, he wrote, " In nearly *Ibid., 9, 3*
all my letters to you I have mentioned the subject of leopards.
It will be a disgrace to you if, when Patiscus [2] has sent ten to

[1] Cibyra was a place in Cicero's province in S. Phrygia near the
borders of Caria and Lycia. Cælius' phrase is, *ut Cibyratas accersas*—
to summon, call up, the Cibyrates. What Cicero understood him to
mean will appear later.

[2] Patiscus was a Roman knight in business in Cilicia.

Curio,[1] you don't get many more. Curio has made me a present of those ten, and of another ten from Africa. . . . If you will only remember to set the Cibyrates to work, and to write to Pamphylia—for they say that more are caught there —you will get what you want done. I am the more anxious about this now, as I think I shall have to make all my preparations independently of my colleague.[2] Do please see that you attend to this. You like taking trouble—as I like still more taking no trouble. In this affair the trouble for you is only to talk—I mean, to issue orders officially and to give commissions (*imperandi et mandandi*). For as soon as the leopards are caught, you have my people, whom I have sent about Sittius' bond,[3] to look after the animals' keep and bring them to Rome. I think, too, if you write encouragingly, I shall send some more men of mine to your part of the world."

Ibid., 8, 10   Early in October Cælius wrote : " Curio is treating me generously, and his present has given me work to do. For if he had not given me some African beasts, which had been brought here for his shows, I might have done without such things. But now, since I must give a show of that sort, I should like you to attend (as I have been all along asking you to do) to

Ibid., 6, 5   my having some beasts from your province." And in February of the next year, Cælius ended a letter, " It will be a disgrace to you if I don't have any Greek leopards."[4]

Unfortunately for Cælius, Cicero was anxious to be a model governor, and was not at all inclined to harass the people of his province to furnish his friend with wild beasts. Evidently, so long as it was not quite certain that Cælius was to be ædile,

---

[1] C. Curio, the famous tribune of 50 B.C., had been collecting animals for the *ludi* which he was to give to the Roman public in memory of his father, who had died in the year 53.

[2] The colleague of Cælius in the curule ædileship was M. Octavius. A pair of ædiles might or might not combine to give entertainments in their joint names. See Suetonius, *Div. Iul.*, 10, 1.

[3] A matter of business in which Cælius was interested, and which he was repeatedly recommending to Cicero's attention.

[4] *Pantheras Græcas*. It has been suggested that *Græcas* has got into the text from a marginal gloss on Κιβυράτας.

Cicero had avoided giving any definite answer to the requests
and reminders about leopards. But in the middle of February,
he wrote thus from Cilicia to Atticus, when by some mischance
he had only just received a letter which Atticus had written
on 21 September : " The only new thing in that letter was *Ad. Att*, V,
about Cibyrate leopards. I am very grateful to you for reply- 21, 5
ing to M. Octavius [1] that you didn't think I would do what
he suggested. But henceforth give a definite refusal to all
improper requests." A few days later he was writing again *Ibid.*, VI, 1, 21
to Atticus, " As for M. Octavius, I reply, as I have done once
already, that you answered him rightly ; only I wish your
answer had been a little more confident. For Cælius sent
me his freedman with an elaborate letter about leopards
and about getting subscriptions to his shows from the communities of my province.[2] On the latter point my answer
was that I should have been displeased at his request even
if my governorship had been wrapped in obscurity, and the
report had not reached Rome that not a penny was being paid
in my province unless it was owed ; and I told him that it was
illegal for me to collect the money and for him to receive it.
. . . About the other matter, I said that it was not consistent
with my reputation that the Cibyrates should hold a municipal
hunt on official orders from me (*Cibyratas imperio meo publice
venari*)." On 4 April Cicero, in a letter to Cælius, tried to
soften his refusal : " About the leopards, the professional *Ad. Fam.*, II,
hunters are busy, acting on my commission.[3] But there is 11, 2
an extraordinary scarcity of the beasts, and it is said that those
that there are complain bitterly that they are the only living
creatures in my province against whom any harm is meditated.

---

[1] The colleague of Cælius, and clearly after leopards on his own
account.

[2] Reading *de civitatibus* for *a civitatibus*. At any rate, what Cicero
means is made clear by what follows.

[3] *De pantheris per eos, qui venari solent, agitur mandatu meo diligenter.*
The phrase *mandatu meo* implies that Cicero had given commissions,
rather than official orders, to procure leopards. Cælius had hoped
(*Ad. Fam.*, VIII, 9, 3) that Cicero would undertake the work of giving
both official orders and commissions (*imperandi et mandandi*).

So they are said to have decided to leave my province and move into Caria. Still, the business is being carefully attended to, and particularly by Patiscus.[1] Whatever is got will be for you, but what there is to get, we do not know." Nor does posterity know how many leopards from Cilicia Cælius obtained for his shows.

There was of course a good side to the collecting of wild animals from the provinces for the Roman Shows, in so far as it meant a decrease in the numbers of destructive beasts. And this side is referred to by Strabo in his remark that Numidian agriculture had been promoted by the Roman taste for beast-fights. But it is clear that in the time of the Roman Republic the capturing of wild animals might be made a burdensome *corvée* for provincials, or for the subjects of those kings under Roman protectorate who would wish to stand well with important persons at Rome. Cælius' proposal to increase his staff in Cilicia, if the leopard catch warranted it, suggests that transport of the animals when captured often proved, then as in later times, burdensome to the inhabitants of the towns and districts through which they were taken ; but to that point a return will be made later in this chapter.

Strabo, II, 5, 33

Capture under the Empire

If we turn to the period of the Empire, there seems to be almost no evidence as to how the imperial administration obtained animals for the shows which the Emperors gave at Rome. Many of the methods of capture described by contemporary writers are given below and to them we may safely add all the hunters' tricks of any age. Science has made slaughter easy and has simplified transport, but capture depends on cunning and patience wherein no progress has been made. Presumably the imperial officials who were charged with this work employed professional hunters, and made contracts with, and purchases from, such dealers in wild animals as the *negotia-*

---

[1] It will be observed that Patiscus, who has been mentioned already as supplying Curio with ten leopards, seems to have made it part of his regular business to get animals for the Roman shows.

tores ursorum mentioned by Symmachus. Probably the Symmachus,
Epp., V, 62 inhabitants of districts where animals wanted could be found were sometimes pressed for this service. It is likely too that soldiers were sometimes employed in it (as they were employed on the construction of public works, and in the collection of goose feathers in Gaul), especially as hunting was recognized as useful training for war. It may well have been that corps stationed on the frontiers had their *venatores immunes* (soldiers with special duties as *venatores*), and their *vivaria* attached to camp-amphitheatres, as the Prætorian Guard had its *venatores* Dessau, *Inscr.*
Lat. Sel., 2091 and *vivarium* at Rome in the third century A.D.[1] It has been noticed already (p. 134 above) that when Julian's army found in Babylonia a collection of wild beasts belonging to the Persian King, the cavalry destroyed the animals with " hunting spears and missiles." And at the beginning of the fifth century A.D. the preserving of lions in the provinces where those animals were found, and also the transport of wild beasts Ammianus
Marcellinus,
XXIV, 5, 2 for the imperial shows were the concern of the departments of the military governors (*duces*). Local collectors would *Cod. Theod.*,
XV, 11, 1–2 help to supply imperial shows given in the provinces.

How the Roman noble Symmachus towards the end of the fourth century A.D. collected animals for shows at Rome through his agents and friends in the provinces, and with the help of government officials, has been described on pp. 95–97 above.

It seems that under the Empire licences from the imperial government were needed for the taking of elephants, and at Ælian, *N.A.*,
X, 1 some time became necessary for the hunting, killing or capture of lions.[2] In 414 A.D. the government permitted the *killing* *Cod. Theod.*,
XV, 11, 1

---

[1] A centurion of the VI Legion *Victrix* carried out the fencing of a *vivarium* at Cologne (Dessau, *Inscr. Lat. Sel.*, 3265). An *ursarius* of a legion is recorded in an inscription from the Rhineland (*Ibid.*, 3267, note 1). It seems to have been the rule that a legionary fortress should have its amphitheatre. On exhibitions of beast-fighting given by men of the Prætorian Guard at Rome under Claudius and Nero, see p. 69 and p. 70 above.

[2] This is to be distinguished from the need to obtain the permission of the imperial authorities to give a *venatio* of *Libycæ feræ* in the arena : Symmachus, *Epp.*, II, 46 ; IV, 12 ; VII, 59 and 122.

of lions without special licence, " since," as the Emperors Honorius and Theodosius II are made to say, " the safety of our provincials must be preferred to our own pleasure." But at the same time it was expressly declared that this was not a general permission to hunt lions or sell them. It was no doubt meant that inhabitants of countries where lions were to be found should not be penalised for having killed these animals in self-defence or in protecting live-stock.

The professional hunter or trapper who worked in wild countries on or beyond the borders of the Empire was probably often of a type common among men of his kind in other ages and to-day—shy, sullen, and morose, short-tempered and quick to quarrel, shunning society and growing savage among savages. Of such men, perhaps, Philo of Alexandria was thinking when he wrote that Nimrod (whom he took to have been a " mighty hunter," not, as our translation of the Bible has it, " before the Lord," but " against the Lord ") was the type of all great sinners, because the hunter's profession was detestable, being utterly removed from a rational existence ; " for who lives with wild beasts chooses to live the life of a beast, and to be on a level with the brutes in the vices of wickedness."

Philo Judæus, Quæst. et Sol. in Genes., II, 82(166)

The two chief means of capture were the pit and the net.

The ordinary form of pit used for taking a lion or a leopard had in its centre a pillar of earth or stone or wood, on the top of which was tied a kid or a lamb or (for leopards) a puppy so fastened as to make it howl from pain. Round the outer edge of the pit was built a wall or wooden fence. The lion or leopard, attracted by the bleating or howling of the decoy, would leap this barrier in trying to reach its prey, and would fall into the pit. A cage would then be let down into the pit, baited with a piece of meat, and the beast so caught would be hauled up.[1]

Xenophon, Cyn., 11, 4
" Oppian," Cyn., IV, 77–111 ; 212–29
" Oppian," Hal., III, 386–95

---

[1] In pits like those used for leopards (which were smaller than the pits for lions) were taken θῶες ἀναιδέες—bold hunting-dogs—*not* jackals. In Book III of " Oppian's " *Cynegetica*, line 337, θῶες are described as κρατερόφρονα φῦλα. Jackals are timid creatures, and would have been frightened by the howls of the dog. They sneak on

In Africa pits were ordinarily used for taking elephants. Pliny mentions, moreover, that " Kings " (probably Numidian) used to organize elephant-hunts in which horsemen would drive a herd into an artificial hollow (*vallem manu factam*), where the animals would find themselves shut in by the steep sides of the depression and by ditches. The taking of wild elephants by means of tame animals was known to Pliny as an Indian device, but it seems not to have been practised in Africa in Roman times. It appears from Pliny's account that starvation mitigated by barley juice (*hordei sucus*) was the African way of taming captured elephants [1] —a method which probably caused the death of many animals.

Pliny, *N.H.*, VIII, 8(8), 24–5

Also Strabo, XV, 1, 42, for the *Keddah* method

The driving of a herd of wild animals into an enclosed hollow or chasm may be regarded as an extension of the method of capture by the pit. It was used not only for elephants, but also, according to Pausanias, for taking European bisons (the wisent), which he confuses with Pæonian bulls that were probably really musk-oxen (p. 86, *n.* 1). In that case, the device was to enclose a hollow with a strong fence, and to cover both the bottom of it and the slope to the bottom with slippery fresh or oiled skins. Horsemen drove the buffaloes to the hollow, and the animals slipped on the first skins they came to, and rolled down to the bottom. After four or five days of starvation, trainers went among them with pine-kernels,[2] the only food which they could be persuaded to eat. Frazer, in his note on this passage in Pausanias, quotes a description by Raphael Volaterranus of a similar method (though without the slippery hides) used in Lithuania in the

Pausanias, X, 13, 2

their prey, and never jump for it. The hunting-dog (*Lycaon pictus*) is one of the most noxious of African carnivora, a terror alike to antelope and to lions.

[1] Capti celerrime mitificantur hordei suco . . . Inclusos ripis fossisque fame domabant.

I suggest for " *hordei suco* " fermented barley, i.e. beer, which elephants drink with pleasure.

[2] Cones of the " cultivated " pine. Perhaps cones from pine enclosed and thinned for special purposes, e.g. making masts.

Cæsar,*B.G.*,
VI, 28

fifteenth century. Cæsar mentions that the *urus* (aurochs) was taken in pits in Germany.

Nets were much used in ancient hunting when the purpose was to kill, and also when animals were to be taken alive. Probably most of the wild animals exhibited at Rome had been captured by this means. Of the collecting of beasts for Stilicho's shows Claudian writes,

Claudian,
De Cons. Stil.,
III, 272–3

Retibus et clatris dilata morte tenendæ
Ducendaeque feræ.

Anthology,
VII, 626

The animals are to be caught in nets and transported in cages (*clatris*). A Greek epigram says that Cæsar has taken in nets a vast number of African wild beasts for a single show.

" Oppian,"
Cyn., IV,
354–424

In the *Cynegetica* ascribed to Oppian there is an account of how bears were taken alive in Armenia. When the bear had been marked to its lair, nets were placed at the end of a run or alley, which was lined on one side with groups of men in ambush, and enclosed on the other by a rope hung with coloured ribbons and feathers—the very common device used in ancient hunting for keeping an animal moving in a certain direction—

Seneca, *De Ira*,
II, 12, 2

the Latin name for it was *formido*, a scare.[1] The bear was roused by a blast on a trumpet, and when it had left its lair, it was driven by beaters down the alley into the net, whereupon men hidden on either side pulled the cords by which the mouth of the net was closed. The question then was whether the bear would break the net and escape. More nets were piled on it, and an attempt was made to catch its paw in a noose, after which it could be tied to wooden logs, and finally got into a strong wooden box.

But in the large captures needed for the Roman animal-shows the driving of many beasts at once into a net or netted enclosure must often have been practised.

" Oppian,"
Cyn., IV,
112–46

In the region of the Euphrates lions were taken in a curved line of nets, towards which they were driven by horsemen who

---

[1] It has been used in other ages and regions besides those of the Greco-Roman world ; as by North American Indians in their deer-hunts.

scared them with lighted torches and a rattling of shields; evidently the method was of almost universal application.

In a Roman villa at Bona, in Algeria, was found a large and well-preserved picture, dating from about A.D. 300, of an African hunt. Its main effect is a representation of a drive of carnivora. There are mounted Numidian beaters, the horses have curious designs painted on them (probably amulets), and have their breasts protected with trellises of wood or leather. The horsemen have driven the beasts towards a place where a long line of nets is spread behind a fence of prickly ficus, a ring of Roman hunters on foot, each bucklered and carrying a flaming torch, is closing in, preventing the escape of the hunted, and forcing the beasts towards the nets. The artist has chosen the tense moment when the lions and leopards perceive the snare, and make a bold and dangerous dash for liberty. One of the details in the picture is a two-muled cart with boxes for the captured animals. More will be said about such boxes later.

Deer, antelope, and wild boars might be taken in nets. In the British Museum is a representation of a water-trap, with nets spread in the shallows (see p. 9). The catch comprises deer, ostrich and boar.[1] Deer might be driven to the nets with the help of long lines of rope hung with feathers and ribbons, as described above.[2] Or they and other animals—ostriches, for example— might be driven, not into net-entanglements, but into corrals and netted enclosures. In the picture found at Bona, Numidian horsemen are driving ostriches, gemsbok, and beisa antelopes, while the curious hartebeeste (the so-called cow-faced antelope), and the aoudad, or Barbary sheep, are shown already corralled. The use of the lasso is illustrated in the same picture, where

Loisel, *Ménageries de l'Antiquité,* I, 96, and Plate

---

[1] The Boers of South Africa, when game was plentiful, used to drown great herds by driving them into the elbow of a river.

[2] A device known to-day in Africa, and possibly in the Roman Empire, is that of attracting deer to a place where there is brushwood by food placed for them there, and now and then scaring them and letting them escape, till they feel sure of their line of retreat, and congregate in large numbers, when nets are set in the brushwood, and the animals are thus trapped.

a Numidian, riding bareback and stirrupless, is throwing one at a wild ass.

The wild birds that were sometimes to be seen in the shows at Rome would usually have been taken in nets, and the same
means might be used for capturing the crocodiles that were now and then exhibited in the Roman arena, and the great snakes that were sometimes on view as rarities.

The calthrop (ποδοστράβη, ποδάγρα, pedica dentata), a trap so arranged that a beast might catch its foot in a noose which was set in a frame and attached to a log, with the result that its flight would be hampered, was much used by those who hunted the elephant, antelope, deer or boar, at any rate to kill.

A number of other devices for capturing animals are described by ancient writers as practised, either in the wilder parts of the Empire or in countries beyond its borders. Some of these accounts are clearly fictions, others are possibly or probably true.

It may well have been that leopards, as Ælian says, were taken in Mauretania by a rope-trap placed in a stone hut and baited with rotten meat, by the smell of which the leopard was attracted. Lions would be even more likely than leopards to be taken by such a bait, for they return to their kill until it is totally consumed.

In the poem on hunting ascribed to Oppian, it is said that leopards were taken in Africa by drugging water-holes with wine. I have never heard of this as a way of capturing leopards, but it is sometimes used for taking small carnivora in the East, and, generally speaking, animals are fond of intoxicants.

In the same poem there is an account of how Ethiopians armed with shields, their bodies thickly covered with sheepskins, and their heads well protected, exhaust a lion by harassing him with whips, till he is weak enough to be bound " like a sheep "
—a fiction no doubt.[1] It may be true that, as Pliny relates, an

---

[1] Lions being imperial beasts the account of a killing would have meant death to all the actors. Substitute spears for whips and there is the famous Masai lion hunt as practised to this day.

African herdsman in the time of Claudius stilled by fright a lion, by throwing his cloak over its head, and that exhibitions of this trick were afterwards given in the arena at Rome. But that it became a common way of taking lions, as Pliny seems to suggest, is incredible. At most it may have been found useful for quieting a lion that had been drawn out of a pit or already taken in a net.

The exciting method of bringing down an elephant,[1] practised, according to Diodorus and Pliny, among a Sudanese people, by dropping from a tree on to the animal's back, grasping the tail, sliding on to the left hind leg, and thence hamstringing the right, was clearly not a way of taking the animal alive. And the same might be thought of the account in Diodorus of harpooning the hippopotamus ; an animal which was probably taken alive in pits. Nevertheless, the first hippopotamus received by the London Zoological Gardens was held by a harpoon as it slipped from the hunters, and a hippopotamus belonging to my family also bore the tell-tale mark.

Diodorus, III, 26
Pliny, N.H., VIII, 8(8), 26

Diodorus, I, 35, 10

Since the tiger was not an inhabitant of the Roman Empire, romantic stories of how it was taken were easily believed. The mirror-trap may indeed have been used in capturing tigers and other beasts, though an animal sees in a mirror an enemy rather than (as the ancients thought) a cub. But the favourite idea in the Roman Empire of a tiger-hunt was of a raid on the tigress' cubs, and a flight of the mounted hunters from the swift pursuit of the tigress—this animal being associated in the minds of the Greeks and Romans particularly with speed. Pliny makes the hunters drop a cub now and then, to delay the mother, and finally escape on ship-board, leaving the tigress howling on the shore. These are travellers' fictions. There seems to have been even a popular idea that animals of this kind were all females, sired by the winds. " Oppian " probably with reason, accounts for this notion by the theory

St. Ambrose, Exaemeron, VI, 4, 21
Claudian, De Raptu Proser- pinæ, III, 263-8
Pomponius Mela, III, 43

Pliny, N.H., VIII, 18(25), 66
Martial, VIII, 26, 1-2
Claudian, loc. cit.
Solinus, 17, 4-7

" Oppian," Cyn., III, 355-63

---

[1] Diodorus (III, 27) furnishes for elephants in Ethiopia a parallel to Cæsar's story of how elk were taken in Germany by sawing half through trees against which they leant (B.G., VI, 27.) Neither tale has any foundation in fact.

that the tigress would stand by her cubs and so be taken in the hunters' nets when the male escaped.[1]

Ælian, N.A.
XVII, 25
(quoting
Cleitarchus)

Probably fictitious were the stories of how Indian hunters took advantage of the imitative ways of monkeys.[2] The hunters, it was said, when they knew that they were being watched by the monkeys which they wished to trap, went through the action of putting on their shoes, and then moved away, leaving other shoes, with nooses attached to them and leaden soles, in which the beasts clogged themselves. Or again the men smeared their faces with a black pigment, and then left a bowl of it mixed with birdlime, the result being that the monkeys sealed their own eyes, and so were taken. In any case, as it seems that Indian monkeys were not brought to the Roman Empire (p. 128 above), these tales have probably no direct bearing on my subject.[3]

After the taking of a carnivorous animal, there would be a need to keep it for sometime in a dark, narrow box. The darkness quiets the beast, which, if placed in a cage with iron bars, would soon break its teeth on them, and would probably die in its struggles. Boxes for newly-taken beasts are represented in the picture of an African hunt already mentioned ; they are of wood strengthened with iron, and seem to be insufficiently ventilated ; but the sliding door is neat and worthy of imitation.

Lucan, X,
445–6

The first fury of a newly caught wild beast in its narrow box is perhaps described by Lucan, though he imagines the animal breaking its teeth, whereas in fact the use of the box would be a precaution against its doing so. Of Cæsar, caught in the

[1] The word *tigris* is said to be always feminine in the poets, but it is found in the masculine gender in prose.

[2] These large variegated monkeys are probably langurs (*Semnopithecus entellus*). There is a white and a black variety, but each is self-coloured.

[3] Birdlime may have been used in the Roman Empire for taking certain quadrupeds. A bear which had birdlime on its paw would rub its paw over its head, and so might close up its eyes. It may have been such a device for capturing bears that suggested the use of birdlime to reduce a bear to helplessness in the arena (Martial, *De Spectaculis*, 11)—a sight which the spectators probably found amusing.

royal palace of the Ptolemies by a rising of the Alexandrians, and closely beleaguered, it is said,

> Sic fremit in parvis fera nobilis abdita claustris,[1]
> Et frangit rapidos præmorso carcere dentes.

But animals could hardly have been kept in such boxes throughout long, slow journeys from the places of capture to Rome. Usually, no doubt, they were transferred to cages, of which one side was barred, and could either be left open or closed with a movable shutter. (Thus Symmachus speaks of animals brought to Rome *ferreis caveis*, meaning, apparently, iron-barred cages.) A cage of this sort when shuttered is kept warm by animal heat, and the close and fœtid atmosphere does no harm, unless confinement in it is very prolonged. The change of scene on a journey keeps animals interested and alert, and when once they are reconciled to captivity, they retain their health and condition in their portable cages. In our modern travelling shows lions and tigers may live for years in a space of 8 × 4 feet ; and they breed more rapidly and look more healthy than in the large cages and dreary monotony of a zoological garden. Many animals, like the bears of Demochares mentioned below, must have died before they were either accustomed to captivity or killed in the arena. But it may be supposed that what skill the age had in tending wild animals recently captured would be usually available for the care of beasts which were meant for imperial shows at Rome.

Herbivorous beasts could be kept and carried in solid-bottomed crates barred with planed wood. Inoffensive animals might be given the freedom of the ship on a sea-voyage, or tamed to go at liberty with the caravan.

Travelling dens for bears are low and rather narrow to pre-

Symmachus,
Epp., II, 77

---

[1] Possibly the word *claustra* was regularly used for such a box as distinct from a cage (*cavea*). Thracians in battle are described as *haud secus quam diu claustris retentae feræ, ira concitati* (Livy, XLII, 59). Pliny the Younger in the *Panegyric* (81, 3) speaks of Emperors who hunted only *domitas fractasque claustris feras ac deinde in ipsorum quidem ludibrium emissas*. The Greek equivalent to the Latin *cavea*, in the sense of a wild beast's cage, was γαλεάγρα, as in Strabo, VI, 2, 6.

vent the animal using its strength effectively ; and lighted only through the barred front ; if the slightest crevice be left elsewhere the strongest timbers are often ineffective against the strength and iron-hard nails of the huge paws. This gives an air of plausibility to the story told on page 172 where success depended on passing off a robber dressed in a bear skin as the real thing.

Claudian,
De Cons.
Stilich, III,
325-32

Claudian thus describes the transport of animals to Rome for the shows to be given by Stilicho : " Some went on laden craft by sea or river : the pale rower's hands are numbed with fear, and the sailor dreads his own merchandise. Others are carried by land on wheels, and waggons full of the spoils of the hills block the roads in long files. Uneasy bullocks bear the captive beast that once sated his hunger on their kind, and whenever they turn their necks and catch sight of him they start away trembling from the pole." A poetic conceit." neither sight nor scent would for long terrify the bullocks.

Pliny, N.H.,
XV, 18(20), 74 ;
XIX, 1(1), 4

Land-transport would be usually by slow-going ox-cart (transport by river would be available chiefly in Gaul) ; and though with a favourable wind the sea-passage from Africa to Puteoli or Ostia might take only two or three days, and though it was not impossible to make the voyage from Alexandria to Puteoli in eight or nine days,[1] yet what with bad weather interrupting navigation or closing land-routes in the winter, and winds in summer blowing for days together so as to hold up sailings for Italy (as did the so-called etesian or annual winds of the Eastern Mediterranean), months might elapse between

Cicero, Ad.
Fam., II, 11, 2

the capture of animals for the Roman shows and their arrival at Rome. It may be noticed, however, that Cicero writes from Laodicea on 4 April, 50 B.C., as though it were still worth

---

[1] It may be noticed that marine communications under the Roman Empire benefited by the progress in ship-building, and the increase in the size of ships, which had been achieved in the Hellenistic age. In the first two centuries A.D., the exceptionally large merchant ships of which we have record must have been well over 1,000 tons. Very much earlier the Carthaginians found no difficulty in transporting over a hundred elephants to Sicily.

while trying to get leopards in Southern Asia Minor for a *venatio* at Rome to be given by Cælius as curule ædile, presumably in September at the *ludi Romani*—the other *ludi* managed by the curule ædiles being in April and the first few days of May.

Probably on the whole the transport of animals was quickest in the first two centuries A.D., especially when it was a matter of getting them to Rome for shows to be given by the Emperor. But no doubt there were many disappointments like that of the friend of the younger Pliny, whose " African beasts " did not arrive in time for their purchaser's show at Verona owing to bad weather (*tempestate detentæ*). Pliny, *Epp.*, VI, 34, 3

We have indications of slow transport of animals at the end of the fourth and the beginning of the fifth century A.D. Mention has been made in another chapter (pp. 96–97 above) of the anxieties and disappointments of Symmachus when he was trying to obtain animals for his son's Quæstorian Games in A.D. 393—the loss of some of his purchases through shipwreck, and the arrival, when he was expecting his bears, of only " a few starving and weary cubs." It has also been remarked (p. 95 above) that he began collecting in the year 398 for *ludi* which he expected would be given in the year 400. Here it may be noticed that he wished some horses which he was getting from Spain for chariot-races to spend the winter on the estate of a friend of his in the neighbourhood of Arles. He may have desired this after finding that of 16 horses sent to him by a friend in Spain, 5 died on the way, and others soon after arrival. Horses can easily be walked to death. Symmachus, *Epp.*, IX, 117; II, 76 *Ibid.*, IX, 20 *Ibid.*, V, 56

In A.D. 417 an imperial order was made in response to a complaint, about the transport of beasts in the region of the Euphrates. " We learn, from a complaint made by the civil governor's department in the Euphrates province, that those who are entrusted with the transport of wild beasts by the military governor's department remain at the city of Hierapolis [between Aleppo and the Euphrates] for three or four months instead of seven or eight days, thus contravening the rules for official missions, and that after the expense which they cause by staying for so long they even requisition cages, the supply *Cod. Theod.*, XV, 11, 2 of which is not authorized by any custom (*post expensas tanti temporis etiam caveas exigere quas nulla præberi consuetudo permittit*). We therefore order that wild beasts, which are being transported to the department of the *Comes Domesticorum* from any military governor of a frontier district, are not to be kept in any one municipality (*intra singulas civitates*) for more than seven days." Military governors and their subordinates were to be fined for disobeying this order.

Possibly Hierapolis had been used as a collecting-centre by those who were obtaining beasts for the Government.

The phrase *etiam caveas exigere quas nulla præberi consuetudo permittit* seems to show that the preceding words *post expensas* (sc. *pecunias*) *tanti temporis* do not refer to a waste of the Government's money, but to the expenses which the inhabitants of Hierapolis were forced to incur. And the special mention of the requisitioning of cages, as something irregular, suggests that persons in the Government's service, who were transporting wild beasts for the Emperor, were authorized to live at free quarters on the inhabitants of the towns through which they passed, and perhaps to demand free food for their charges, so long as they did not stay at any one place for more than a few days.

There is apparently no evidence to show how long this had been the rule under the Empire. As regards the Republican period, it seems that one can only say, that the attempts made by Roman magistrates to extort subscriptions to their shows from provincials [1] are expressions of a temper which may well have displayed itself at times in the infliction of expense, and much inconvenience, on the inhabitants of places through which animals were transported for those shows. When in 48 B.C. the Megarians tried to loose on Roman troops the lions belonging to Cassius, which had been held up on the way from Syria to Rome at Megara by the Roman civil war, they may have had some idea of avenging themselves for the plague that the lions had been to them.

Plutarch, Brutus, 8

The Roman law of the imperial age as to damage done by

[1] See p. 139 above, Cicero, *Ad. Att.*, VI, 1, 21.

captive wild beasts was derived from ordinances of the Ædiles, who in the Republican period had charge of the ways and markets of Rome. It was the law that a dog, tusked boar or smaller wild pig, wolf, bear, leopard or lion, or any other noxious animal, whether loose or tied,[1] should not be so kept on any public way (*qua vulgo iter fiet*) that it might harm or cause loss to any person. If a breach of this rule led to the death of a free man, a fine was due, in Ulpian's day, of 200 *solidi* ; if it led to injury to a free man, the judge was to assess compensation ; if it led to damage to property (including slaves), double the value of the property lost was to be paid.

Digest, XXI, 1, 40-2

Against the owner of a domestic animal which did damage, an action would lie for *pauperies* (defined as *damnum sine iniuria facientis datum*), resulting, if successful, in surrender of the animal or compensation equivalent to the damage. But for damage done by a captive wild animal which had escaped from control, this action would not lie, because such an animal, when no longer under control, was considered no longer to have an owner ; it might be killed by anyone, and the body would belong to whoever killed it.

Digest, IX, 1, 1-10

Customs were levied on the frontiers of the Empire, and also on certain lines within it. Lions, lionesses, and animals of the leopard class (*leones, leænæ, pardi, leopardi, pantheræ*—see Appendix I, p. 187) were dutiable ; and in the fourth century, at any rate, there was a duty on bears. But Symmachus says that Quæstors at Rome had " never " paid the *portorium ferarum* on animals for their shows ; and no doubt this rule applied to other magistrates who had to manage official *ludi* at Rome.

Digest, XXXIX, 4, 16, 7

Symmachus, *Epp.*, V, 62

Animals newly arrived at Rome by river from Ostia might be seen at the Docks (*Navalia*) on the Tiber bank. Towards the end of the Republican period, the sculptor Pasiteles, *diligentissimus artifex*, was working at the Docks on the figure of a lion, and was intent on his model, which was in a cage before him, when he was nearly killed by a leopard, which had escaped from another cage.

Pliny, *N.H.*, XXXVI, 5(12), 40

---

[1] *i.e.* either tethered or loose in a pen.

CHAPTER X

DEVELOPMENT OF THE ARENA

THE earliest animal shows at Rome were given in the Forum or other large space, with the exits blocked ; similar temporary enclosures were used for the occasional shows given in Italy in the Middle Ages, and must have been adopted for the exhibitions in the smaller towns of the Empire, and indeed in Rome itself, when games were given, as by Augustus, in the forum or for the various wards of the city. Their arrangement and the sport provided are set forth in this short description of a show not given in an amphitheatre.

Suetonius, Div. Aug., 43, 1

ὡς δ᾽ ὅτε θηροφόνων τις ἀνὴρ δεδαημένος ἔργων,
λαῶν ἀμφιδόμοισιν ἐναγρομένων ἀγορῇσι,
πόρδαλιν οἰστρηθεῖσαν ἐνὶ ῥοίζοισιν ἱμάσθλης
ἐγχείῃ δέχεται ταναήκεϊ δοχμὸς ὑποστάς·
ἡ δὲ καὶ εἰσορόωσα γένυν θηκτοῖο σιδήρου
ἄγρια κυμαίνουσα κορύσσεται, ἐν δ᾽ ἄρα λαιμῷ
ἠΰτε δουροδόκῃ χαλκήλατον ἔσπασεν αἰχμήν·

"Oppian," Hal., II, 350–6

English trans. from Loeb ed.

" As when a man skilled in the work of slaying wild beasts, when the people are gathered in the house-encircled market-place, awaits the Leopard maddened by the cracking of the whip and with long-edged spear stands athwart her path ; she, though she beholds the edge of sharp iron, mantles in swelling fury and receives in her throat, as it were in a spearstand, the brazen lance."[1]

[1] As a leopard would have to be confined to a very small space if it was to be made to charge by the cracking of a whip, I believe that we have here a picture of a performance by a small travelling show.

Itinerant troupes of gladiators could be hired, and it is likely therefore that the showman's business was conducted on the same lines. A travelling menagerie might be hired by a local notable who was giving a show either as a municipal magistrate or as a private individual, but on occasion it might make its profit from the entrance-money of the spectators.

The *arenæ* throughout the Empire were limited in number and of the one type—the ellipse—with very few exceptions, but they belonged to communities varying extremely in wealth and they were all compromises, meeting opposite demands— the display on the one hand of the skill and subtleties of men, and on the other of the unreasoning ferocity of wild beasts, from which the spectators required protection : for the one little was required beyond a flat surface with a firm foothold ; the other called for all the skill of the architect, and the desire for realistic representation of wild-life made his task still more difficult. Some architects, probably the majority, refused to make the effort, contenting themselves with a temporary cage in the middle of the arena. The arena at Pompeii seems to belong to this class and that of Nîmes certainly does ; the scene in the Corinthian theatre (described by Apuleius) gives a good idea of this restricted exhibition. Cities more wealthy, or more enterprising, such as Arles, met the difficulty in various ways, changing their methods from time to time as experience dictated. *Venationes* were given in the circus, forum or amphitheatre ; in Rome there was never only one centre for exhibition. Temporary structures gave ample opportunity for experiment. There are no details of the internal arrangement of Scaurus' theatre, but it must have had some sort of open-work protection in wire or wood, through which the leopards could be seen if they were exhibited there, and high enough to prevent their escape. Across the front of a theatre the open work must have been continued to the ground level ; round an arena, this was not quite so important and a solid wooden base had many advantages for enclosing cattle, wild boars, bears and other heavy animals. Leopards can leap

Apuleius, *Metam.*, X, 18-19.

Claudian, *De Sext. Cons. Honorii*, 618-20

Friedländer, Vol. IV, pp. 194-5 (English translation)

13 feet high, and a roughly boarded fence 20 feet high would not contain them long ; but a strong, solid wooden fence 6 feet high, with nets fastened to the top of it and overhanging the arena to a maximum height of 11 or 12 feet would be ample, when protected by the arena-guard, to contain any of the carnivora and the other animals I have mentioned. Against elephants such protections were useless—a fact discovered when the populace feared that the frightened animals would break through iron gates at Pompey's Games, 55 B.C.

(Elephantes) universi eruptionem temptavere non sine vexatione populi, circumdatis clathris ferreis ; qua de causa Cæsar dictator postea simile spectaculum editurus euripis harenam circumdedit quos Nero princeps sustulit equiti loca addens.

Pliny, *N.H.*,
VIII, 7(7), 21

Cæsar, to meet the difficulty, surrounded the arena of the Circus Maximus with a ditch, *euripus*, 10 feet wide and 10 feet deep.[1] That ditch must have been between the seats and the inner barrier, otherwise the bulls that were

Suetonius,
Div. Iul., 39, 2
Dionysius
Halic., III, 68, 2

sent into the ring maddened with thirst would have drunk at the water and the bull-fighting would have been spoiled.

The barrier gave temporary relief to a hard-pressed performer of sufficient agility and so increased the variety and excitement of the show and was perhaps the fortuitous cause of that sustained interest in bull-fighting from horseback which was the only innovation of Julius Cæsar that survived him.

The elephants, if they blundered through the barrier, being deep in the water, were not dangerous to the spectators and could scramble out again to the arena.

Cæsar's *euripus* throws much light on the development of arenas in general and the Colosseum in particular. Though

---

[1] These dimensions are given by Dionysius of Halicarnassus. The sides of such a ditch would have to be perpendicular to afford security from elephants. The year in which the *equites* were given special seats in the Circus, and the *euripus* was therefore abolished, was A.D. 63 (Tacitus *Ann.*, XV, 32, 2). The Senate had its reserved seats in the Circus from the time of Claudius (Suetonius, *Div. Claud.*, 21, 3).

it was suppressed by Nero, it was no doubt in the minds of the designers of the Colosseum, and accounts for the 15 feet wide *podium* which is supposed—probably without reason—to have been necessary to counteract the inward thrust of the building. The style of it is reproduced at Verona in the third century and at Capua, but in most provincial arenas, however high the *podium*, e.g. 4 feet 6 inches at Nîmes or 11 feet 6 inches at Arles, it is not particularly strong. *Podium* is technically a parapet or balcony, and in most cases the first level of the seats has on it a wall, about 15 inches wide and of convenient height, to form an elbow-rest for the front line of spectators. But in Rome, and a few other places, this did not exist, and the word was applied to the chief place in the amphitheatre, a flat surface about 15 feet wide on which the spectators sat at ease, or could at their discretion stroll and converse with their friends.

The words " *podio adaperto* ", in the account in Suetonius of how Nero used to watch spectacles, refer, I think, to the removal of the low wall, a change which, as is obvious, extended and improved the view of all the spectators. Suetonius, *Nero*, 12, 2

The circle of this inner barricade[1] was the limit of the arena " as arranged by Julius Cæsar, and in the perfected Colosseum." The masts for the *velarium* or awning were either flush with it or served to support it from the rear. The nets against the carnivora were a necessity and the poles for the *velarium* could be used for carrying wire stays to the ends of the projecting tusks referred to below. Safety would require for the *velarium* masts 12 inches in diameter, not more than 18 feet apart ; planks to a height of 6 feet would be laid between them. Near each mast there would be a V-shaped block behind the top plank furnished with a clamp hinged at one end and fastened over a staple by a simple peg ; these would form obvious and perfect supports for the iron rods, or, as Calpurnius says, the elephant-tusks that carried the nets. Being all of one length, and a slight sagging being of no detriment, these nets were interchangeable ; by means of rings of suitable size fastened Calpurnius, VII, 48 ff.

[1] See note 1 on next page

at one edge they could be slipped on to the supports in a few minutes, the other edge would hook into the next net; looped on nails behind the topmost plank, the inner edge could not slip forward, and the rings binding on the ever-widening support held the net taut in the other direction. The time for fixing was not important; removal, which was important, could be done very quickly by a process such as this: the barrier end might be freed and the hooks on the edge unfastened; the net now hanging vertically would be drawn slightly inwards so that the top ring could be pushed off. The support, relieved of the greatest strain, could be then drawn backwards, releasing the net, which would fall to the ground and could be carried away by two men with ease; the supports, now standing behind the barrier, would be either lodged on brackets there or taken below.

This permanent barrier would be returned to the *podium*-wall at the entrance gates at the ends of the larger axis which, Calpurnius
Ecl., VII, 23 ff. being of necessity unnetted, were made unscaleable by revolving ivory wheels. An interior fence of this kind is well adapted for the arrangement of scenic cloths, so often used in conjunction with rocks, water and trees, to heighten the effects of the animal shows, and it permits of endless variety in entrances[1] for the beasts " as from a natural lair," whereas the *podium*[2] of the Colosseum —which was very broad and solid—could at the best have

---

[1] At Nîmes and Arles the *podium* is not wide, but the first has only two, the second six openings, which may have been used as entrances to the surrounding ring, as they are to-day at the bullfights. The amphitheatre at El Djemm in Algeria has such a fence in stone, with the *podium* outside it. Arles with a *podium* and parapet, 14 feet high, would leave most of its wild beasts invisible to many spectators if there were no inner ring. Middleton found the base plates of this fence in the Colosseum. Ch. Dubois at Puteoli, *Pouzzoles antiques* Paris, 1907. Hoffbauer at Paris: Hoffbauer (F) *Paris à travers les ages*, 2nd edit. Paris, 1885, pp. 117, 170, 173, 174.

Dio, LIX, 10, 3 [2] The wickedness of Caligula supplies a curious bit of evidence in support of what follows. A large number of persons of the lowest Eusebius, *Eccl. Hist.*, V, 1 class always managed to gain admittance to the underworld of the amphitheatre; their ribald jests and callous cruelty embittered the last moments of the poor wretches going to their death. Kicks and

had only a few, if any, openings and these at fixed places. Before the building of the permanent Colosseum the chief guests sat on the front row of benches and the beasts were brought from beneath them in cages into the various passages between the blocks of seats and along the inner corridor to the place of entry.[1] In the permanent building the animals were kept either in cages under the arena and thence drawn up by windlasses, obliquely or perpendicularly to the surface, or were transferred to a series of cages underground, whence, at the proper time, they were released into a passage and forced along it to the surface, or into a square well with a moving base that could be raised to deliver them quite unsheltered on the sand. There remained also the older method of running the cages round the inner corridor, garaging them in recesses,[2] and releasing the animals at the desired spot. At Probus' show this method was largely used—the animals wasted with disease refused to leave the *claustra* which were then carried into the arena and broken open "*e posticis contificiis interempti sunt.*" The question is of extreme interest to naturalists because of the difficulty experienced in moving large carnivora from their quarters into new surroundings, even in a menagerie. When done with care and in quietness it is often a matter of hours ; it would be much harder to drive beasts suddenly into the glare of the arena and the presence of a shouting mob. Often enough when released the animals

Hist. Aug. Probus, 19
Ammianus Marcellinus, XXVIII, 1, 10. Maximin let loose his natural ferocity " ut sæpe faciunt amphitheatrales feræ diffractis tandem solutæ posticis "

blows were showered upon them by this frowsy mob who, following on, crowded the passages and beyond to catch a glimpse of the show to the great annoyance of the distinguished company in the best seats, including the Emperor, with whom they were almost in contact. I have no doubt that a fit of irritation caused by this unseemly intrusion explains the brutal order of Caligula to throw some of them into the arena.

Cf. Tertullian, *de Spect.*, 3, 6

[1] See preceding note.

[2] There are 14 such recesses in the *podium* wall of the Colosseum, 4 feet deep 6 feet high and 6 feet 4 inches long, well adapted for animal claustra. There is one in the arena (Rue des Arènes) at Paris. This small arena is worth examination for that, and for the inlet staircase with gate giving access to the principal seats.

J. H. Middleton, *op. cit.*

Martial, *De Spectaculis*, 19

took refuge under the barricades, and burning straw was needed to drive them from this poor retreat.

Corippus Africanus, *In laud. Iustini. Augusti minoris*, III, 249–50 Cf. Claudian, *In Rufinum*, II, 394-9

Feræ populorum milia circum
Suspiciunt magnoque metu mitescere discunt.

The wild beasts, looking up mistrustfully at the thousands of spectators, become tame under stress of fear.

Long before I found these verses I had felt assured of the fact. Hot irons or fire must have been always at hand to make them leave their boxes or cages or the poor shelter of the barrier : this fact is exceptionally strong evidence for the existence of the wooden barrier, and it gives us some idea of its construction ; there must have been a narrow opening below the lowest plank, through which the torture could be immediately and effectively applied, for it is clear that slaves carrying burning straw would not have been tolerated among the distinguished company on the *podium*. At Puteoli and under the Colosseum the cages were built on a common plan with this end in view ; the fronts were made to open wide, and at the rear of the roof there is a small square aperture, not for feeding purposes, as has been surmised, but for the blazing straw.   J. H. Middleton has an excellent plan of the cages which

J. H. Middleton, *The Remains of Ancient Rome*, 2 Vols, 1892, Vol. II, p. 107

were built in the Colosseum (see p. 173) : they were inside the *podium*, under the arena area, and consist of a series of arches in two tiers, the lower one, provided with water, and cleansing traps, alone being used for the beasts.   The arches are about 8 feet deep, 7 wide and 7 high ; the lower floor is 20 feet below the arena ; between the upper arches there was a 5 foot passage giving access to the bases of the masts—which were fixed between the lower pair of cages—and to the square openings in the top of the dens.   Along the front of the dens at distances of about 5 feet are a row of tufa pillars supporting the roof ; the passage is not wide enough to turn an animal-box, and therefore the partition—which I imagine was of iron bars—must have been fixed on the rear of the pillars.   The Roman travelling-cages opened with a slide at the end, therefore the iron cage fronts must have been flush with the face of the arch.   The animal was probably introduced by a narrow door formed in the cage-front : for its release a different method would be needed, or an animal might be badly burned before it found the exit. Probably the whole front swung on a centre : a keeper, using a hook through the barrier across the passage, would swing it open as the burning straw fell, and close it as soon as the animal was in the passage.

A whole row of cages could be opened almost simultaneously, each being closed as soon as its occupant fled. Fire in the passage would drive the creatures forward : a movable shield prevented return, and the whole crowd could be gathered in the chamber, the door closed, and a rising floor would then carry them into the arena ; or they could be driven up a slope or along a passage to the desired exit. At Arles there are grooves on the arches which suggest temporary hoardings to make a narrow regular passage ; without that precaution the beasts would have crouched low down at the edge of the arch. A partition such as is used now by the Scottish Zoological Society, with catches to prevent any backward movement, could be pushed along the passage, forcing the animals before it and delivering them in the arena at the required moment— a difficult matter but very important, as the Games were worked to time. Claudius, indeed, made carpenters or other attendants fight as gladiators in the arena, if anything went wrong with the apparatus of the performance.

In the arena at Puteoli the beast-exits are very numerous square traps, far from the wall, and one supposes there were many small lifts each devoted to a few of the many underground cages. They all have the small opening in the roof, to be used for the same purpose as at Rome. The Colosseum passage is roofed with tufa, pierced for light and air and covered by gratings which come just on the arena side of the barricade. Ventilation was a serious problem.

The row of masts supporting the *velarium* make perfect supports for the barricade : these masts, I surmise, were on the outside of the barricade, and provided with steps for the sailors who had to adjust the ropes continually and needed protection from the beasts. The masts being 60 feet or more

Suetonius, *Div. Claud.*, 34, 2 Cf. Caligula who had his beast-master beaten to death with chains. Suetonius, *Caligula*, 27, 4

The ventilators are shown in the Diptychs of Anastasius A.D. 517 and of Stilicho under Theodosius Magnus, reproduced in Gorius, Vol. II, Plate 1, p. 129

in height, the distance from barrier to *podium* must have been about 10 feet to insure shade to the spectators on the *podium*. How the central *velarium* was carried is a vexed question, the width, 176 feet, is too great to be spanned, the sag of the sheet would be excessive.

In my opinion there was a skeleton structure in the centre of the arena parallel to the longer axis. The width of it would be about 20 feet, the length about 72 feet. The poles forming it would rise about 65 feet above the sand, be strongly braced at the top, and furnished with a pent-roof as a protection for the furled strips of the very light *velarium* ; at about 60 feet from the ground the masts would be firmly joined, and the whole space floored, as a platform for the workmen [1] and artistes who took part in the shows, and the sailors who would be required to haul in and stow that part of the velarium that covered the arena.

The guess as to length is made advisedly. The friction marks still visible on the wall show that the poles round the arena were 18 feet centres distant from each other, and that *one was omitted* in front of the Imperial Box and its opposite counterpart to give a clear view across the arena. The two sets of four poles on each side, required for the scaffold we have mentioned, would be 36 feet apart at the middle and 18 feet at either end. To these central posts, at a height of about 60 feet, ropes led from all the encircling masts in the arena, which were also fastened to one another, laterally, and to the masts on the outer wall of the building, the whole being a perfect adjustment of great strength, and capable of bearing with safety the strain either of the stretched *velarium* [2] or the localized weight of a bull or other heavy animal, hauled, as they often were, to the simulated sky. Cupids and the like were swung in the air continually, which implies platforms on the masttops for the scene-workers. The *velarium* over the seats was

Claudian, *Paneg. Manl. Theod.*, 325–6

---

[1] For workmen arranging spectacular effects.

[2] Other arrangements were of course possible. See, for instance, p. 164 for a different kind of *velarium* which a graffito has shown to have been in use at Pompeii.

worked from the highest point of the building by sailors from the fleet, who hauled the ropes from a special platform which gave to the poorest people the only rain-proof seats. It has been objected that such a structure of poles could not have been present, being too great an obstruction, but they are nothing like so serious a block as the row of poles, say 12 inches in diameter and less than 18 feet apart, which at the best shut off one-seventeenth of the view. The Colosseum may be compared to a modern football ground surrounded by thick poles ; no modern crowd would accept the amount of obstruction that the senators were forced to endure ; to the common people on the top benches at either end of the ellipse of seats the *velarium* and the poles excluded the view of half the arena. This handicap is the most likely explanation of their marked preference for the animal turns over the gladiatorial contests which, on the contrary, appealed more strongly to the well-placed richer classes.

The omission of one mast on the inner ring on either side of the arena, leaving an opening corresponding to the arch in the centre, would make for effect. There would be an uninterrupted view from the two *suggesta* (of the Emperor and the giver of the show) either of processions or of the gladiatorial duels. A similar arrangement at each end of the longer axis would make for homogeneity and for more imposing entrances. Further exploration at Puteoli, Capua and other provincial arenas would give much valuable information on the question of masts ; for these amphitheatres were at places of popular resort, and very likely there was a charge for seats, in which case the show would be given at the most suitable time, and be of short duration, and the question of shade would then be simplified.

A recent guide to Pompeii states that the awnings were stretched between the towers of the eastern wall of the town and a row of masts stepped in holes of the stones behind the women's (that is the highest) gallery. A show at Pompeii is advertised to begin in the morning ; and we have a record of one at Panormus, in Sicily, which began at noon. In

Guide to Pompeii, W. Englemann, Leipzig, 1925

C.I.L., IV, 1200 ; X, 7295 (Dessau, 3055)

M

either case the time was unusual for the short shows in the provinces and may have been arranged to take advantage of the facilities for shading.

Every arena was built to suit the comfort of the great in this respect. They sat with their backs to the sun at 3 p.m. At Rome where the spectacle lasted many days the animal show began at 6 a.m. but the important contests of the gladiators were staged in the afternoon, as they were in the provinces. It is to be noted that at Pompeii masts are expressly mentioned for the May show but not for that of November, whence we may assume that on some occasions they were not provided and could be unstepped and so a better view would be given. At Dove, in Poitou, there was one upright mast and about six round it, rising like the ribs of an umbrella, all stepped in large holes cut in the supporting stones, whence removal was quite simple. There is no reason why this course could not have been taken in the Colosseum at winter shows.

"Morning,"
see Seneca,
Epp., 70, 20 ;
De ira, III, 43, 2;
and best of all
Epp., 7, 4,
*Mane leonibus
et ursis homines
obiciuntur*,
Martial, XIII,
95
References to
awnings in
Friedländer,
Vol. IV
(English
translation),
p. 519 (Notes
on Vol. II,
p. 59, l. 30)
Lipsius, *De
amph.*, VI
(a fine
illustration)

THE *VELARIUM* AT POMPEII

CHAPTER XI

PROVINCIAL AMPHITHEATRES

THERE are evident remains of more than 70 arenas in the Roman Empire, and this figure is, in all probability, very far from the total number that once existed. It was the custom, particularly in the later period, to construct them on, so as to form part of, town walls and defences, wherefore many are likely to have disappeared totally, either by the will of some conqueror or in the natural expansion of a progressive town. The amphitheatre was a passion in all parts of the Empire, whence we may conclude that the importance of a town is the best guarantee for the possession of such a place of amusement, its construction being affected largely by the wealth of the leading citizens and its strategic value if the town were besieged. Some of the strongest stone amphitheatres will not accommodate more than 6,000 persons. Twice that number can be accommodated at a comparatively small expense round three sides of an ordinary football ground, whose playing space is larger than the arena at the Colosseum. With the fourth side built of wood, with suitable gates or sliding doors, the gladiators and the beasts would be introduced with the maximum of effect. The accounts of various serious but infrequent accidents show that the Romans were adepts at building wooden stands ; these would endure about 30 years without much attention, and the total expense of a large stand need not have been more than £5,000. A mountain-side or bank of earth as at Fréjus made a fine viewpoint for the common people. Such an enclosure was well within the means of a magistrate, or pro-

Tacitus, *Ann.*, IV, 62, 63 (collapse of a stand)

curator of a province desirous of obtaining popularity during his short term of administration

What was at first merely vanity became, under the weak administration of Claudius, a scandal requiring stern measures. One of the earlier edicts of Nero enacted that " No magistrate or procurator who has obtained a charge in any province shall exhibit a spectacle of gladiators, or wild beasts or any other popular entertainment whatsoever." " Before this," says Tacitus, " they had, by such acts of munificence, no less afflicted those under their jurisdiction than if they had plundered them of their money, whilst, under cover of such court to the multitude, they sheltered their arbitrary delinquencies and rapine."

A.D. 57
Tacitus, *Ann.*,
XIII, 31, 4–5

Remains of a stone-built amphitheatre have just been discovered at Chester, a fortress required by the necessity for efficient protection against the Welsh. At Dorchester and many other places there are remains of a more primitive nature. One can hazard the assumption that the grassy enclosures were without subterranean passages, such as existed in all the stone buildings, and they would not have any facilities for aquatic displays.

Picture in
*Manchester
Guardian,*
August 1929

The shows in the amphitheatres in all parts of the Empire were like those of Rome though on a much smaller scale ; the presence of even one lion is extremely rare, a dozen leopards very unusual. Pliny compliments a friend on having bought *plurimas Africanas* for a show at Verona ; but it may not mean much in a polite letter ! Pompeii has but one or two leopards, though an old painting now lost shows lions, tigers and leopards, also bears, wolves, wild boars, bulls and gazelles at the opening of its theatre. In the most diverse parts of the Empire—Britain, Africa, Spain, France, Palestine—the martyrs are threatened or confronted with wild beasts of four kinds, leopards, bears, wild bulls and wild boars.

Tertullian, *De
Spect.*, 7, 2

Pliny, *Epp.*,
VI, 34, 3

H. Thédenat,
II, 95, 96
Eusebius, *Hist.
Eccl.*, VIII,
Cap. 7, 1

Leopards (*pardi*, not *leopardi* which were maneless lions) were the carnivorous animals commonly used for shows in the *municipia* and the provinces. Bears were common everywhere except in Africa.

Wild boars, each after its kind, were found everywhere. The bulls were domestic animals trained to truculence and rendered savage by irritation and torture before they entered the arena. The *urus* and the bison, respectively the aurochs, i.e. wild cattle of Europe, still existing in a debilitated state in the herds of Chillingham and other parks, and the European bison (wisent), which was extinguished in its last reserve in the Caucasus as lately as the recent war, also appeared from time to time as instruments of death in the arena, but as we find them specifically described under their own names, one may conclude that they were not usually comprehended in the term *tauri*.

Lions are mentioned very rarely, and, as far as I am aware, only in the East, but it is hard to believe that they were never shown in Carthage, a city through or near which probably nine-tenths of the Mauretanian lions would pass on their way to Rome. The city and province were both wealthy and important, and the people were so given to gladiatorial displays and shows of beasts that the *sacerdotium provinciæ Africæ* was a great burden. If these great cats never appeared there nor in the arenas in Spain, which were almost as well situated to receive a cheap and ample supply, it is a wonderful testimony to the strict hold kept on the beasts by the central power, but it is difficult to reconcile their absence in this part of the Empire with their appearance on the islands of the Ægean and in the seaboard provinces in Asia : e.g. at Antioch, one of the largest cities and particularly given to such amusements, at Smyrna, in the island of Lesbos where sculptured stones at Mitylene show *bestiarii* fighting with lions and in the province of Cilicia, where a lioness refused to attack Saint Tarachus and his companions, and in Palestine according to that curious Jewish law of the second century, forbidding the sale of bears, lions or other harmful creatures to the heathen. Lions as well as other animals were tamed and trained at Alexandria. Philo, writing in the earlier half of the first century A.D., says, " I have frequently known instances of lions and bears and

Eusebius, *Hist. Eccl.*, VIII, 7, 1
Martial, *De Spectaculis*, 19
Ruinart, *Acta Martyrum*, p. 171
Borghesi Mosaic, *C.I.L.*, X, 1074
Cicero, *Pro. C. Cornel.*, I, 3 (Teubner, VIII, 408)

Tertullian, *De Spectaculis*, 2, 1

Friedländer, Vol. IV, p. 241 (English translation, and references here given)

Conze, *Reise auf der Insel Lesbos*, p. 5

Acta martyrum

Friedländer, Vol. IV, p. 534

Philo Jud., *De Decem Oraculis*, 23 ; cf. *De Animalibus*, 23-4, 90 leopards being made gentle not only to those who feed them by reason of their gratitude for necessaries, but also to others, on account, in my opinion, of their resemblance to the feeders." [1]

Alexandria probably supplied the whole Roman world with men for animal-breaking. It was a wild beast market through the Middle Ages, it remained important after the discovery of the sea route to India, and is still a small but recognized centre of the animal trade, though the opening of the Suez Canal has greatly decreased its usefulness.

Déchélette, J.,
Les vases
céramiques
ornés de la
Gaule Romaine,
Vol. II, 642,
3, 4, 5, Paris,
1904, IV, 15
Loisel, Vol. I,
p. 127, quoting
Déchélette,
Vol. II, fig. 641

That the tiger was shown elsewhere than at Rome is doubtful. Certain vases found in Roman Gaul picture naked women surrounded by lions, tigers and leopards, but there is no certainty that they represent any local event. On another vase a woman bound in a car is shown pursued by a lion, a rather common form of exposure at Rome, but the representations of lions are so few as rather to lay stress on the cost and rarity of this animal.

Eusebius,
Hist. Eccles.,
IV, 15, 23

When the threat of the wild beasts did not produce submission or they were not available, burning could be resorted to. At Smyrna A.D. 169 the people asked for a lion to be loosed against St. Polycarp who had withstood the threat of beasts. It was the property of the Asiarchs and not of the governor —the request was refused on the ground that the *venationes* were over, and Polycarp was burnt. In the martyrdom of Tarachus, Probus, and Andronicus the governor, in a white heat of anger, ordered a lioness to be teased and turned upon them. She fled to her cage frightened by the shouts of the mob:

Acta Martyrum,
also see
Salmasius, ad
Vopisci Probum
c. 19, p. 675
(Hist. Aug.
Script., VI ed.
1671, Tom. II)

Præses confusus et ira excandescens mandavit suis leanam provocare : quæ magno rugitu posticam aggreditur et transiit. Clamat populus timens magna voce : Aperietur : et sic postica destructa est.

Executions of this kind usually took place in the amphitheatre, but the stage of a theatre was often used for lack of a

---

[1] It is recorded that Firmus, who in Aurelian's day held Egypt for a time, owned and rode on a tamed hippopotamus (*Hist. Aug.*, *Firmus, etc.*, 6, 2).

more suitable place. It was temporarily barred round, the victim was bound to a stake in the centre and the wild beast's wooden cage was introduced parallel to the bars. One end, loosened in advance was opened through the bars with chisels and crowbars,—" *Postica diffracta*." As soon as the beast emerged, the wooden end still held by the bent nails on its lower edge, was pushed up again and roughly fastened. This method is often employed to-day. In a modern menagerie, where there is neither noise nor a crowd of spectators, one must move quietly and quickly to prevent a beast's return after he has been turned out of his cage ; in front of the stage there was continuous noise, developing into yells that often drove the wild things mad with terror, and impelled them to claw their way back to the dark box. Sometimes the animals refused to come out. That there were so many successful executions is more remarkable than the number of failures. Only extreme hunger could bring success, and this was pushed to such a point, that often the executioner rolled over and died at the feet of the victim. This did not mean pardon—but at best a reprieve and that often only momentary.

Cf. Ammianus Marcellinus, XXVIII, 1, 10 (posticis diffractis)

Passio SS. Perpetuae et Felicitatis, c. VI (Migne, Patr. Lat. III, 14–59) Cf. Libanius Or., V, 14 (Vol 1, p. 309, ed. Förster) Eusebius, V, 1, 41 ; 53; VIII, 7, 2 ; 6

Criminals were treated very harshly in the Roman World ; on the way to death they had to run the gauntlet of insults and blows from the common crowd in the underground of the arena ; if the beasts spared them, man was less kind. The best they could hope for was a speedy execution by the ready sword of some callous gladiator—the worst and most usual a later submission to a more terrible doom.

Eusebius, V, 1, 7. Torturing of Blandina and others at Lugdunum

In the provinces criminals were begged or bought from the Governor by those who wished to add a choice " extra " to their entertainment. These items were incidentals—much of the show was simple and pleasing. The occasion made a local re-union of rank and fashion.

Tertullian, De Spectaculis, 25, 2–3

The whole scene is excellently described by Apuleius as follows : " His name was Thiasus ; he was born at Corinth, which is the principal town of all the province of Achæa ; he had passed all offices of honour in due course according as his birth and dignity required, and he should now take upon

Apuleius, Metam., X, 18–19 (16th cent. translation in Loeb edition)

him the degree Quinquennial [1] : and now to show his worthiness to enter upon that office, and to purchase the benevolence of every person, he appointed and promised public joys and triumphs of gladiators, to endure the space of three days. To bring his endeavour for the public favour to pass, he came into Thessaly to buy excellent beasts and valiant fighters for the purpose, and now when he had bought such things as were necessary, and was about returning home, he would not journey into his country in his fine chariots or splendid wagons, which travelled behind him in the rear, some covered and some open, neither would he ride upon Thessalian horses, or jennets of France [*iumentis gallicanis*] which be most excellent (by reason of their long descent) that can be found ; but caused me [i.e. the hero of the tale, who had been transformed into an ass] to be garnished and trimmed with trappings of gold, with brave harness, with purple coverings, with a bridle of silver, with pictured clothes, and with shrilling bells, and in this manner he rode upon me lovingly . . . [When we arrived at Corinth,] the people of the town came about us on every side, not so much to do honour unto Thiasus as to see me : for my fame was so greatly spread there, that I gained my master much money : for when the people was desirous to see me play pranks, he caused the gates to be shut, and such as entered in should pay money ; by means whereof I was a profitable companion to him every day . . .

[23] . . . at length they obtained for money an evil woman, which was condemned to be eaten of wild beasts, with whom I should be set in a cage before the people . . .

[29] . . . But when the last sound of the trumpet gave warning that every man should retire to his place from those knots and circlings about [in a dance with which the show began], then was the curtain taken away and all the hangings rolled apart, and then began the triumph to appear.

[30] First there was a hill of wood, not much unlike that

---

[1] When, once in every five years, a local census was held in a municipality, the two chief municipal magistrates for that year were called *quinquennales*.

famous hill which the poet Homer called Ida, reared up exceed-
ing high and garnished about with all sort of green verdures
and lively trees, from the top whereof ran down a clear and
fresh fountain, made by the skilful hands of the artificer,
distilling out waters below. There were there a few young
and tender goats, plucking and feeding daintily on the budding
grass, and then came a young man, a shepherd representing
Paris . . .

[34] . . . [After a representation of the Judgement of
Paris] from the top of the hill through a privy spout ran a flood
of wine coloured with saffron, which fell upon the goats in a
sweet-scented stream, and changed their white hair into yellow
more fair : and then with a sweet odour to all them of the
theatre, by certain engines the ground opened and swallowed
up the hill of wood. Then behold there came a man-at-arms
through the middle of the space, demanding by the command-
ment of the people the woman who for her manifold crimes
was condemned to the beasts."

The show of Demochares at Platæa, also described by
Apuleius, gives a still better idea how the beasts were obtained, one slight indication of their cost and an interesting
view of the sordid condition of the common people.

" [At Platæa] we found great fame concerning a man named Apuleius,
Demochares that purposed to set forth a great game, where *Metam.*,
IV, 13 foll.
should be a trial of all kinds of weapons ; he was come of a
good house, marvellous rich, liberal, and well deserved that
which he had, and had prepared many shews and pleasures
for the common people : in so much that there is no man can
either by wit or eloquence shew in fit words all the manifold
shapes of his preparations, for first he had provided gladiators
of a famous band, then all manner of hunters most fleet of
foot, then guilty men without hope of reprieve who were judged
for their punishment to be food for wild beasts. He had
ordained a machine made of beams fixed together, great towers
and platforms like a house to move hither and thither, very
well painted, to be places to contain all the quarry : he had
ready a great number of wild beasts and all sorts of them,

especially he had brought from abroad those noble creatures that were soon to be the death of so many condemned persons. But amongst so great preparations of noble price, he bestowed the most part of his patrimony in buying a vast multitude of great bears, which either by chasing he had caught himself, or which he dearly bought or which were given him by divers of his friends, who strove one with another in making him such gifts : and all these he kept and nourished to his very great cost. Howbeit for all his care of the public pleasure, he could not be free from the malicious eyes of envy : for some of them were well nigh dead, with too long tying up ; some meagre with the broiling heat of the sun ; some languished with long lying, but all (having sundry diseases) were so afflicted that they died one after another, and there were well-nigh none left, in such sort that you might see their wrecks piteously lying in the street and all but dead : and then the common people, having no other meat to feed on, and forced by their rude poverty to find any new meat and cheap feasts, would come forth and fill their bellies with the flesh of the bears. . . .

We, Babulus and I, killed a bear, sewed Thrasyleon in the skin, and put him in a cage which we bought cheap ; then we feigned letters as though they came from one Nicanor which dwelt in the country of Thrace, which was of great acquaintance with this Demochares, wherein we wrote that he had sent him, being his friend, the first-fruits of his coursing and hunting. When night was come we took cover of the darkness, and brought Thrasyleon's cage and our forged letters and presented them to Demochares. When Demochares wonderingly beheld this mighty bear, and saw the timely liberality of Nicanor his friend, he was glad, and commanded his servant to deliver unto us who brought him this joy ten gold crowns . . .   We offered to attend the bear all night, but he answered, ' Verily, masters, you need not to put yourselves to such pains : for I have men, yea, almost all my family [i.e. staff of servants] that serve for nothing but for this purpose of tending bears.' "

Here there are several notable facts—the great sum spent, the frequency of such shows as proved by the fact that cages could be bought in a small town in Greece, whereas they could with difficulty be procured to-day in London, and lastly such store set on a fine bear that the servants of the donor received as a tip 10 golden crowns, which would mean almost 10 guineas in our money, without allowing for gold being more valuable then than now. From such a figure, a guess at the purchase price of a bear may be hazarded, and £30 would seem to err on the lower side—a price higher than was usual for any bear delivered in England in the pre-war years. They cost from £40 to £60 to-day.

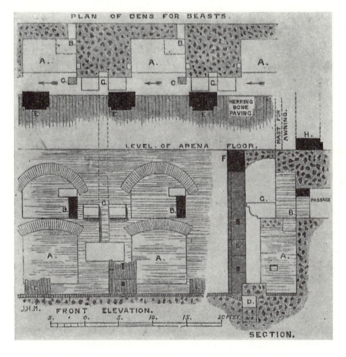

ANIMAL DENS IN THE COLOSSEUM (*see p.* 160)

CHAPTER XII

STOCKYARDS FOR THE BEASTS

St. Chrysostom, 59th Homily

Id. Hom. in Matth., 28, 5

Tertullian, Ad. Martyres, 5

Paul. Diac., Historia Miscella, Book XVI, 23rd year of Justinian

Libanius Or., Artemis, 14 (Vol. I, p. 309, ed. Förster)

Dessau, Inscr. Lat. Sel., 2091

THE animals destined for the arena were kept in remote parts of the city from fear of the danger and terror that followed their not infrequent escapes. St. Chrysostom says that the *vivaria* where the beasts are kept shut up in cages are far from the senate-house, law-courts and palace, lest the beasts breaking out should put anyone in danger. And again, " Just as the wild beasts that break out of their cages spread panic through cities " (καθάπερ θηρία χαλεπὰ ἀπὸ γαλεαγρίας φυγόντα τὰς πόλεις θορυβοῦσιν). Tertullian says : " How often have wild beasts escaped from their cages and devoured men in the middle of cities." In a chronicle we find :

Mense Martio exsiluit elephas e stabulo noctu et interficit multos, alios vero debilitavit.

The risk was indeed great, if the fear was excessive. As Libanius says, " When a long-starved ravenous creature finds itself at liberty, the mere sight of it spreads panic—everyone seeks shelter and shuts fast his door."

The chief enclosure for wild animals at Rome was outside the Praenestine Gate ; Domitian had an exercise school for *bestiarii* on the Caelian Hill. Between the site of the Praetorian Camp and the rampart of Servius there was discovered a votive tablet, of the year A.D. 239, on which is recorded a keeper of the *vivarium* of the praetorian and urban cohorts. This was the *vivarium* attached to the praetorians' own amphitheatre, the *amphitheatrum castrense*, which lay on the eastern side of Rome, not far from the Prænestine Gate. There may have been two or more *vivaria* in that neighbourhood. In late imperial times there was certainly a repository for wild beasts on that side of the city (ἀμφὶ πύλην Πενεστρίναν, ἐπὶ μοῖραν τοῦ περιβόλου ἦν ῾Ρωμαῖοι βιβαρίον καλοῦσι). It was in an enclosure formed by a wall built on to the city wall, in a poor and thinly inhabited district near the Prænestine Gate ; thus it could receive long trains of animals at any time, day or night, without causing inconvenience, and the broad road through the city gate direct to the Colosseum facilitated the speedy carriage of stock to the arena. The exact position is nowhere defined, but the explorations of Paolo Maffei, the account in Procopius, and the contour of the city walls as built by Aurelian, enable us to place it with tolerable accuracy, and to deduce its form, structure and special purpose.

Paolo Maffei in the *Giornale dei Litterati* says " The remains of an old wall with some big windows, which formed a square to the right of the Porta Maggiore, belonged to the *vivarium*, indeed until recently (*circa* 1712) it kept that name. In a small subterranean chamber used as a prison there were found in 1547 three very fine pictures of all sorts of strange animals ; and Panvinius mentions a similar find in a cell [1] under the Via Tiburtina ; which proved that the *vivarium* was extensive." But the explanation may be that these were the keepers' rooms of different *vivaria*.

The whole coincides with the detailed account in Procopius and elucidates the obscurities. That the *vivarium* was to the right of the Porta Maggiore (the former Prænestine Gate) and that it was rectangular are particularly interesting facts. About 70 yards beyond the gate on that side the wall takes a right-angled turn ; consequently the outer weaker walls enclosed a space 70 yards wide and if to the next bastion about 440 yards long.

Procopius says that the ground here was flat, and had been enclosed by the Romans of old, as a depot for the ferocious beasts used in the amphitheatre. That it was narrow is proved by the fact that Belisarius, after allowing the Goths to break and climb

Procopius, Hist.Bell.,Goth., I, 22-3

Giornale dei Litterati d'Italia, Venezia, XII, c. 4, p. 103. Pictured by Fogli del Sadeler and Domenico de Rossi, Grævius, De Antiq. Roman. Panvinius, De ludis circ., lib. 6, cap. 6

Procopius, loc. cit.

---

[1] Probably the keeper's room.

the outer wall, armed his sortie party with swords only—the immense slaughter proves that the enclosure was extensive. It was a large rectangular yard surrounded by high walls, its flat floor unrelieved by any amenity ; in no respect, then, a zoological garden, but eminently suitable for its specific purpose.

From this depot the beasts were brought to the amphitheatre in the night preceding the show. Box-cages for lions, or leopards need not be large for so short a passage as that from the *vivarium* to the arena, and several might be packed on a single waggon ; many recent arrivals, however, would be sent down in their heavy travelling dens, two to a waggon, for these carnivora are the easiest to move. Bears require much stronger and heavier boxes ; deer and bulls occupy cumbersome cases, and each elk, hippopotamus or rhinoceros makes a load very difficult to handle. We must consider, too, the great herds of tame cattle that were driven in for " padding " ; and the delay when special " properties," such as growing trees, were taken down (to appear in all their freshness on the morrow as a forest), and it will be easy for us to picture the bustle and activity, the seeming confusion, that marked the night before the show, and made the purlieus of the Colosseum a rendezvous for the curious sightseer and therefore for people of ill-repute, who were a mine of wealth to tapsters and brothel-keepers. The work began at sundown and had to be finished before 6 a.m. when the animal shows commenced. They finished before midday, the afternoons were always devoted to the far more important gladiatorial combats—the amusement of the cultured classes.

CHAPTER XIII

THE SHOWS IN THE ARENA

IT would be a waste of time to repeat the account of " turns " described under the reign wherein each began. So, after I have discussed the important question of how animals who had done their " turns " were recaptured, my task will end with a full description of that lighter class of entertainment towards which there was an ever-growing tendency.

My readers have perhaps marvelled at the huge numbers of animals shown and slain—numbers much underestimated if we consider the vast majority of unrecorded exhibitions, but always too many for the occasion in question. In the words of Dio, " anyone who cared to record their number would find his task a burden, without being able in all probability to present the truth : for all such matters are regularly exaggerated in a spirit of boastfulness." He speaks of those slain. ^{Dio, XLII, 22, 4}

Evidently many of the animals that entered the arena left it alive : the victor in a contest was not always killed ; the lion in Statius (p. 79), for example, had many victories to his credit. Nor can one eliminate the difficulty by the mere statement that it was a tame lion. Such a beast—full of the blood lust— would be as dangerous for the moment as the savage creature fresh from the wilds, probably more so, from having no fear of the light and the shouting crowds.

A regular system of recapture must have existed ; that it should have been in force is natural. Imagine a broiling August day in Rome—the crowded seats—the blood-soaked arena and the swarms of flies, and the reader must agree that economy in blood was as important as economy in beasts.

As all the animals were presumed to have been killed, the writers of the *Acta diurna* avoided all reference to the subject and passed unnoticed the flagrant untruth, and we have to rely almost entirely on a chance remark of a Christian writer in the provinces—at Lyons, to be exact—for full light on the subject.

There, a certain Bessus, a centurion, obtained permission to remove the body of a woman—a Christian martyr—from the stake in the arena : " The slaves with their seven-thonged whips, each loaded with hard clay balls, drove off the bear." We must imagine that the same system was in vogue in Rome. The reader's attention has already been drawn (p. 73) to the words of Martial, " the lion would not face him but sprang on the spears." Armed men fully accoutred drove the animals together for fights or urged them towards their human quarry. Eusebius, an eyewitness of the martyrdoms at Tyre, says that the leopards and bears turned upon those who were goading and exciting (παρώρμων αὐτά) them to attack, neglecting the victims at the stake though they were nude and defenceless.

Eusebius, *Hist.*, VIII, 7, 2

With that information we can reconstruct the scene. The grand spectacular finale has ended ; some hundreds of beasts are in the arena, the carnivora feasting on dying sheep or bullocks. The seats empty but the show never stops ; yet all must be in readiness for the great entertainment—the Gladiatorial Show at 3 p.m.

From the great gate issues a century of pikemen, and form up along the edge of the arena. Under their protecting spears are slaves with the loaded whips, they advance slowly, without great danger, driving the beasts forward and turning them, as occasion offers, to suitable exits at the sides or in the centre of the arena.

The Bestiary (original in University Library Cambridge) M. R. James, Oxford University Press Picture of elephant. The keeper has such a whip

To the blood-stained space behind the advancing spears, half-trained men are sent to kill one another to keep the show alive. It is the blackest hour in a sport that is all murky darkness. They have no skill in thrust or parry—quality is of no consequence—the seats are empty save for some brutes who gloat on pain and suffering and the sight of gaping wounds : all is mere butchery. At other times there is a rag of hope, not now !

" In the morning men are thrown to lions and bears ; at noon to the spectators, who order slayers to be thrown to those who will slay them, and the victor to be kept for another slaughter." Seneca, *Epp.*, 7, 4

Work goes on regardless of their agony, the lions and bears are driven underground and the arena is cleansed. But the beast-master's work has only begun : he will need all his ingenuity and experience to clear his underground passages, and get his charges caged in a manner not too harmful. Water would help him most : thirst would be torturing the beasts ; but there must have been a long exciting time for the keepers standing behind the barred passage, ready with their hooks to slam the front as each cage got a suitable tenant.

As wealth decreased the big battues diminished, and the Christian religion, though it could not kill the shows, yet managed to soften them considerably. " There are in the shows some turns purely pleasant, simple and modest." " One mixes," says Tertullian, " poison with sweet, not with bitter. Beware the devil ! " In the fourth and fifth centuries the comical side of the entertainment was developed—the spectators were more pleased with the tricks and skill of the performer than by his death. Even criminals had some weapon of offence left to them, although they had no bodily protection ; sometimes naked, and with never more than a loin-cloth, they can be distinguished at a glance from the *venatores*, or athletes on the diptychs of the fourth and fifth centuries. These have long loose dresses and wear protective amulets, or they may be in full armour, or, at least when fighting with lions, have good protection on chest, back and legs.

Tertullian, *De Spectaculis*, 27

Daremberg and Saglio, *Dict. d' antiquités*, II. 273, Fig. 2456

Gorius, *Thesaurus veterum diptychorum*, Vol. II, p. 281 Tab. XI, XII ; Vol. II, Tab. p. 218

The scenes portrayed are for the most part in Constantinople, but a single diptych of Stilicho's second consulate proves that the games were similar in the Eastern and Western Empire. There are bulls pitted against lions and bears, as of old, and there

Op. cit., Vol. II, Tab. I, p. 129

is a contest in which a lion is badly defeated by a horse (*videre solemus inter matutina arenæ spectacula tauri et ursi pugnam inter se colligatorum*) ; there are combats of gladiators versus lions, bears, leopards and elk : there are athletic displays with the Contobolon or Jumping Pole, there is a great increase in the use of the Cochlea—three being erected at one time to help the performers in dodging the lions—and Cassiodorus in the sixth century grows enthusiastic in his praise of their agility. There is a see-saw of two men in baskets, who are swung up and down to avoid the beasts. And the Canistrum has come into vogue : it is a safe and amusing device, a hollow iron sphere, well pitted with holes through which some contortionist twisted inside it can prick and irritate the beast. The infuriated animal falls upon it, bowls it fast and far over the arena, amid the laughter of the spectators—redoubled when the uncanny case rolls slowly and steadily back again to attack the baffled enemy. Danger is not eliminated, a leg or arm may fall to teeth or claws, but the risk of death has almost gone. The Master of the Games is in the arena with helpers, under his command, ready with their lassoes to distract or drag away the beast. There is now an obvious solicitude for the safety of the performers. Round the arena, at short intervals, strong doors stand ajar, each with a handle of rope spliced on two rings. Behind stands a doorkeeper to let the hard-pressed performer pass, and to hold the door against the pursuer. Even these precautions did not satisfy the public ! Though a law of Justinian regulating the entertainments to be given by consuls speaks of the pleasures which the public derives from the daring of beast-fighters and the killing of beasts, the population of Constantinople had not the old Roman passion for *venationes*.

But the interest in wild beasts was in no whit diminished. The zoological garden of Constantinople had begun, and it continued as long as the Empire. When that fell the next garden rose to greater fame, for the conquering Turk kept in his new capital the finest animal-collection in the world.

Long before this, the rulers of the city states of a revivified Italy were adorning their Courts with rare beasts ; the wealthy

Margin notes:
Seneca, *De Ira*, III, 43, 2

Cassiodorus, *Var.*, V, 42

See Diptychs of period *supra*

Justinian, *Nov.* CV, Chap. I

kings of Western Europe imitated, and surpassed Florence and Genoa in collections, which reach their height in the royal menagerie of Louis XIV, placed in and around the former menagerie or farm of Louis XIII, at Versailles,—the forerunner and type of the modern zoological garden.

Ménagerie, whence menagerie

APPENDIX I

LEOPARD

πάρδαλις πάνθηρ πάρδος λεόπαρδος λεοντόπαρδος.

Panthera, pardus, varia, leopardus.

IN attempting to disentangle the meanings of the above words I propose to use the English words :

Leopard (*Felis pardus*), the large spotted cat of Asia and Africa.

Cheetah or Hunting leopard (*Cynælurus jubatus*), Asia and Africa.

Caracal (*Felis caracal*), the unspotted lynx used so largely for hunting in the East. Found in Asia and Africa.

Lynx (*Felis lynx*) the spotted short-tailed lynx of Europe and Asia.

Serval (*Felis serval*), a spotted cat with a moderately long tail found in Africa.

Genet (*Genetta vulgaris*), the common genet, a small, long-tailed, much spotted viverrine of S. Europe and N. Africa.

Lion (*Felis leo*), the lion of Asia and Africa.

Maneless lion (*Felis leo*), a lion which has little or no mane.

Panther will not be used ; it is a word in very common use, loosely applied to a leopard, and the usage has a growing tendency to limit itself to the black leopard of the East Indies. The panther, however, does *not* exist in English zoological nomenclature.

Ancient writers were faced with two great difficulties in putting correct names to these spotted cats great and small ; they believed in the breeding of hybrid forms in nature, and the Romans had the additional difficulty of naming a foreign animal. That the consequent confusion has subsisted to our own day is evinced by the startling fact that both the popular and scientific name of the largest of these animals is wrong ; the leopard has no connection with leopardus, but I must keep the word, and use it in my explanation. It may be said at once that πέρδαλις (or πόρδαλις), when it is used for a quadruped, and not for a sea-monster, may be generally assumed to mean leopard ; though in a passage which will be noticed at the end of this Appendix the cheetah seems to be referred to as a kind of πάρδαλις.

183

Leopards probably came to Rome at first from Africa. I think

Pœnulus, 1011 leopards are referred to in the *Pœnulus* of Plantus as *mures Africani*, just as giraffes were called African sheep. This is mere conjecture, but it is certain that leopards were called *pantheræ* at Rome in the Republican age, receiving what was probably a common Latin word for a spotted animal.

Panthera was derived from the Greek πάνθηρ, as *cratera* from κρᾱτήρ. Now πάνθηρ, though it is found meaning a cheetah, was certainly also used for a small animal. Thus in the poem on hunting ascribed to

"Oppian," *Cyn.*, II, 570-3

Oppian we have, " Dear Muse, it is not for me to sing of small creatures. Leave the vermin which have no strength in them, the grey-eyed πάνθηρες and the destructive αἴλουροι which make war on the nests of domestic fowls." Here the πάνθηρ is a small animal associated with the αἴλουρος, which I take to be, not the domestic or any other

Aristotle, *H.A.*, VI, 580a, 24-7

cat, but the pine marten (*Mustela martes*) : Aristotle says that the αἴλουρος lives for six years—true for the marten, not nearly long enough for the cat. Of the πάνθηρ Aristotle only says (mentioning it after the αἴλουρος and the ichneumon) that its young are born blind like those of the wolf, and that they are never more than four at a birth.

Galen, quoted by Gesner, *Physiogn.*, VIII, 4

Galen seems to mean by πάνθηρ the sort of animal meant by " Oppian ". There are some men, he says, so bestial that they eat the flesh of lions and leopards, others who eat that of dogs or πάνθηρες or foxes.

This small πάνθηρ seems to have been bright and variegated in its

Strabo, XVI, 4, 16. For the bright colours of the κῆπος, Ælian, *N.A.*, XVII, 8

colouring. Strabo says that the bright-coloured κῆπος (or κῆβος) monkey has the face of a lion, and the body of a πάνθηρ, and is the size of a gazelle.

These passages suggest that the Greeks used the word πάνθηρ for the genet, a small spotted carnivore, of a lustrous, ever-varying hue, found in large numbers in the woods of Greece and Italy. The application of its name to much larger spotted animals would be paralleled by the way in which the κροκόδειλος, the little lizard of the Grecian wall, gave its name to the mighty crocodile of the Nile.

Ælian, *N.A.*, XV, 14 Dio, Epitome, LXXVI, 1

The use of πάνθηρ for cheetah by Ælian (who mentions πάνθηρας τιθασοὺς among the presents made to Indian kings by their subjects), and perhaps in Dio, may have been influenced by the fact, which will be explained below, that the Latin *panthera* came to bear the meaning cheetah in the Roman imperial age. But a contemporary account of a

Athenæus, V, 201c

great procession at Alexandria in the first half of the third century B.C. apparently placed πάνθηρες or πάνθηροι between leopards and lynxes ;

Xenophon, *Cyn.*, 11

and these animals are not likely to have been genets. Xenophon in his

---

[1] *Variare*, to stripe or spot, and *varius*, striped or spotted, were slaves' slang for " to beat " and " beaten." See Plautus, *Pœnulus*, Prol. 26, and *Pseudolus*, 145.

treatise on hunting says that lions, leopards, lynxes, πάνθηρες, bears, and other such wild animals, are caught in foreign countries (ἁλίσκεται ἐν ξέναις χώραις). He is clearly speaking of large, or fairly large, beasts hunted in mountainous wilds. Here, therefore, πάνθηρ does not mean genet, but some large spotted animal, though hardly the cheetah, which is not fond of mountains.

Panthera, then, may have originally meant a genet in Latin. In a conversation between two slaves at the beginning of the *Epidicus* of Plautus, we have : *Epidicus, 17–18*

EP. Quid agis ? Perpetuen valuisti ? TH. Varie. EP. Qui
            varie valent,
Capreaginum hominum non placet mihi neque pantherinum genus !
Here I would translate *pantherinum genus* by " the genet kind."

From this little animal, the *panthera*, the larger animal, our leopard, got its name. We can see from the correspondence of Cicero that *panthera* was ordinarily used for leopard in the middle of the first century B.C. Before the end of Nero's reign *pardus* had come into literary use. It is found in Lucan. But its first reception into vulgar Latin may have been much earlier, perhaps soon after the Eastern conquests of Pompey had led to a great increase in the number of leopards brought to Rome. It may be supposed that πάρδος, for πόρδαλις, was in use among Greek traders, and so found its way into Latin as *pardus*.[1] Its adoption may have been due in some degree to the convenience of having a word of masculine form for the male leopard. *E.g. Ad Fam., II, 11, 2 ; VIII, 4, 5 Lucan, VI, 183*

It seems that in the time of the Elder Pliny there was a tendency to use *panthera* for cheetah and *varia* and *pardus* for leopard, or, more widely, for any large spotted animal of that class. This limitation of the use of *panthera* may have had its origin in an idea that leopard and cheetah were the male and female of the same species of animal[2]; but Pliny says that *pardus* was used for the male of the *varia*. His words are, *Pantheris in candido breves macularum oculi. . . . Nunc varias et pardos, qua mares sunt, appellant, in eo omni genere creberrimo in Africa Syriaque. Quidam ab iis pantheras candore solo discernunt, nec adhuc aliam differentiam inveni*. His description of the *panthera* as having small spots on a white ground suggests the cheetah. Elsewhere he says that the lynx (*chama quem Galli rufium vocabant*) has the spots of the *pardus*. The spots of the lynx are on a reddish ground. *Pliny, N.H., VIII, 17(23), 62–3*

Ibid., 19(28), 70

---

[1] Animal-dealers to-day speak invariably of chimps, monks, hippos, rhinos on the one hand, or of pigs (meaning guinea-pigs) on the other.

[2] The masculine form *panther* occurs once in later literature : *Panther caurit amans, pardus hiando felit* (*Anthol. Lat.*, Riese, No. 762). The cheetah's cry is an exaggerated mew ; the leopard gives a short coughing sound.

That Pliny's white-coated *panthera* was the snow leopard, i.e. Ounce, may, I think, be dismissed from our calculations. The animal may have been known to a few Greeks, but is unlikely to have reached Rome. Its habitat is about or above 10,000 feet in the mountain ranges of Northern India ; and at sea level it rarely lives more than a few weeks.

In a seventeenth-century commentary on Solinus it is asserted that *leopardi* were so called because they were supposed to be the offspring of *pardi* and lionesses. The name *leopardus* was probably in fact derived from such a belief. But it was not originally a name for the leopard. On the contrary, it was at first applied to a lion—a lion of a particular kind. This appears from a passage in Pliny : *Leoni praecipua generositas tunc cum colla armosque vestiunt iubae. Id enim aetate contingit leone conceptis. Quos vero pardi generavere semper insigni hoc carent, simili modo feminæ.* That is to say, lions born from lions will at a certain age get a full mane, but this is never acquired by lions born from the pard—they are maneless like the lioness. Pliny thought that breeding together by pard and lioness was quite common. *Magna libido coitus*, he says, *et ob hoc maribus ira.* The lion discovers the adultery by the smell of the pard, and to remove this smell the lioness bathes. Solinus, writing probably in the third century A.D., repeats Pliny's assertion that there were maneless lions in Africa born of lionesses and *pardi*.

Leopardus, therefore, is a species of lion of which the male has practically no mane. And in spite of Pliny's remark that *pardus* and lioness bred together mostly in Africa, where owing to the lack of water different sorts of animals gather at a few rivers, we may suspect that *leopardi* were found in fairly well-watered districts. Solinus speaks of *ignobiles leones*, the offspring of *pardi* and lionesses, in Hyrcania.

The mighty well-maned lions were few in Roman times as they are to-day, and came as a rule from desert or mountain—those from the neighbourhood of the Tigris, says " Oppian," " are not so valiant." He speaks of these latter as maned. (" From neck and jaws springs flowing hair.") But it is probable enough that many lions from well-watered plains in the world known to the Romans were like those in the moist and lightly wooded territory just south of Uganda, in Tanganyika Colony. Not only are the lions there small and almost maneless—they are often faintly striped or spotted, and the females are almost all spotted, sometimes as fully as a leopard, but more faintly.

Thus *leopardi*, though spotted, are still lions—*leones qui iubis carent.*

The lioness and leopard have bred together in Europe quite recently. I have seen the hybrids in the animal groups of Carl Hagenbeck. And so, in view of the facts above stated, we may excuse, though we cannot approve, the ancient belief that this union took place frequently.

Elagabalus turned among his guests, as a practical joke, animals which

Pliny, *N.H.*, VIII, 16(17), 42–3

Solinus, 27, 13

Solinus, 17, 11

Martial, *Ep.*, VIII, 53 (55), 6–10
" Oppian," *Cyn.*, III, 20–8
Safari, Martin Johnson
Lions, Martin Johnson (Putnam, 1929), pp. 98, 138, 179, 221, 237, 240
In the Land of the Lion, Cherry Kearton (Arrowsmith, 1929) ; illustrations, pp. 45, 52, 54

are called in the *Historia Augusta*, first *leones et leopardos et ursos*, and then *leones, ursos, pardos*. But this does not, of course, show that *leopardi* were really a sort of *pardi*. In an account of a *venatio* given by Probus *leopardi* from Africa and from Syria come next after maned lions (*iubati leones*) and before lionesses and bears ; but there is no separate mention of leopards here. However, in a list of dutiable articles in the *Digest* appear *leones, leœnœ, pardi, leopardi, pantherœ*—lions, lionesses, leopards, maneless lions, cheetahs.

Lastly it may be noticed that the author of the poem on hunting ascribed to "Oppian," a very trustworthy guide, distinguishes two sorts of leopard, a larger and a smaller. The larger sort has the smaller tail. They are probably the leopard and the cheetah. He goes on to mention two notable lynxes. The larger, saffron and like sulphur in colour, is the caracal. The smaller has a ruddy hide, and is the serval.

Hist. Aug. Elagabal., 25, 1

Hist. Aug. Probus, 19, 5 and 7

Digest, XXXIX, 4, 16, 7

" Oppian," *Cyn.*, III, 63–73

Ibid., 84–95

APPENDIX II

THE DATE OF CALPURNIUS

THIS is a battle of the dons, those of the seventeenth century believed him to have written under Carinus (A.D. 283) the modern for philological reasons place him in the reign of Nero.

On the evidence of the seventh eclogue I have no hesitation in placing him at the later date. The animals and the entertainment were altogether foreign to the usual shows of that ruler, and none of the former has received even a passing reference from writers of his time. Nero, we know, killed off hundreds of carnivora, even hazarded against them the Pretorian Guard—in this show all is peace. The single lion is dismissed in a single word and even that little is doubtful—the word may be a gloss : "Martichoram "(line 59). Martichora (Persian Mard-khora, man-eater), the fabulous beast described by Ctesias (400 B.C.), often spoken of, never before seen, this lion-like creature with a spiked tail, this eater of men, to appear in a show under Nero without a victim ! The thing is unthinkable. But it would figure as a most appropriate gift to Aurelian from his friends at the Persian court. The other animals were worthy of any show at any time, but doubly wonderful in the time of Nero. The hippopotamus alone had appeared previously in Rome. Slowly one by one the others came before the Roman public, often much lauded, but no word of them occurs under Nero. The variable hares attracted Martial's pen, the elk first appeared in the reign of Commodus. Pliny had heard of it, knew that its legs were stiff and that it had an elongated upper lip, but makes no mention of its broad distinctive antlers. It was a native of Scandinavia, he says, and had never been seen in Rome. Although his description is decisive, it is a difficulty that he calls it *achlis* (*Alces machlis*) and he has just described the *alces*, " elk," as " similem iuvenco, ni proceritas aurium et cervicis distinguat." The scientific term *Alces machlis* assumes that he is speaking of the same beast, perhaps at an earlier stage of growth, but this is doubtful. It may be added that Pausanias in the next century speaks as if he had not seen elk, although he had seen two-horned rhinoceroses and other rarities of Rome. There were also the gnu from Africa, the dwarf-zebu from Asia

Pausanias, IX, 21, 4, gives Ctesias' account of this beast.

Pliny, VIII, 15(16), 39

Pausanias, IX, 21, 3

Minor, the bison and aurochs, none of which is mentioned by any writer on the Neronian shows. Nor do they find even a passing phrase for Rome's unique marvel that no one could miss, nor, seeing, fail to praise.

THE POLAR BEAR

This animal may be deduced from the passage. " Nec solum nobis silvestria cernere monstra Contigit ; *æquoreos ego cum certantibus ursis Spectavi vitulos . . .*" *Eclogue,* VII, 43–6

This is the only reference to bears associated with seals in the whole history of the entertainments and is in itself most valuable evidence that these were not ordinary bears, for bears had appeared in hundreds from early days, and seals were numerous on the coast of Italy. Bears do so well without baths that the provision of a tank for them in zoological gardens is exceptional, but the polar bears' pool is always an attraction. The seal is their chief prey, and they stalk it cat-like on the ice or as stealthily from the water.

The bold *negotiator ursorum* (bear dealer) who picked up these treasures, possibly on the Baltic, would be aware of their habits ; seals were easily obtained, and what better show could he suggest than a few seals in a large and ornate pool, as prey for the hungry bears ? What a delightful study in varied natation, with the certainty of a noisy fight, and bloodshed when one brought its prey ashore !

No writer mentions them. Pliny did not so much as suspect the existence of the great white bear from the frozen north. He writes with knowledge and at length on bears in general, without a hint of one that swims : he knew their habit of hibernation, how they emerged from hidden caverns ill, unkempt and wasted in the spring, and passes on without comparing them with the fierce, thick-coated snow-white monarch that braved the fury of an Arctic winter. That thick snowy white pelt would have sold for fancy prices in the Capitol, but there is no record of it.

The polar bear remained unknown until the beginning of the third century, at the end of which, if our surmise be correct, it appeared in the Roman arena.

It seems to be mentioned by " Oppian," a reliable authority, and his text introduces another animal still more wonderful, the walrus, which, so far as we know, never reached Rome alive.

> φώκην δὲ βλοσυρὴν καὶ ἐπὶ χθονὶ χαιτήεσσαι
> ἄρκτοι πεφρίκασι καὶ ἐς μόθον ἀντιόωσαι
> δάμνανται·

"Oppian," *Hal.,* V, 38, 40 (Loeb translation)

" Before the dread-eyed seal the maned bears on the land tremble and, when they meet them in battle, they are vanquished."

Calpurnius is generally considered to have lived under Nero but this detailed explanation proves, I think, that he is antedated. The show came late in the history of Rome, the exact date is not material.

APPENDIX III

THE GOLD-FINDING ANTS

HERODOTUS, BOOK III, CHAPTER 102, ETC.

THE story is so simple that the naturalist can have no difficulty in naming the gold-finding ant, nor in explaining the historian's lapses from accuracy.

Strabo, XV, 1, 44, quoting Megasthenes (*circa* 300 B.C.)
Even the exact area of this novel form of place-mining—the country 3,000 stadia, i.e. 375 miles in circumference, threaded by the numerous feeders of the Yarkand River in the South West of Eastern Turkestan, can be stated with tolerable certainty. Many historians consider Tibet is indicated, but we would adduce two potent reasons for thinking that they are in error.

1st, This plain of East Turkestan is almost 9,000 feet lower than the plateau of Tibet, and therefore much warmer.

Herodotus, III 102
2nd, " The Persian King has a number of them, the Ants (actually the Indian Pangolin, *Manis pentadactyla*), which have been caught by the hunters in the land whereof we are speaking."

Turkestan was close to Persia ; Tibet was separated from that land by more than 500 miles of the most mountainous country in the world.

Ælian, *De Natura Animalium*, XVI, 6
Ælian describes the pangolin under the name φαττάγης. It is an animal found " among the Indians " about the size of a Maltese (a toy dog) ; in shape like a lizard with a skin tough enough to be used as a file. It can cut brass or eat through iron.

Jennison, *Who's Who of the Animal World*, p. 320, Black & Co., London
There are several varieties of Pangolin extending from North of the Himalayas through India proper as far as Malaysia. They are found among rocks at the foot of hills, and burrow in a slanting direction to a depth of 8 or 12 feet below the surface, enlarging into a chamber some 2 feet in diameter, where they live in pairs with one or two young. The burrow is closed with earth when the animals are in it. The food is ants and termites, whose nests are torn open by the powerful claws of the pangolin ; the long tongue is thrust into the passage ways and withdraws the ants, which adhere to it.

INDIAN PANGOLIN (*Manis pentadactyla*).

Where found.—India, Tibet.

Size.—Length of body 24 inches. Height 8 inches. Tail 1 foot 6 inches. Weight 25 lbs.

Physical features.—Head short and narrow. Muzzle long. Mouth minute. No teeth. Tongue very long and extensile. Eye small. Ear minute. Head, back, flanks, outer side of legs and tail covered with horny overlapping scales increasing in size towards the rear. Nose, cheeks and underparts without scales. Legs short and strong. Toes 5 on each foot. Slight hair between the scales.

Colour.—Shiny dark brown.

Length of life.—Short.

Food.—Ants.

Young.—One.

Referring to the story in Herodotus, readers will note that the camel riders belong to a warlike tribe bordering on the city of Caspatyrus which is on a river that flows due east and afterwards due west. This is the Kabul River and the Indus. Some may have doubts whether this city lay in Kashmir ; we have none—not because of the topographical facts, but from the well-known fact that the Afghans are born camel-keepers, whose services have been, and are to this day requisitioned all over the world.

These warlike camel riders were sent a great distance from their country to gather the treasure. The gold land is well defined—a sandy desert—open to the east, evidently flanked on the south by very high mountains which alone could account for the abnormal temperature, lower at noon than at 10 a.m., and a country well watered, in spite of the sand, for otherwise the inhabitants would not have been accustomed to use the douche to counteract the heat.

The tract referred to is the Turkestan desert bordered on the south by the Karakorum mountains. It is full of rivers, many of which lose themselves, and the gold they carry, far under the sand. Here enters the gold-finding ant. This is the pangolin, a scaly creature, not without a rough resemblance to an ant, and in size between dog and fox, as Herodotus says. It is nocturnal and burrows deep, say 8 to 12 feet to its den, and, if necessary, goes deeper for the water it requires. Its habits dispose of the fable that it rushes out upon the marauders—it does not, and if it did, it would be outdistanced in a hundred yards. Nor was it dangerous, otherwise the hunters would not have caught numbers of them. They were quiet and inoffensive, and were numerous up to the Indian boundary.

These near ones were neglected by the gold seekers ; their holes had long been worked out—the Afghans had to ride or drive [1] a long

---

[1] I think they drove a cart exactly like the Russian *troika* of the present day, having the female camel in the centre, the males pulling too, attached on either side.

distance on to the sandy desert, keeping their eyes open for pangolin mounds, which would show the course of the hidden stream and from time to time auriferous deposit. These rich deposits were put in the sacks, and no doubt the Afghans dug down further as best they could to make the most of their opportunities, keeping an eye the while on the wandering Kirghiz in the desert, " who [and not the pangolins] are so swift that there is nothing in the world like them." These tribes slept in their tents through the period of greatest heat (here we get the transition from the ants to the other defenders of the treasure)—consequently the camel riders starting before daybreak had about five hours to examine approximately 40 miles of suitable country, as a camel can travel easily 12 miles per hour. Undiscovered they could load at leisure, but if seen they fled. On this point there is a nice balance of advantage and disadvantage in the use of camels ; horses smell them (the narrative speaks of the ants smelling the enemy), and may thus have given the alarm, but, on the other hand, they outran easily the small horses of the tribesmen, who could only hope to catch them by a series of spurts that would wear down the camels, spurts that could only be given by a large number of horsemen attacking furiously in successive parties. The Kirghiz camp in scattered parties, they required time to come together, which explains the last statement in a plain narrative, only slightly vitiated by condensation.

Herodotus, III, 105

Strabo quotes Megasthenes on the subject only to discredit that writer, whose other marvels are nearly all easily explained and obvious truths ; the accounts in other writers are based on Herodotus, and each, including Pliny, adds something which confirms and strengthens his story. Pliny, as is well known, begins his account thus. " In the temple of Hercules at Erythrae the horns of an Indian ant were to be seen—an astonishing object." On that remark all kinds of surmises have been founded, for example that the ants were mythical and that these horns were the picks of miners who worked underground. Probably there were miners who used antlers as picks ; that would be evidence sufficient to ease the conscience of the temple attendants, who were showing and describing the greatest marvel in the Museum. But his own account, and that of most of the others, show that the horns and the ants were in no way connected. A creature, the size of a small dog, that lived in a burrow and yet had large antlers would be indeed a marvel, and the antlers could scarcely have escaped the notice of Herodotus's informant, who saw the living animals (not men) at the court of the Persian King, or of Nearchus who had examined many skins.

The criticism is only mentioned to be dismissed as ill founded, and the suggestion that the whole story is derived from the Sanskrit word Pippilika, or ant-gold, is only valuable in so far as the specks of gold would be about the size of ant eggs, and so would help in giving a name to the animals, that threw them out of the earth. Thus far criticisms. Confirmation comes in several forms.

Pliny supplies the valuable information that " this gold which they throw up in winter the Indians contrive to steal in the summer." Why wait until summer? Let us imagine what we know to be a fact, that every winter the high tableland lies deep in snow—not much chance then of spotting gold-flecked soil. There is the reason that brooks no argument.

The " ants " produced the gold, of that there is no doubt, and, as Arrian says, who treats the subject soberly and wisely, they did it by chance while making for themselves a home.

AUTHORITIES

Herodotus, III, 102, 104, 105.
Strabo, II, c.1, 9   ; XV, c.1, 37, 44
Pomponius Mela, III, 62.
Pliny, *N.H.*, XI, 31(36), 111
Arrian, *Indica*, XV, 5
Ælian, *N.A.*, III, 4 ; XVI, 6

APPENDIX IV

TRAINING MAN-EATERS

Eusebius, *Hist. Eccl.*, VIII, 7, 2, quoted by Friedländer, Vol. IV, p. 527 (English translation)

"THE martyrs standing naked and defenceless incite the beasts to attack them by moving their hands, for they were ordered so to do."

This is the usual method of irritating wild animals, the movement being simultaneous with a rush to the cage, which generally frightens the animal. It recovers in a short time, replying by a counter-attack, but there is no certainty that this would be carried beyond the limits of its cage. Usually, escaped animals are only too eager to return there.

The school for *bestiarii* established or enlarged by Domitian was also a school for beasts. The Pompeian frescoes show the manner of training—there a youth is attacked by a leopard which is fastened to a bull and thus restricted in its movements. Such beasts as were eager and ferocious would be chosen as man-eaters, but even then their training was far from complete. Many, terror-stricken and fearful, would fail in the open area of the practice ring, and no doubt many *bestiarii* died there while perfecting the education of themselves and their savage opponents.

The *bestiarii*, in the beginning just criminals cast to the beasts, soon became a class of trained men valuable, like the gladiators, for Cicero, *Ad. Quintum Fratrem*, II, 4, 5 skill in their profession. Their education implies nothing of charity, merely a desire for a more sporting entertainment.

In the later days of the Empire they had almost attained the status of *venatores ;* they were of several classes—runners, dodgers, pole-jumpers, etc., and provided much amusement by their skill and agility.

The *venatores* were always skilled men who ran perhaps no greater risk than a Spanish toreador. They often fought the wild creatures without weapons, killing them by strangulation or suffocation.

Carpophorus of Domitian's time, a young man of huge bulk and enormous strength, killed 20 wild beasts on one day. This human power seems marvellous, but it has been, if not equalled, certainly approached by animal trainers of the present time, e.g. by Mr. John Hagenbeck who, I was informed by one of his relatives, was wont to force his charges by brute strength to take up the positions he desired.

APPENDIX V

AFRICAN AND INDIAN ELEPHANTS

ELEPHANTS were not used in warfare in Africa or Europe before the campaigns of Alexander, from which time they are often mentioned.

The Ptolemies immediately began to examine the possibilities of the new arm, and the Carthaginians soon followed their example.

The débâcle at the battle of Raphia (217 B.C.) in which Ptolemy's African elephants were so inferior to the Indian beasts, has raised the question whether the former were employed afterwards. There are several reasons why they were unsuitable for the purpose. First and principally because the number captured was too small for any effective selection of suitable animals. Secondly, the treatment of newly captured animals was not properly understood. Lastly, the large ears obstruct the rector, or mahout.

All these criticisms are well founded—very few African elephants reached maturity, and as a consequence those that went into battle were much smaller than the Indian animals opposed to them.

But in spite of these drawbacks, the Carthaginians, and *a fortiori* the Numidians may be said, for lack of evidence to the contrary, to have used only the native animal.

That they used African elephants is proved by an article of the treaty of peace between Carthage and the Romans after the battle of Zama 202 B.C. :

Livy, **XXX,** 37
" Traderent elephantos . . . quos haberent domitos : neque domarent alios."

They were to give up their tame elephants, and not break in others.

Elephants that had travelled from India must have been tame beasts.

Appian,
Rom. Hist.,
VIII, 9, 13
Livy, XXXVII,
37, 39, 13
Also, in 205 B.C., Hasdrubal the son of Gisco headed an expedition that captured 140 wild elephants.

L. Scipio, in the battle of Magnesia against Antiochus III of Syria

(190 B.C.) recognized that his African elephants were inferior to the Indian beasts of the enemy, in quality as well as in number, and therefore he kept them in reserve. Appian, *Rom. Hist.*, 31

At the battle of Thapsus in 46 B.C. the elephants of King Juba were not thoroughly broken to fight, and were but lately taken out of the woods, as Florus says. Florus, II, 13 (IV, 2), 67

There is certain evidence of the use by the Romans of elephants received from Numidia.

These facts do not preclude the possibility that Indian elephants also were employed. But of this there is no clear evidence (*cf.* page 58). And the coins and medals testify to the contrary. With the exception of elephants known to have come from Asia, such as those captured from Pyrrhus and Antiochus, all those figured in the British Museum catalogue of Roman coins, including the *biga* with elephants of Augustus, which is supposed to have been an honour decreed because of the gift of a white elephant from the Seres, are African.

The African elephant has very large ears, and usually the tusks are much longer than those of the Indian beast, but the ignorance or exaggeration of the artist is apt to magnify these features, and so make an Indian animal appear to be African : but there are two points on which there is never any doubt.

1st. Seen *en face* the African elephant is very tall and slopes sharply to the rump.

2nd. In profile the back of the African animal is concave—in the Indian it is convex. In one or other of these positions elephants are usually engraved.

Figure 824 in the *Dictionnaire d' Antiquités* of Daremberg and Saglio is an excellent cut of an African elephant in profile, which may help in the examination of other coins. The denarius of L. Caecilius Metellus recording his victory over the Carthaginians at Panormus 251 B.C. is an equally fine picture of 2 African elephants seen *en face*. It is figured in the British Museum Catalogue of Roman Coins, Vol. I, page 182, Plate XXX, 8.

In Otto Keller's *Die antike Tierwelt*, Plate II, 18, at the end of Vol. I, is particularly interesting as it shows how the Numidians sat sideways on the necks of their elephants, and the form of goad required for driving them (see next page). Plate II, 16, an Indian elephant of Antiochus, shows at a glance the characteristic difference between the races.

We learn from Ælian that the performing elephants that gave a famous display at Rome in the last years of Augustus were born in Italy. In another passage Ælian says " I gather that the period of gestation for the elephant is two years, but some say that it is only eighteen months." It is actually about 650 days. Ælian, *N.A.*, II, 11 ; IV, 31 *Herc. and Pomp*, H. Roux ainé, Firmin Didot, Paris, 1861, Vol. I, Plate 28

The elephant with young, shown on the walls of a house at Pompeii, is a tame beast, and the very large ears of the calf prove it to be of the African race.

The figures of a few Indian armies give the clue to the superiority of Indian over African elephants in war.

Infantry.	Cavalry.	Elephants.
70,000	1,000	700
50,000	5,000	400
150,000	5,000	1,700

No Power in the Western Mediterranean ever put 150 elephants, African or Indian, into one army.

NUMIDIAN ON ELEPHANT (see p. 197)

INDEX